Louise Imogen Guiney, James Clarence Mangan

James Clarence Mangan

Selected Poems

Louise Imogen Guiney, James Clarence Mangan

James Clarence Mangan
Selected Poems

ISBN/EAN: 9783744714273

Printed in Europe, USA, Canada, Australia, Japan

Cover: Foto ©Thomas Meinert / pixelio.de

More available books at **www.hansebooks.com**

Norwood Press

J. S. Cushing & Co. — Berwick & Smith

Norwood Mass. U.S.A.

The Dedication

Dear Sir Charles Gavan Duffy, the new Mangan begs to be yours, partly for the gratification of its editor, one of the many who revere you; much more for the sake of the poor poet who helped to endear your distinguished name when he saluted it, fifty years ago, as that of his kindest friend. What the book has tried to be, you will know best. Far away, in your late southern sunshine, among distances, with the old clear-seeing mood ever upon you, may you read it gently!

Editor's Note

MANY thanks are due the Reverend J. H. Gavin of S. Charles Seminary, Overbrook, Pennsylvania, for the loan of books, prints, and manuscripts, while this edition of Mangan was in progress. For other favors, and much general furtherance, warm acknowledgments are tendered to the Reverend William Hayes Ward, D.D.; to Mr. Theodore Koch, Esq., of Cornell University Library; Mr. Theodor Guelich of Burlington, Iowa; Messrs. Robert Waters of Linden, and Francis Nugent of Peabody, Massachusetts; Dr. J. J. Mangan of Lynn; Mr. D. J. O'Donoghue; and Miss Dora Sigerson, now Mrs. Clement Shorter, who, besides, drew the portrait used as frontispiece. Owing to the courteous permission of Messrs. Houghton, Mifflin & Co., the Editor is able to reprint the Study, contributed some five years ago to *The Atlantic Monthly*, and since greatly revised and enlarged.

Auburndale, Massachusetts, January, 1897.

Table of Contents

	Page
James Clarence Mangan : a Study . . .	3

MY DARK ROSALEEN, AND OTHER TRANSLATIONS
FROM THE GAELIC

My Dark Rosaleen	115
Prince Aldfrid's Itinerary through Ireland . .	118
Kinkora	121
St. Patrick's Hymn before Tara	123
O'Daly's Keen for O'Neill	128
The Fair Hills of Eiré, O	129
The Geraldine's Daughter	131
A Lamentation for the Death of Sir Maurice Fitzgerald	133
Ellen Bawn	135
O'Hussey's Ode to The Maguire	137
A Lament for the Princes of Tyrone and Tyrconnell .	141
A Love Song	150
A Lullaby	152
The Expedition and Death of King Dathy . .	156
The Woman of Three Cows	159
A Farewell to Patrick Sarsfield, Lord Lucan . .	162

Page

The Ruins of Donegal Castle 166
Sancta Opera Domini 171
Kathaleen Ny-Houlahan 173
Welcome to the Prince 174
The Song of Gladness 177
The Dream of John Mac Donnell 179
The Sorrows of Innisfail 182
Leather Away with the Wattle, O! . . . 184
Lament for Banba 186
The Dawning of the Day 188
Dirge for The O'Sullivan Beare 190

TRANSLATIONS, CHIEFLY FROM THE GERMAN

The Maid of Orleans 195
The Fisherman 196
Mignon's Song 197
Nature More than Science 198
The Dying Flower 199
Gone in the Wind 202
The Glaive Song 205
Alexander the Great and the Tree . . . 210
Strew the Way with Flowers 213
The Erl-King's Daughter 215
The Grave, the Grave 218
A Song 219
To Ludwig Uhland 220
The Poet's Consolation 221
The Love-Adieu 222

Page

A Drinking-Song 222
Swabian Popular Song 223
Holiness to the Lord 225
The Ride around the Parapet 226
My Home 234
The Fairies' Passage 235
The Last Words of Al-Hassan 238
And Then no More 241
Mother and Son 242
Two Sonnets from Filicaja 244
The Mariner's Bride 245
To Don Rodrigo 247
Dies Irae 248

ORIGINAL POEMS

*I. Those purporting to be Translations from
the Oriental Languages*

The Karamanian Exile 253
The Wail and Warning of the Three Khalandeers . 256
Relic of Prince Bayazeed 260
Advice against Travel 260
Adam's Oath 261
Night is Nearing 262
To Mihri 263
The City of Truth 264
An Epitaph 267
Good Counsel 268
A Ghazel 268

	Page
The Time of the Roses	270
The Time Ere the Roses were Blowing	273
To Amine, on seeing her About to veil her Mirror	275
The Howling Song of Al Mohara	275
Sayings and Proverbs	278
Lament from the Farewell-book of Ahi	281
Love	282
Trust not the World, nor Time	283
Relic of Servi	286
Jealousy	286
The World: a Ghazel	288
The Time of the Barmecides	289

II. Pro Patria

Irish National Hymn	295
An Invitation	297
Soul and Country	299
A Highway for Freedom	300
To my Native Land	302
Hymn for Pentecost	304

III. Those on Miscellaneous Subjects

Pompeii	309
Twenty Golden Years ago	311
To Laura	313
Sonnet	316
Curtain the Lamp	316
The Dying Enthusiast	318

Page

To Joseph Brenan 319
Lines on the Death of C. H. 321
The World's Changes 323
The Departure of Love 326
Bear Up 326
Two Sonnets to Caroline 328
Enthusiasm 329
The Lovely Land 330
Fronti Nulla Fides 332
Siberia 332
A Vision of Connaught in the Thirteenth Century . 334
The Saw-mill 337
The One Mystery 339
The Nameless One 340

Notes by the Editor 343

James Clarence Mangan

A Study

JAMES CLARENCE MANGAN:

A Study

" *Noi siam vermi*
Nati a formar l'angelica farfalla."
Purgatorio : Canto X.

I

ON the principle that "it has become almost an honor not to be crowned," the name of James Clarence Mangan may be announced at once as very worthy, very distinguished. He is unknown • outside his own non-academic fatherland, though he bids fair to be a proverb and a fire-. side commonplace, much as the Polish poets are at home, within it. Belonging to an age which is nothing if not specific and departmental, he has somehow escaped the classifiers; he has never been run through with a pin, nor have his wings been spread under glass in the museums. It was only yesterday that Mangan took rank in *The Dictionary of National Biography*, in Miles' *Poets of the Century*, and in a new edition of *Lyra Elegantiarum*. In Allibone's *Dictionary of Authors* he has but hasty mention, and a representation as unjust

3

as possible in H. F. Randolph's *Fifty Years
of English Song*. He is absent from the *Ency-
clopedia Britannica*. Even Mr. J. O'Kane
Murray's obese volume, *The Prose and Poetry
of Ireland*, has contrived to live without him.
Palgrave, Dana, Duyckinck, and the score of
lesser books which are kind to forgotten or in-
frequent lyres, know him not; Ward's *English
Poets* has no inch of classic text to devote to
him.   Nor is Mangan's absence altogether or
even chiefly due to editorial shortcomings.
The search after him has always been difficult.
During his lifetime he published only a collection of translations, and his original numbers
were left tangled up with other translations,
by his own exasperating hand.   A large mass
of his work, good, bad, and indifferent, lay hid
in old newspaper files, whence some of it has
been injudiciously rescued by John McCall, a
devoted fellow-countryman ; and what was, for
a very long time, the only collection drawn
from Mangan's store, bearing a New York
imprint, and prefaced by John Mitchel's beautiful memoir, has never had a revised issue.
In 1884, the Rev. C. P. Meehan brought out
a small two-volume reprint of Mangan, better
than Mitchel's, and with some freshly-discov-
ered songs.   The text in all these books is in
an imperfect condition.   Beyond them, Man-

gan's work was not accessible in any form, until some of it was put into the Library series brought out by Mr. Duffy and Mr. McCarthy: cheap volumes, intended for the people. Mangan is hardly yet a Book. So it is, and so, perhaps, it must be. Our time adjusts merit with supreme propriety, in setting up Herrick in the market-place, and in. still reserving Daniel for a domestic adoration. Apollo has a class of might-have-beens whom he loves; poets bred in melancholy places, under disabilities, with thwarted growth and thinned voices; poets compounded of everything magical and fair, like an elixir which is the outcome of knowledge and patience, and which wants in the end, even as common water would, the essence of immortality. The making of a name is too often like the making of a fortune: the more scrupulous contestants are

" Delicate spirits, pushed away
In the hot press of the noonday."

Mangan's is such a memory, captive and overborne. It may be unjust to lend him the epitaph of defeat, for he never strove at all. One can think of no other, in the long disastrous annals of English literature, cursed with so monotonous a misery, so much hope-

lessness and stagnant grief. He had no public ;
he was poor, infirm, homeless, loveless ; travel
and adventure were cut off from him, and he
had no minor risks to run ; the cruel necessities
of labor sapped his dreams from a boy; morbid
fancies mastered him as the rider masters his
horse ; the demon of opium, then the demon
of alcohol, pulled him under, body and soul,
despite a persistent and heart-breaking struggle,
and he perished ignobly in his prime.

We know nothing of his ancestry ; and can
trace to none of its watersheds the stream of
tendency in one so variously endowed.   There
are Mangins buried in the old Huguenot
ground in Dublin, from whom Edward Man-
gin, a writer of much charm, but unknown to
fame (1772–1852), was descended. Was our
poet possibly derived from the Manians, or
clan of Hy-Many, descendants of Maine Mor,
who was in the line of Cairbre Liffeachair,
King of Ireland in the third century ?   Or
we may, with reason, conjecture that Mangan
had some Norman blood ; for his features were
of a decided Norman cast. He was born at
number 3 Fishamble Street, the ancient Vicus
Piscariorum of Dublin, on the first day of
May, 1803. He was the eldest of four children, an early-dying family; his brother, the
only one who survived him, was destined to fol-

low him to the grave during the same month. The father belonged in Shanagolden, Limerick, and was a grocer in fair circumstances when his son was born. The house and shop were the property of the mother, Catherine Smith, a comely member of a respectable farmer's family near Dunsay, in the County Meath. The shop seems to have been soon resigned by the elder Mangan to a brother-in-law, whom he beguiled over from London; and into the receptive hands of the new-comer he is said to have delivered his elder son, and all responsibility for him. James Mangan was a nervous, wilful, tyrannous person, of whom his little ones were afraid. He retired from his business on a competency, but ran through his new estate from excess of hospitality, made his small investments which failed, and died prematurely of the superior disease of disillusion and vexation. The poet, in a posthumously published autobiographical fragment, half-fanciful, half-literal, thus describes him, and exalts or debases him into a Celtic type: "His nature was truly noble; to quote a phrase of my friend O'Donovan, he 'never knew what it was to refuse the countenance of living man'; but in neglecting his own interests (and not the most selfish misanthropes could accuse him of attending too closely to those), he unfortunately forgot

the injuries which he inflicted upon the interests of others.   He was of an ardent and for-
ward-bounding disposition; and though deeply
religious by nature, he hated the restraints of
social life, and seemed to think that all feelings
with regard to family connections, and the ob-
ligations imposed by them, were beneath his
notice.   Me, my two brothers, and my sister,
he treated habitually as a huntsman would treat
refractory hounds.   It was his boast, uttered
in pure glee of heart, that we would run into
a mousehole to shun him!   While my mother
lived, he made her miserable; he led my only
sister such a life that she was obliged to leave
our house; he kept up a continual succession
of hostilities with my brothers; and if he spared
me more than others, it was, perhaps, because I
displayed a greater contempt of life and everything connected with it. . . .   May God assoil
his great and mistaken soul, and grant him
eternal peace and forgiveness!   But I have an
inward feeling that to him I owe all my mis-
fortunes."

Mangan's judgments were gentle.   He was
never heard to criticise nor blame any one but
himself.   Yet the experiences of his tragic in-
fancy must have affected the fountain-springs
of human feeling.   Perhaps he remembered his
own nameless antipathy, by contrast, when he

came to render the wistful thought of a dead father in August Kuhn's lonely little wildwood boy:—

> "I would rather
> Be with him than pulling roses."

An odd moody child, he was sent to school in Swift's forlorn and formal natal neighborhood, in Derby Square, off Werburgh Street. There was a master there who had baptized him in Rosemary Lane Chapel, and who loved him; and from him he learned, among other things, the rudiments of Latin and French. But at thirteen or at fifteen (it is impossible to know which), he had to enter the bitter workaday lists of the world, for the support of a family of steadily-sinking fortunes, who, once they found him productive of so many shillings a week, had no mercy for him, and preyed upon him like a nest of harpies. As early as 1817 the talent within him was visibly astir, venting itself in the charades and whimsical rhymes proper to deservedly obscure Diaries and Almanacs. But before he was sixteen, he had printed some noteworthy verses, with all of the faults, and some of the virtues, of his maturer work, and dark already with settled melancholy. This is a fine imaginative passage from the pen of a child:—

" A dream fell on me, fraught
    With many mingled images ascending
    Up from the depths of slumber :
    Gigantical, voluminous, inblending."

For seven weary years he toiled at copying,
from five in the morning, winter and summer,
until eleven at night, through a boyhood which
knew no vacations.   Mangan shared this hard
boyish experience with Samuel Richardson,
bound out at thirteen as apprentice to a printer
in Aldersgate, and undergoing for seven years
an intolerable drudgery.   He never uttered,
then or after, Mangan's " lyric cry " of protest;
perhaps because he knew that Pamela and her
prose were conspiracy-proof, and not to be
snuffed out in him.   For three years succeed-
ing, the young Mangan was an attorney's clerk,
in close air and among vulgar associates, so tortured in every sentient fibre of his being that he
affirmed nothing but a special Providence preserved him from suicide.   The circumstances of
this slavery gnawed into his memory.   Isolation
of mind was his habit then as afterwards, and long
walks at night were his sole relaxation.   As he
looked back upon the spectacle of his innocent
and stricken youth, he was able to record the
anguish at which the outer willingness was
priced.   " I would frequently inquire, though

I scarcely acknowledged the inquiry to myself,
how or why it was that I should be called
upon to sacrifice the immortal for the mortal;
to give away irredeemably the Promethean fire
within me, for the cooking of a beefsteak; to
destroy and damn my own soul that I might
preserve for a few miserable months or years
the bodies of others. Often would I wander
out into the fields, and groan to God for
help: *De profundis clamavi!* was my continual
cry."

These were the years when first he took
comfort, five minutes at a time, in delightful
study; when from pure single-hearted passion
he made himself an Oxford out of nothing, and
won what is rightly called his "profound and
curiously exquisite culture"; when toward the
unlovely home, anon removed to Peter Street,
and again to Chancery Lane, or the yet un-
lovelier office, at 6 York Street, he would go
softly reciting some sad verses of Ovid which
had a charm for him at school, and keeping his
mind alive with bookish reverie: a solitary
young gold-haired figure, rapt and kind, upon
whom no gladness ever broke, and who was
alone in any crowd. His genius led him in-
stinctively into scholastic ways. Mr. T. H.
Wright, with equal truth and pathos, has thus
sung of him: —

—" Not with rude
Untutored hand Apollo's lyre he smote,
Tho' by the Furies oftentimes pursued
In dull delirious flight thro' wastes remote."

In the parlors of 2 Church Lane, College
Green, he found his earliest encouragers; intellectual tipplers, like Tighe and Lawrence
Bligh, stood ready to be Mangan's colleagues
in worldly paths. A friend betrayed his confi-
dence in some way, and helped him to a sick-
ening foretaste of what his lot was to be. We
have no reason to infer, however, that the blow
was dealt to so trustful a heart by any of the
radiant and erratic Comet Club, of which that
interesting person, Samuel Lover, was then a
member. Sometime between 1825 and 1835,
Mangan had a calamity of the heart. Mitchel's
too romantic statement, generally followed, is
that Mangan's first love was given to a girl
much " above him," according to our strange
surveys; that she encouraged his shy approaches, and he was tremblingly happy; that
for the pleasantest period of his life he was in
frequent contact with those who made for him
his fitting social environment; and that at the
moment when he feared nothing, he was scornfully " whistled down the wind." And the
natural inference is that his harsh disappoint-

ment warped the poet's life, and fastened on
him his air of irremediable suffering. There is
every reason why Mangan should have had a
hard lot, and a heavy heart to carry, without
being crossed in his affections. In *Grant's
Almanack* for 1826, is a poem addressed to him,
signed by his old friend Tighe, reproaching
Mangan for "the dole that hath too long o'er-
cast his soul." He was then twenty-three.
It hardly follows that the event in question was
already past. All adolescent thinkers, whether
lovers or not, experience "dole." In the October of 1832 died Catharine Hayes, of Re-
hoboth ("the quaint old house with the Syrian
name"), a young girl, almost a child, to whom
he taught German. It has been said that this
was she to whom he was engaged, that the
breaking of the tie was an amicable affair of
mutual heroism, and that the girl perished,
shortly after, of consumption. Let us look
into the poetic chronology; for though Mangan, orally, was a most uncomplaining person,
he was not altogether reticent, upon paper.
*Elegiac Verses on the Early Death of a Beloved
Friend* first appeared in *The Comet*, on the tenth
of February, 1833. They were unearthed and
reprinted by John McCall. Beginning

"I stood aloof; I dared not to behold,"

these tender lines were clearly written out of
no vital destroying grief. Ten days later, and
also in the columns of *The Comet*, appear from
Mangan's pen *Two Sonnets to Caroline*, adorned
later by bantering adjectives: *Two Very Interesting Sonnets to Caroline.* They are a-quiver
with something: one knows not whether with
strong feeling in the perfect tense, or with that
dramatic semblance of strong feeling which
Childe Harold had made easy to his contemporaries. They are not love-poems. The curious circumstance connected with them is that
they figure anew in *The Dublin University
Magazine* for January, 1839, as translations
from Gellert! and the elegy for C. H., with
six stanzas eliminated, emerges, in the April
number following, tagged "from the Irish";
and with a colophon in genuine Gaelic superadded. Furthermore, we have to consider a
prose paper by "Clarence" in *The Weekly
Dublin Satirist*, dated October of 1833. It is
called *My Transformation*; the heroine is one
Eleanor Campion; a bitterly-conceived sketch,
ending in burlesque, it affords minute description of "life's fitful fever." Clearly, Mangan
was in a very black Byronic mood indeed *circa*
1832–3. Little Miss Hayes was in no wise
responsible for it; but her dying coincided
neatly with the *a posteriori* suspicions of his-

toriographers. As we have seen, he reprinted these melodramatic compositions in 1839: a year when he recurred afresh to the pseudo-subjective vein. Amid the clumsy machinery of the dialogue *Polyglot Anthology*, Mangan produces some rather imprecatory stanzas *To Laura*, or, as afterwards amended, *To Frances*, beginning with a plagiarism from Burns:—

"The life of life is gone and over,"

which would seem to indicate that he stood in no awe of his victress; nor does he fail to mention, with his usual mendacity and presence of mind, that the lyric reproach is taken from the Italian. Beautifully does it close:—

"Adieu! for thee the heavens are bright,
    Bright flowers along thy pathway lie;
The bolts that strike, the winds that blight,
    Will pass thy bower of beauty by.

"But when shall rest be mine? Alas,
    When first the winter wind shall wave
The pale wild flowers, the long dark grass,
    Above my unremembered grave."

It has been taken for granted by some, since the version entitled *To Frances* is less inaccessible than the other, that Frances was the true name of the cruel maid: a most unlikely deduction. A recent writer, " R. M. S.," in *The Catholic World* for October, 1888, gives a thoughtful vote of accusation to one Frances Stacpoole. Stackpole, too, is the name independently rescued by Mr. W. B. Yeats from the reminiscences of an aged Anglican Archdeacon. Says Miss Susan Gavan Duffy, in a private letter to the editor (1896): " Margaret, not Frances Stacpoole, was the name of the lady beloved by Mangan; and my Father says you are right in surmising that his blighted-love episode was not so overwhelming a grief as it has been represented to be; for when it was all over and past, Mangan repeatedly took my Father to visit Margaret, and her mother and sister. Of course there is no doubt that the poet was a wrecked and broken-hearted man, though Margaret Stacpoole may be not in the least accountable for his misery." Charles Gavan Duffy had met Mangan, through Carleton the novelist, in 1836. During the very time, therefore, when the poet was still gladly visiting the gentlewomen who kept their kindness for him, he was putting together the highly-colored maledictions which could not possibly have represented his real feeling. That he was, in some sense, disillusioned, and thrown back upon himself, is sure. It is piteous that he had ever hoped for common domestic happiness : his fate could neither achieve it nor sustain it, for an hour. He was ineffably unhappy, and in his loneliness poured his unhappiness into verse. It would be unjust to call his attitude a pose; for he was sincere. Yet he must have expressed a little more than he felt, as did every poet of that melodramatic generation. And there is some evidence that he knew his lack of discipline. *Stanzas Written in Midsummer* (1839) he rechristened as *Stanzas Which Ought Not to Have Been Written in Midsummer.* They are gruesome pictures of

—" an undeparting woe
Beheld and shared by none :
A canker-worm whose work is slow,
And gnaws the heart-strings one by one,
And drains the bosom's blood, till the last drop be
    gone ! "

We must remember that a poet's despair cannot gracefully charge itself to dearth of beef, unpleasant kinsfolk, and headaches out of a morphine phial. Hence woman, and the love of woman, come in as the *causa rerum*, irrespective of proof, even with a Mangan. After his rebuff, he worked back into some show of moral courage and indifferentism ; and it is said that no fair face ever appealed to him again. Other, and more mocking faces, walked

c

by his side; for his ruin had begun, and the
fatal friend of sin clung to him, when the
white visions he adored had, one by one, withdrawn.

Henceforth it is not so easy to track him;
he seems to have vanished into smoke. His
bright hair blanched of a sudden during his
first withdrawal from the upper world, and from
the fire which burned his fingers. Whatever is
known of him has been gathered only with
extreme painstaking; his personal history is
quite as vague as if he had lived in a hermit's
cell eight hundred years ago, when as yet the
fine arts of spying and reporting were in the
germ. Even to the men who saw him close
at hand, he was a stranger. He passed
through their company like the ghost of a
séance, with Dryden's "down look," with
soundless speech and gait; whence and whither
none could discover. Mangan was a loving
student of the mediæval alchemists, and he
took for his own the black art of shooting
out of darkness into a partial light, and vanishing as soon. He would disappear for
weeks and months at a time, and baffle search.
It was evident that he mingled, meanwhile,
with those who had snapped all links with
human society. Nor is he the only poet in
English letters over whose head the tides of

despair rose and rolled, that he might so sink, and float, and sink again. We have not forgotten Dr. Johnson's heartfelt lament over Richard Savage, who, not without an inner battle, retired occasionally into chaos, his pension-money in his pocket. "On a bulk, in a cellar, or in a glass-house, among thieves and beggars," says that illustrious friend, "was to be found the author of *The Wanderer,* the man of exalted sentiments, extensive views, and curious observation; the man whose remarks on life might have assisted the statesman, whose ideas of virtue might have enlightened the moralist, whose eloquence might have influenced senates, and whose delicacy might have polished courts." Into such lowest deeps of partial insanity did Mangan also die, and out of them, ever and again, he was born, humble, active, clean of heart, by some reparative miracle, his eyes fixed (they, at least, never wavered) on eternal beauty and eternal good.

II

It is plain on the face of things that he was going the dark way of the opium-eater. Yet this point has been greatly obscured. As early as 1833, Dr. Wall being the Librarian of

Trinity College, Mangan, through the friendly offices of Dr. Todd, who had been attracted by the poet's verses, obtained employment for which he was fitted, and in an atmosphere which came as near as anything could, to making him happy. Trinity was then drawing up her vast new catalogues, and appreciated "the admirable scribe's" assiduity, until, alas, he forfeited her regard. At large among rare folios, Mangan copied for his living, and read for love; losing himself, during the intervals for lunch or exercise, in Matthew Paris, and Calmet's *Dissertatio in Musicam Veterum Hebræorum*. Mitchel's Carlyle-like pen so paints him for us. "The present biographer being in the College Library, and having occasion for a book in that gloomy apartment called the Fagel Library, which is the innermost recess of the stately building, [an acquaintance pointed out to me a man perched on the top of a ladder, with the whispered information that the figure was Clarence Mangan. It was an unearthly and ghostly figure, in a brown garment: the same garment, to all appearance, which lasted till the day of his death. The blanched hair was totally unkempt, the corpse-like features still as marble; a large book was in his arms, and all his soul was in the book. I had never heard of Clarence Mangan before, and

knew not for what he was celebrated, whether
as a magician, a poet, or a murderer: yet I took
a volume and spread it on the table, not to
read, but, with pretence of reading, to gaze on
the spectral person upon the ladder." This
striking description of a man who, it is strange
to remember, was then only in his early thir-
ties, is everywhere corroborated, even by those
who did not see, as Mitchel did, what the description implied. Mr. James T. Fields once
wrote of his meeting with De Quincey:
" When he came out to receive me, at his garden gate, I thought I had never seen anything
so small and pale in the shape of a great man,
nor a more impressive head on human shoulders. The unmistakable alabaster shine, which
I had noticed in other opium-eaters, was on his
face." Mangan, as reported by all who remember him, as implicated (if one may use
that word) in a pathetic posthumous portrait,
done in black-and-white, had also "the unmistakable alabaster-shine." All his fitful recluse
habits pointed to the same cause. That he
had gorgeous visions, his fixed eyes, "lustrously
mild, beautifully blue," his strangely-colored
poems, his rapt and reticent personality, were
so many witnesses. Nor did he escape the
penalties intertwined with stolen dreams. "The
Gorgon's head," he wrote, "the triple-faced

hell-dog, the handwriting on Belshazzar's pal-
ace-wall, the fire-globe that burned below the
feet of Pascal, are all bagatelles beside the
phantasmagoria which evermore haunt my
brain, and blast my eyes." Mangan is looked
upon as a drunkard. To what is this singular
misconception due? To his own denial of his
real folly, and to his complaint that William
Carleton had circulated the statement that he
(Mangan) was an opium-eater; and likewise to
the denial of the Reverend Charles Meehan,
who knew the poet well, who survived him
until the spring of 1890, and had always a positive statement or two to make, concerning him.
Every one knows that the opium practice is
never admitted by its victims; secretiveness is
its sign-manual. As to the second testimony,
it is true so far as it goes. The kind priest
never knew Mangan to touch the drug. But
then, he knew him rather late. Said Dr.
George Sigerson, F. R. U. I., in a recent lecture
before the Irish Literary Society: " It has been
stated, in a letter given to the public some
months ago, that Mangan's writing was extremely irregular and erratic, owing to his drinking habits. O'Daly also had said that the versions of the Munster poets were often brought
to him in different-colored inks, indicative of
different hostelries or public-houses in which

they were composed. Now the specimens here shown prove that Clarence Mangan wrote a clear, legible, elegant hand, manifest in his earliest and latest manuscripts. The writing in these versions of the Munster poets was all in black ink. Very possibly, they were written in various public-houses, for Dublin offered little open hospitality, while there were no free libraries, and all the squares were closed. In Paris, and in London, many writers have used the coffee-houses. . . . Mangan's handwriting does not present the signs of one whose nervous system is shattered by alcohol." An American physician, a great lover of Mangan, has come to the same conviction, by the process of pure induction. He writes to the present editor (May 17, 1896): "How vain it is to try to see in Mangan the fiery, sensual, besotted look of the alcoholic victim! Opium, too, explains his strange manner of life to any medical mind, which alcohol certainly does not; and I should dearly like to see him freed from the stigma of drunkenness, even though by so doing he had to take his unhappy place with Coleridge and De Quincey." One other point has to be disposed of. In *The Nameless One*, Mangan deplores his own fall into

— "The gulf and grave of Maginn and Burns."

The confession is most inaccurately phrased.
It is by poetic license, indeed, that the conse-
quences of other drugs are so visited, before
all men, on the known scapegoat head of
whiskey. But *The Nameless One* was written
in 1842. By that time Mangan had learned
intemperance. It is pathologically impossible
that a man should be a drunkard and an
opium-eater at the same time. The general
testimony is that the very smallest quantity
of spirits was sufficient to send Mangan on
the road to madness. He could never have
gratified an appetite for strong drink, did he
possess it; for his physical forces were ruined.
He may have begun in his youth, on a few
occasional grains of opium, with the intent to
deaden the pangs of hunger and dejection.
Such things have been. And he must have
tasted of liquor in the end, as part and parcel
of a resolve to break off at any cost from
life-long slavery. Between De Quincey, who
struggled successfully, and Coleridge, who
struggled hardly at all, stands this lonely Irish
poet, who struggled in vain. Sometime between his twenty-eighth and his thirty-fifth
year he stopped on his downward course, and
entered on a new life. Feeble, but not overborne, eager for any help, though it were full
of danger, he fell presently on the neck of one

evil, seeking deliverance from another. And
whereas, in his former misery, he had cried out
in no human ear, he began now to pour forth
impotent plaints and promises, after the manner of dipsomaniacs. These are too painful
to quote. One marvels how his patient and
compassionate friends endured him at all; and
that they stood by him even while he evaded
and disheartened them, proves that in Mangan,
repentant for the moment, survived a spark
of the immortal he was, some nameless divine
quality which never forfeited reverence. Sighing over him, they may have anticipated the
mournful final verdict passed by Stevenson on
Burns. " If he had been but strong enough
to refrain, or bad enough to persevere in evil!
. . . there had been some possible road for him
throughout this troublesome world; but a man,
alas, who is equally at the call of his worse and
better instincts, stands among changing events
without foundation or resource." It is the one
atoning circumstance, in Mangan's favor, that
though his attempt was a foregone defeat, it
was a brave fight; he broke himself to pieces
in the effort to save his soul alive. His occasional regularity of living, and his deepening
religiousness, show that some very powerful
influence was at work within him. Is it a
stretch of fancy to recur to Margaret Stac-

poole? She must have refused him prior to
1837, and the refusal was perhaps conditional.
It may well have been that she was the witness
to his vow of reform; and that afterwards,
while he came and went with other literary
men, in her mother's house, she was gazing
through tears, in the pauses of his losing battle, on her poor shattered knight. At any
rate, the supposition harmonizes with what we
know of his restless, ever-remorseful, light-ador-
ing, and "gloom-o'erdarkened" spirit. Had
his passion indeed ended in the short pang
of a rude dismissal, as some of his biographers
contend, it would have left him more of a man.
A hope of marriage, " subdued and cherished
long," eclipsed a thousand times by horrible
folly and weakness, and flickering on in con-
valescent dreams, would be the explanation
both of much of Mangan's poetry, and of the
moral turmoil of all his latter years. Love
the saviour was not strong enough to save
him. The men who guessed nothing of his
true heart-history, and who saw him often and
near enough to connect his squalor and despair with a mere common dissipation, were
natural contradictors of that earlier allegation,
Carleton's or another's, concerning opium.
Still less did they disentangle the thing Clarence Mangan was, from the things he kept on

doing. In the sight of the All Wise, he must
have approximated not to the suicide, but to
the martyr.

He is no subject for biography. Paul Ver-
laine is his only parallel, were it not that
Mangan had no such intense moods of religious mysticism, and none of bestiality. "No
purer and more benignant spirit," — it is John
Mitchel, again, who speaks, "ever alighted upon
earth; no more abandoned wretch ever found
earth a purgatory and a hell. There were, as I
have said, two Mangans: one well-known to
the Muses, the other to the police; one soared
through the empyrean and sought the stars,
the other lay too often in the gutters of Peter
Street and Bride Street. . . . In his deadly
struggle with the cold world he wore no defi-
ant air and attitude; was always humble, affectionate, almost prayerful. He was never of
the Satanic school, never devoted mankind to
the infernal gods, nor cursed the sun." Giving what he could, and asking nothing, genial
and gentle to all that lived, he did not lack
affection. In his penury, his eccentric habits,
his irresponsibilities, he found a distinguished
and devoted few to replace his mistaken circle
of Church Lane wits: Mr. George Petrie,
Dr. Todd, and Dr. Anster, the translator of
Faust; the Reverend John Kenyon of Temple-

derry, Dr. Gilbert, and especially Charles Gavan Duffy. *The Nation* paid Mangan in advance for the copy he too often forgot to supply; he had a haven in Trinity Library, and another in the Ordnance Survey Office, where he was at peace awhile among topographers and antiquaries, generally the happiest-tempered of men. He might have lived with those who would have appreciated and protected him, but he, for reasons, was too shy and too proud. It pleased him better to sit in the liberty of a garret by William, his invalid brother, sipping tar-water, and, with his delicate smile, watching the other's consumption of the single egg, which was all Apollo's vassal could afford to buy him for a certain Christmas dinner; or to move from lodging to lodging, with his hand-bag and his "large, malformed umbrella," devising how he could redeem his manuscripts, and his Berkleian tar-water, too, left in pawn for the antepenultimate rent. The poor gifted creature was driven more than once to private beggary. We read of him, at another time, as residing in a hay-loft, and eloquently expostulating with the landlady, a person with a syllogistic eye to conflagrations, because she would allow him no candle to write by! Nothing very definite ever happened to him. Always suffering, always

absent-minded and a prey to accidents, he was
no stranger to hospitals, and cheerfully as-
serted that his intellect cleared the moment
he entered the ward. Lonely, weak, harassed,
scorning precautions, on the ground that there
is no contagion "but thinking makes it so,"
clinging with foolhardy calm to his Bride
Street dwelling during the great cholera epi-
demic, Mangan perished; suddenly and quietly,
as the shutting of a glow-worm's little lamp, on
the twentieth of June, 1849, his life went out, at
the Meath Hospital, Long Lane, whither he had
been removed. He was buried in Glasnevin.
Three persons are said to have followed his body
to the grave. One of these was the Reverend
Charles Meehan. The tardily-raised headstone
was placed by Mangan's uncle, Mr. Smith.

From Mr. Hercules Ellis we have some
distressing details of our poet's last days. "For
twenty years," he says in a sympathetic preface
to his book, *The Ballads and Romances of Ireland*, "Mangan labored assiduously in his art,
gladly accepting for his works payment lower
than that given to the humblest menial; and
the return for this devotion of his noble genius
to the noblest purposes was a life of privation
and wretchedness, and an early death caused by
want, and cold, and hunger, and nakedness, and
every kind of misery."

He goes on to say that, on taking up one of
the Dublin newspapers, he was much startled
by the announcement of the death of Mangan, of whom he had ever been a warm admirer, though a stranger ; and that he reached
the Meath Hospital in time to see his body
before burial, "wrapped in a winding-sheet,
wasted to a skeleton." From the house-sur-
geon he learned that Mangan, alone and ill, in
a wretched room, had been discovered by the
officers of the Board of Health, and removed,
as a probable victim of the cholera, to the
North Union sheds. But the attendant physician recognized him, and found him not
infected, but merely starved. "He was immediately transmitted to the Meath Hospital,
where everything that skill and kindness could
suggest for the purpose of reviving the expir-
ing spark of life was attempted, and attempted
in vain. The unfortunate child of genius sank
hourly, and died shortly after his admission,
exhibiting, to the last, his gentle nature, in re-
peated apologies for the trouble he gave, and
constant thanks for the attentions and assist-
ance afforded him. In his pocket was found a
volume of German poetry, . . . in his hat were
found loose papers. Laboring to the last in
his noble art, striving to obtain a morsel of bread
by the production of the finest compositions,

. . . poor Clarence Mangan died; an honor to his country by his writings, a disgrace to it by his miserable fate."

Father C. P. Meehan, whose kind voice, reciting, by request, the Penitential Psalms, was the last sound Mangan heard on earth, also testified, on being questioned many years after, that Mangan died, not from cholera, but from "exposure and exhaustion." Unattended for the moment, it seems that he arose, and got out upon the street, and in his great weakness fell into a pit dug for a house-foundation, and lay there awhile before being rediscovered. Mr. Ellis's account was thought to be sensational when it was published. But there is a grave fear that it was the truth. The conditions, not of one mishap or one moment, which killed Mangan, were those which have visited poets from the earth's beginning, those which the comfortable world, well-clad, well-dined, with its feet on the fender, finds it hard to believe in at all. Whatever nominal and visible cause appeared to end him, amid the terror and confusion of the great cholera outbreak, we may set him down as a victim, foredoomed from his birth,

— "who on the milk of Paradise
Should have been fed, and swam in more heartsease
Than there are waters in the Sestian seas."

To the tragic testimony of those who stood at Mangan's bedside, may be added an extract from a letter of Miss Jane Barlow to Mrs. Hinkson (Katharine Tynan), since permission has been accorded to quote it here. " The other day I went to see Miss Margaret Stokes, whose acquaintance I made lately. She was talking about Clarence Mangan, whose friend her father was, as no doubt you know. In fact, he was his last friend. For Mangan had been lost sight of by everybody for a very long time, when, one morning, as Dr. Stokes was going his rounds in the Meath Hospital, the porter told him that admission was asked for a miserable-looking poor man at the door. He was shocked to find that this was Mangan, who said to him : ' You are the first who has spoken one kind word to me, for many years ': a terrible saying ! Dr. Stokes got him a private room, and had everything possible done for him ; but not many days after, he died in Dr. Stokes's arms. Immediately after death, such a wonderful change came over the face that Dr. Stokes hurried away to Sir Frederick Burton, the artist, and said to him : ' Clarence Mangan is lying dead at the Hospital. I want you to come and look at him ; for you never saw anything so beautiful in your life !' So Sir Frederick came, and made the sketch which is

now in the National Gallery. I daresay you
have heard all this before." Mr. F. W. Burton, as the painter then was, hurriedly drew
the pallid head as it lay back on the pillow,
old and weary with its forty-six insupport-
able years : hurriedly, because there was some
groundless fear of infection ; and from this first
small sketch, he made the very touching and
striking picture, which Miss Barlow mentions
as among the treasures of the Irish National
Gallery on Leinster Lawn in Dublin. The
original seems to have passed into Father
Meehan's hands ; and by him was given to its
present possessor, the Reverend J. H. Gavin of
S. Charles Seminary, Overbrook, Pennsylvania.
The larger and more perfect head was beautifully reproduced in *Irish Love Songs*, published
by Mr. Fisher Unwin in 1894. There is no
truer relic of its class, in the history of English
letters ; not even among death-masks. And
it recalls to mind, would one seek its fellow,
Severn's heart-breaking little drawing of the
dying Keats. A sad redoubled value attaches
itself to this memorial of Mangan, when it is
remembered that it was his only portrait. He
was too secluded and indifferent to wish his
features perpetuated, too little famous to attract
artists, too poor to pay them. We have to
thank Dr. Stokes and Sir Frederick Burton

D

alone for the broken reflection of his already
vanished spirit.   From this famous vignette
some half dozen copies have been made ; or,
rather, basing themselves upon it, these have
endeavored to represent the poet as he lived,
with no marked technical success, and all, save
one, with a significant misconception.   Mr.
D. J. O'Donoghue, the best authority on
everything pertaining to Mangan, says of these
attempts : " They are not like him.   As they
are all deductions, as it were, from the Burton
in the National Gallery, they make a curious
mistake in assuming that Mangan habitually
showed his fine forehead.   It was only when
he lay dead, with head unsupported, that his
forehead was properly seen ; for his long hair,
which usually fell over it, had then fallen back."
This just criticism cannot be extended to the
sensitively-pencilled sketch by Dora Sigerson
(Mrs. Shorter), which has the tangled locks
shadowing the brow, and the studious stoop of
Haydon's Wordsworth.

" This is the poet and his poetry."

III

In *The Nameless One* Mangan lends us an in-
cidental glimpse of two forerunners to whom
he was attached.   The mention of Maginn has

historic interest ; for he exercised on Mangan's
genius a pronounced, though superficial influence. It seems ironic to recall to the present
generation of readers the Sir Morgan Odoherty
of *Blackwood's*, the star of *Fraser's* and the
Noctes, now *cinis et manes et fabula*,—the joyous, the learned, the amazing William Maginn,
LL.D., who, because he reaped a temporal reward as the most magazinable of men, has all
but perished from the heaven of remembered
literature. The coupling of his name with that
of Burns was, at the given date, obvious. It is
not likely that Mangan would have spoken of
the ultimate blight of Maginn's great powers
while he lived ; and the reference in the poem
itself to the age of the author, would tend to fix
its composition in the year of Maginn's death,
1842. Profound feeling, as of a personal loss,
premonition, as if called forth by the fate of
one familiarly known, hang over these rushing
strophes, written as they are in the third person.
It is clear that Mangan had an enthusiasm for
Maginn, hitherto unnoted. His commentary
in the *Anthologia Germanica*, in the *Litteræ Ori-
entales*, and in all the imitative raillery of his
Dublin University Magazine work, with its offi-
cious instructive foot-notes, testifies how genuine it was. And the midsummer news from
Walton-on-Thames, which struck home to

many who loved wit, and who grieved for
might put to no immortal use, hurt also the
quiet clerkly figure on the library ladders of
Trinity, and added a pang to his opinion of
himself.   Maginn's is the only influence except,
—*longissimo intervallo*—Hunt's and Lamb's,
discernible in Mangan's prose.   As for some
of his early poetry, it is on Coleridge's head.
The Betrothed, beginning

> " A silence reigns in Venice streets,"

has the tone and the motion of *Christabel*.
Mangan assimilated later a note of the "paus-
ing harp" of 1797.   We are told of the knight
who won "the bright and beauteous Genevieve"
that so soon as the story faltered on his lips, he

> "Disturbed her soul with pity."

"The song of the tree that the saw sawed
through," says Mangan, after Coleridge,

> "Disturbed my spirit with pity,
> Began to subdue
> My spirit with tenderest pity."

And there is a palpable echo of two famous
lines of Shelley, imported into Mangan's version of Schiller's *Bis an des Athers bleichste
Sterne* : —

> "Fancy bore him to the palest star
> Pinnacled in the lofty ether dim,"

and a reminiscence of *The Sensitive Plant,* in a mention of the darnel and the mandrake as being unfit sister-growths for

> — "the proud,
> The hundred-leafèd rose."

"Lampless" is a favorite word with Mangan, who had admired it, no doubt, in *Epipsychidion.*

But the man who most powerfully swayed his budding art was not any of these. It seems hardly necessary to state that it was Lord Byron, Byron who once bestrode all young minds,

> "As a god strong,
> And as a god free."

There is nothing more broadly Byronic in the magnific wails of that generation than a certain production of our poet in *The Dublin Satirist* of the fifth of December, 1835. It is amusing to note that the original author's name is given as Johann Theodor Drechsler, one of Mangan's numerous sawdust dollies. He outgrew this influence, as he did every other. In his noble *Pompeii,* lingers the last tone caught from the Childe, already merging into something unlike itself. The *Hymn for Pentecost,* in *The Irish*

Tribune for the eighth of July, 1848, is modelled
naturally on Schiller's and Byron's lines. It is
a pæan of the year of revolution; a plea that
Innisfail might not swoon on, while all Europe
was awakening from

" The nightmare sleep of nations beneath Kings."

Mangan had some theoretical knowledge of
painting and of music. Though the practical
sciences had small attraction for him, in psychic
experimentalists, from Paracelsus to Lavater, he
took deep interest. For the pages of Sweden-
borg he had lasting love. It is said of him
that even as a boy, his reading could not be
prescribed for him. He was a freebooter student, in spirituals and temporals. Of whatever
other comfort he was bereft, he had fabulous
revenues in his .taste for the · best books.
Browsing habitually among the stalls of the
Four Courts, when he could not command a
library, Mangan grew intimate with the fathers
of English literature. It is curious that he
would not, or could not, appreciate the greatness of Burke. His choice of contemporaries
was fallible. He cried up Godwin's *St. Leon*,
and its author's " forty-quill power," and approved of *Contarini Fleming*, while the glorious
Waverleys left him cold. He admired (may he

be forgiven for these vagaries !) Mr. Rogers,
and he did not spare jibes to so good a man
as Mr. Southey.   On the other hand, we find
him quoting Balzac, Charles Lamb, and the
young Tennyson, and affectionately addressing
a friend who sought to uplift him as

    " Thou endowed with all of Shelley's soul,"

at a time when " Shelley's soul " was still rated
below par by the sagacious world which had
not known him.   Mangan thought, however,
that there was " a cloud on Shelley's character."
It is pleasant to think of the small blonde sprite
of 1811 tripping in and out of the Derby
Square school, who may have looked more
than once, unawares, on Shelley's boyish self
as he went crusading with Harriet through the
streets.   For whatever Mangan saw or heard,
it was from his own contracted orbit at home.
He was acquainted with his Dublin

    " As the tanned galley-slave is with his oar,"

and it is doubtful if he were ever out of it,
except on a dull six weeks' visit to his uncle's
farm in Kiltale.   Mangan says, however, that
he found his " Saw-mill " in Rye Valley, Leix-
lip; and he dated some Italian translations
from Liverpool, having apparently induced

Pegasus to ford the Irish Sea for the occasion.
Certain Italian poets were all his life very dear
to him, Petrarca and Filicaja, and Metastasio
in particular.

IV

Deep as was Mangan's hope for the welfare
of all humanity, he could not be accredited
with anything so specific as a political opinion,
even in the seething times of O'Connell, till he
proved, when the crisis came, that his heart
was with the Young Ireland party. In that
season of great intellectual enthusiasm, it was
natural that an impressionable mind like his
should be swept into the wake of Davis, Duffy,
Dillon, O'Hagan, Dalton Williams, Pigot,
D'Arcy M'Gee, Meagher, and Mitchel. But
while the eyes of these men were fixed on their
far-off common ideal, the eyes of Mangan were
fixed only upon them. They had been kind to
him; his soul was sensitively grateful; and he
made their convictions his by an act of faith in
all he knew of
— " that bright band
That on the steady breeze of Honor sailed."

Two among them have written of their uncer-
tainty, lasting for years, regarding their con-
tributor's political feeling; and they were very

careful not to involve his name in their own
hopes and perils. We are happy to think of
him posing as a rebel and a reformer, although
he counts for so little, and looks so oddly mis-
placed. He dedicated to his country a great
deal of middling verse; he meant to conse-
crate to her new-born aspiration the energies in
him which yet survived. Carried away by the
warmth of personal allegiance, Mangan offered
to become a member of the Irish Confedera-
tion, and, later, to follow John Mitchel to
prosecution and exile: measures from which
his wise leaders, as gentlemen endowed with
humor, very gently dissuaded him. Towards
1842, he became touchingly altruistic. ⌄ He
even endeavored to give the benefit of his
interest and criticisms to that incomparably
well-edited paper, *The Nation*. Whatever he
could get, in the way of blocked out translations from the Gaelic, he took, with eagerness,
for his poetic purposes, and obtained, during
his last year or two of life, considerable insight
into his ancestral tongue. Such an ardor,
whether or no its results can be called successful, had, in one apart from the common con-
cerns of men, a distinctive moral beauty. So
Thoreau, wedded to growing leaves and the
golden hues of a squirrel's eye, stood forth
from his happy woods, and spoke promptly and

aloud, in the ear of scandalized New England, for John Brown.

Like all Irishmen, Mangan was by nature something of a commentator on public affairs. Many were the squibs and epigrams from his boyish pen; and in *The Belfast Vindicator* he had all the fun he could out of the eternal English misrule. His highest powers, however, refused to be pressed into service, as the angelic standard-bearers of a cause. Instead of singing *The Nation's First Number* (one knows not what he could have done, with such a low-flying materialistic title as that!), he heartily shouted it. The *Irish National Hymn* has emotion and dignity; *A Highway for Freedom* is a good song of its kind. But there are a dozen kindred themes from Mangan's pen which nobody of frail endurance would wish to read twice. There is opulent speechifying, but little poetry, in *The Warning Voice, The Peal of Another Trumpet* (with its motto " *Irlande, Irlande, ré-jouis-toi,*" from the prophecies of Mademoiselle Lenormand), and in the one strain typical of all, *The Voice of Encouragement : A New Year's Lay.* The last begins oratorically enough : —

Youths, compatriots, friends, men for the time that is
        nearing !
Spirits appointed by Heaven to front the storm and
        the trouble !

You who in seasons of peril, unfaltering still and
  unfearing,
Calmly have held on your course, the course of the
  just and the noble,
You, young men! would a man unworthy to rank in
  your number,
Yet with a heart that bleeds for his country's wrongs
  and affliction,
Fain raise a voice too in song, albeit his music and
  diction
Rather be fitted, alas, to lull to, than startle from
  slumber.

It closes with a lofty abstract image, worthy of
Mangan, and of the spirit of Young Ireland.

Omenful, arched with gloom, and laden with many a
  presage,
Many a portent of woe, looms the impending era;
Not as of old by comet-sword, gorgon, or ghastly
  chimera,
Scarcely by lightning and thunder, Heaven to-day
  sends its message.
Into the secret heart, down thro' the caves of the spirit,
Pierces the silent shaft, sinks the invisible token:
Cloaked in the hall the envoy stands, his mission
  unspoken,
While the pale banquetless guests await in trembling
  to hear it.

Nevertheless, Young Ireland must have found
him a most useless person. His known gen-

ius and admired achievements floated him over
these years of profound stress, when he produced next to nothing of any worth ; and when
his always gently-remote bearing must have
had the value of an anachronism.   Fortunately,
there were those near at hand to supplant him,
the instant he failed.   It is not from Mangan
that we have *Who Fears to Speak of Ninety-Eight*,
and *The Rapparees.*   Best of all, there was
Thomas Osborne Davis, a patrician tribune, a
most lovable and very perfect character, who
made rhymes only as a means to an end, yet
out-reached any rival whomsoever in that
direction, as in others.   With such splendid
popular ballads of his as *Fontenoy, The Sack of
Baltimore, Owen Roe, O'Brien of Ara,* nothing
of Mangan (least of all *The Siege of Maynooth*)
can compete.   Besides, unlike Davis, or his
nearest followers, clear-headed young enthu-
siasts of culture and breeding, Clarence Mangan had no very definite idea of what was the
desirable thing to say.   While in aiming at the
Repeal of the Act of Union, they were content to arouse a manly spirit in the long-
oppressed peasantry, by dwelling on the
antique glories of the isle and the names of
her romantic heroes, nothing would serve
Mangan, the one anointed poet among them,
but prophecy, calamitous preaching, and the

most prosy insistence on concrete agitation.
Worse yet, he was inconsistent: his theories
veered and wobbled. He begets generalities
Continental in application : —

> March forth, Eighteen Forty-Nine!
> Yet not as marched thy predecessor
> With flashing glaive, and cannon-peal:
> Of no law, human or divine,
> Shalt thou be, even in thought, transgressor.
> Strike with amaze, but not with steel!
> Blood enough has flowed, Heaven knows,
> Even at Freedom's holy shrine;
> Not by blowings-up, or blows,
> Shall conquer Eighteen Forty-Nine.

And again, in *Consolation and Counsel :* —

> "'Knowledge is power,' not powder. That man
>   strikes
> A blow for Ireland worth a hundred guns
> Who trains one reasoner. Smash your heads of
>   pikes,
> And form the heads of men, my sons."

Will it do to compare such approved utterances with

> "Your swords, your guns, alone can give
>   To Freedom's course a highway"?

Surely, no more drastic urging ever came from
Mangan's colleague, the young Speranza

(Miss Elgee, afterwards Lady Wilde), in the famous *Jacta Alea Est*. Whether the mood of patience, or that of indignation, at given times, were best for Ireland, is a question apart; what is certain, is that the man who would encourage her simultaneously in both, cancels his value as a public personage, and may well, on the whole, "go back to his gallipots."

It is simple truth to say that Mangan's was a non-conducting mind, up to his very last years. He was "in the sea of life enisled," unwitting of the passions of the human kind. This loneliness of his, this dream-meshed withdrawal, may not have been altogether a congenital condition; for indifferentism is a sure after-growth of the opium garden. Yet he was a born unit. He inhabited a Bagdad of his own, melancholy and fantastic, and with no gates opening on the world of action. No close observer of his earlier life and writing can find in them definite patriotic or religious ardor, or ardor of any sort except the literary. Had Mangan held deep-seated faiths, they could hardly have been in accord, at any rate, with those of *The Dublin University Magazine*, during the years he devoted to its enrichment. That able periodical reeked with the bigotry, arrogance, cruelty, and spite of the dominant social element in the Dublin of sixty years ago.

It was to end such a spirit of faction, *i.e.*, de-
nationalization, that Young Ireland ("Protes-
tant, Catholic, Dissenter: *quis separabit?*")
arose. It endeavored to wake the people
from an enchanted sleep, in the great name of
Justice. It woke Mangan, among others: he
put himself forth, in loyal and honorable
energy, as an Irishman. He had all manner
of new prospects to befit his new character;
for he proposed to devote himself, "almost
exclusively," to the service of his country.
Hence much lamentable prosody: the active
poet's meat is the contemplative poet's poison.
His translations continued to be, in varying
degrees, effective; his original verse became,
for the most part, monstrous flat and foggy.
He belonged in a cell of his own; it was an
artistic error ever to have left it. Yet in leaving it he proved, however feebly, that in his
outworn consciousness was the manly spark,
albeit he could not, out of his accustomed
vaporous abstraction, speak, in the crowd, the
efficacious word. He had been too long a
recluse, a bookworm, and a leaf in the wind.
Poor Mangan, impotently moralizing towards
the last, is not the idler

— "full of health and heart
Upon the foamy Bosphorus;"

but who that loves liberty as well as he loves lyric worth, can be loath to honor him for the fruitless change? It has been remarked concerning Mangan, that though full of personal hopelessness, he was a political optimist. " He always dreamed, mystically enough, after the modern fashion, of a new era just about to dawn upon the world, and of the regeneration of mankind." (And he is a most compensatory singer: "what though," is his ever-recurrent word.) Hungary failed in 1848, Sicily failed, Ireland failed. But there was much healthful havoc. With the final thunder of disparting thrones, dear to Mangan's remote ear, he himself was fated to pass, unconsummated.

V

Mangan, like Cowley, like Southey and Coleridge, like our friend Goldsmith, between his call on the Bishop (in fatal scarlet breeches) and his attacks on medicine and the law, had a yearning for what he is pleased to call

"The dædal Amazon,
    And the glorious O'hi-o;"

and, like Byron, he pays a lofty compliment to "the single soul of Washington"; but the

possibility of his actually taking passage to
Washington's open-doored republic must have
looked absurd even to himself. In fact, he
never struck at anything, nor "put it to the
touch," for the major reason suggested by the
Cavalier poet, that he "feared his fate too
much." His inertia was due mainly, of course,
to the Circean drugs, and partially to his con-
stitutional fragility, and a dull submissiveness
which he took, perhaps, to be his duty. He
had extreme charity for everybody but Clarence Mangan. It seems superfluous to say
that he made no rebellious clutches at life,
had no greed. Thinking once of domestic
peace, debts discharged, and acknowledged personal value to a community, Goldsmith sighed
in a letter to his brother: "Since I knew what
it was to be a man, I have not known these
things." Worldly wisdom is not a gift left in
Irish cradles. It was Mangan's instinct, as it
was Goldsmith's, to "hitch his wagon to a star,"
and presently to discover, without any change
of countenance, that his star had no legs, and
so to stand, a spectacle for the laughter of men
and gods. He was unfair to himself, we know.
And the world was unfair to him, and to his
industry. It is his chief negative merit that
he was duped and driven to the wall. Such
weakness, rather than the "push" which re-

E

ceives superstitious reverence, is advanced civilization ; and yet it must not be recommended
in hornbooks.   Civilized Mangan was, nay,
more : unlike "Goldy," he might be called
genteel.   About the tight coat and the torn
stock was an aroma as of wilted elegance, a
deceptive aroma of what had never been.   His
manner had great charm; his voice and smile
were winning.   With a gliding grace, he wandered around the journalist offices of Trinity
Street; after prolonged eclipse, the outcast ap-
parition alighted again in the doorway, and
heads of curious clerks bobbed up from the
desks.   "He looked like the spectre of some
German romance," said his most appreciative
contemporary.   "He stole into *The Nation*
office once a week, to talk over literary prospects ; but if any of my friends appeared, he
took flight on the instant.   In earlier days, I
had spent many a night, up to the small hours,
listening to his delightful monologues on
poetry and metaphysics; but the animal spirits
and hopefulness of vigorous young men oppressed him, and he fled from the admiration
and sympathy of a stranger as others do from
reproach or insult."   Sir Charles Gavan Duffy
also speaks of him, during *The Nation* years, as
"so purely a poet that he shrank from all
other exercises of his intellect.   He cared noth-

ing for political projects. He could never be induced to attend the weekly suppers, and knew many of his fellow-laborers only by name." And once more, as late as 1893, in the course of a private correspondence with a clerical friend and admirer: "Some of the pleasantest evenings of my life were spent with Mangan in a room in the office of *The Morning Register*, I being then sub-editor. Mangan recited verse with singular power: not with the skill of an elocutionist, but with the *élan* of a man of genius; and his memory was inexhaustible. Great ceremonies, splendid feasts, and distinguished personages have faded away from my mind; but these nights with Mangan are still fresh and vivid." Sometimes, if Mangan talked at all, he indulged in a soft, desultory, uncanny soliloquy, in the ear of an old friend. "It was easy to perceive that his being was all drowned in the blackest despair. . . . He saw spirits, too, and received unwelcome visits from his dead father, whom he did not love." In spite of destiny he would anon be gay. There was nothing in him of the roisterer, but his speech was full of sudden witticisms, sly fooling which drew no blood. He could not forbear a bit of satire at the expense of his countrymen, as in his charming claim of the discovery of fire, by Prometheus, five thousand six hundred years ago, in Kilkenny! The grimmest poem he wrote has its play upon words, at which melancholy game he takes rank with Heine and Thomas Hood, invincibles like himself. "Poor Clarence Mangan, with his queer puns and jokes, and odd little cloak and wonderful hat!"—so his old deskmate in the Ordnance Survey Office, Mr. W. F. Wakeman, paints him, not without a handsome reference to the huge inevitable umbrella. This implement, says Father Meehan, was "carried like a cotton oriflamme in the most settled weather, and might, when partly covered by his cloak, easily be mistaken for a Scotch bagpipe." Never were clothes so married to a personality; they were as much a part of Mangan as his shining blue eyes, or his quiet, rapid, monk-like step. He had a brown caped cloak in which he seemed to have been born; and the strange antique dismaying hat aforesaid, fixed over his yellow silken dishevelled hair, is set down, to our great satisfaction (in the preface to O'Daly's *Poets of Munster*), as broad-leafed, steeple-shaped, and presumably built on the Hudibras model! Stooped, but not short; wan, thin, and bright; powdery with dust from the upper shelf; equipped with the scant toga precariously buttoned, the great goggles, and the king-umbrella of Great Britain and Ireland,—such was Mangan, so ludicrous and so endearing a figure that one wishes him but a thought in Fielding's brain, lovingly handled in three volumes octavo, and abstracted from the hard vicissitudes of mortality.

VI

A lecture on Mangan was lately delivered in Glasgow by Mr. W. Boyle. We learn from a newspaper report that after giving the date of birth, May Day of 1803, this gentleman said further: "You will all remember that some four and twenty years before, upon another May morning, another poet, named Thomas Moore, had been born above another grocer's shop in the same old city. . . . To one, the dignified society of all the great and brilliant of his time, the sweetest bowers on the world's sunniest slopes; to the other, the reeking slum, the evil-smelling taproom, the garret, and the lazar-house. To Moore, the loving admiration of all men, high and low; to Mangan the pitying approval of the few, and even in his own city, the all but complete forgetfulness of the many. And yet some of you will be surprised to learn that Mangan, in the intervals of his employment as a scrivener, and during

the active period of a life disturbed by illness,
and not more than half as long, composed almost as many lines of verse as Moore, who
devoted all his time and mind and soul to the
pursuits of literature." In the matter of mere
quantity these two come together, who in all
else stand asunder at the poles of the lyric
world. Mangan, as may be surmised, made
no sustained flights; but there survive from his
pen rather more than two thousand short compositions, about half of which are translations,
or, in some measure too generously acknowledged, inspired by poems in another language.
We may roughly rate his purely original work
(the finer half of which, again, he chose to
call translation), as numbering fully a thousand
pieces. To reprint Mangan in the bulk would
be (and one may count that his first stroke of
luck!) difficult. It would amount, moreover,
to the sin of detraction. The thinnest duo-
decimo, containing at the most thirty-five
poems, would adequately show the quintes-
sence of his gift, to the few whose senses are
quick at literary divination. Slight as is the
body of Mangan's poetry hitherto printed as
his own, he shows in it conspicuous inequality.
It is hard to believe that the strophes of
Enthusiasm, whose opening invocation Clough
might have penned, —

" Not yet trodden-under wholly,
Not yet darkened,
O my spirit's flickering lamp ! art thou,"

belong to the same source as certain numbers
artfully omitted from this book. But Mangan
must have his range: awful when he draws himself up to the Pompeiian or the Karamanian
attitude, and something else when he touches
Ireland and the peasants' famine-year, in

" Understand your position,
Remember your mission,
And vacillate not
Whatsoever ensue ! "

The majority of his fugitive verses were given
to *The Dublin Penny Journal*, from 1832 to 1837;
to *The Irish Penny Journal*, started in 1840, for
which he wrote much; to *The Nation and The
United Irishman ;* and to *The Dublin University
Magazine*, to which, in his intermittent fashion, he was faithful throughout. He is to be
traced under various signatures : The Man in
the Cloak, Monos, Lageniensis, Vacuus, The
Mourner, A Yankee, Terræ Filius, Wilhelm,
J. C. M., Clarence, Clarence Mangan, and James
Clarence Mangan. " Throughout his whole literary life of twenty years," says his patriot friend
Mitchel, " he never published a line in any Eng-
lish periodical or through any English bookseller.

He never appeared to be aware that there was
a British public to please." Mangan, modest
by nature, had schooled himself to the neglect
of the critics; no selfish zeal was able to fire
him, and he would not have crossed the street
to advance his interests. He says roguishly of
one of his home-made German poets, " Selber's
toploftical disdain of human applause is the
only great thing about him, except his cloak."
It is just to reflect, also, that he kept from the
agreeable ways of publicity in London, because
his feelings and associations, so far as they were
defined, were republican and hostile, and on the
side of his country in her storms of fifty years
ago. At any rate, he never burned the per-
missible candle to Mammon. London, and
through her, posterity, are the losers; there
would have been, sooner or later, no doubt of
his welcome. He was not uncritical. He
likened his genius to "a mountain stream," and
no analysis could be better, on the whole. His
home is on untrodden highlands, in rough pre-
cipitous places, where only the Munster shep-
herd-boys pass with their flocks, and drink of
the gushing water, and dream not but that all
water tastes the same, the wide world over.

Miserable as Mangan was, he had comfort
in his art. On this subject, where so many are
loquacious enough, he is dumb. We know

very little of his literary habits, save that he wrote fitfully, and often failed, in his earlier years, to get a farthing's pay. He apologizes for gaps in his various *Anthologiæ*, once by pleading that he had mislaid the last leaves of his manuscript, again by saying that he had not of late found a peaceful hour in which to resume his task. He belied himself by letting men think that this irregularity was due to too convivial nights. On that subject he gives us an epigram.

"Thinkers have always been drinkers, and scribblers
    will always be bibblers;
Waiter! I solemnly charge you to vanish, and make
    yourself handy!"

VII

His work, at its worst, has the faults inseparable from the conditions under which it was wrought: it is stumbling, pert, diffuse, distraught. What Mr. Gosse has named the "overflow," the flux of a line-ending into the next line's beginning, so that it becomes difficult to read both aloud, and preserve the stress and rhyme,—this bad habit of good poets, completely ruins several of Mangan's longer pieces. He had in full that racial luxuriance and fluency which, wonderful to see in their

happier action, tend always to carry a writer off
his feet, and wash him into the deep sea of
slovenliness.   Mangan's scholarship, painfully,
intermittently acquired, never distilled itself
into him, to react imperiously on all he wrote,
smoothing the rough and welding the disjointed.
Again, his mental strength, crowded back from
the highways of literature, wreaked itself in
feats not the worthiest : in the taming of un-
heard-of metres, in illegal decoration of other
men's fabrics, in orthoepic and homonymic
freaks of all kinds, not to be matched since the
Middle Ages. ʼ   .
He delights in creating oceans of this sort of
thing (1835) : —

"Besides, of course, heroically bearing
  The speech, half-sneer, half-compliment, of Baring,
  And standing the infliction of a peel
  Of plaudits from Lord Eldon and Bob Peel."

Or this (1839) : —

"The wretch, who rescued from the halter, still
        Will kill,
  Or he, who after trampling tillages,
        Pillages villages,
  Has less of guiltiness than one who when
        Men pen   ·
  Such rubbish as the dullest must despise,
        Cries ' Wise ! ' "

What he alleges, with truth, in a posthumous fragment, of Maginn, may be reverted to himself: "He wrote alike without labor and without limit. He had, properly speaking, no style; or rather, he was master of all styles, though he cared for none." The legerdemain he shows in handling our flexible language, is hardly so admirable as it has been said, on excellent authority, to be. His compound rhymes, his unearthly opulent metres, are indeed extraordinary; but their effect is often gained by illegitimate means. Mangan has no philological scruples, no "literary conscience," whatever. Does he need a rhyme, he invents a word, chooses one which is archaic, or gives to a known one some grotesque turn; he has prefixtures and elisions ever on duty; his musicianly ear cannot be relied upon to keep him always clear of English sibilations; he frequently loses his sense of the place and time to stop; and when he attempts recognized forms, as in the sapphics (with breath-catching rhymes!) of his own *Lurelay*, or the alexandrines of Freiligrath's spirited

"Bound, bound, my desert barb from Alexandria!"

the result is somewhat fearsome, to say the least. While a poet subdues technical difficulties by overriding their laws, success so ob-

tained must be ruled out of court.   However,
a born metrist he was, though a perverse one.
From his very first appearances in print, as a
young boy, he displays as his essential charac-
teristics, imagination, and the greatest verbal
dexterity.   A good proportion of his poems
are informal exhibitions by a virtuoso, a game
of all miracles known to writing man.   His
best burlesque rivals Butler's and Thomas
Hood's, which is the same as saying that it
attains the front rank.   But we cannot endure
mediocre burlesque in the author of *Dark
Rosaleen*.   His prose, nearly always, is forced,
and defaced with tedious puns.   The painful
mummery of some pages (of which, it is but
fair to recall, their author had never the revi-
sion, and which should not have been, nor
should be reprinted) is not representative of
anything but the awkwardness that comes at
intervals over Mangan, and stands between
him and his angel,

" When the angel says, ' Write.' "

As an essayist, despite some fine flashes, he is
hardly worth preserving.   Nor can it be denied that the same element of restlessness and
strain, a sort of alloy from the frightful pov-
erty and degradation nigh it, gets at times

even into much of Mangan's golden poetic
work. "Hippocrene may be inexhaustible," he
says quaintly, "but it flows up to Us through
a pump." Did ever the Virgilian distinction
spring from a houseless Muse, half-fed? The
marvel, rather, is that the spirit in Mangan so
often surmounts the most appalling obstacles
known to the human mind.

Mitchel, who had unerring literary acumen,
detected in him the conflict of "deepest pathos
and a sort of fictitious jollity." At times, he
says, the poet breaks into would-be humor,
"not merry and hearty fun, but rather grotesque, bitter, Fescennine buffoonery, which
leaves an unpleasant impression, as if he were
grimly sneering at himself and all the world,
purposely spoiling and marring the effect of
fine poetry by turning it into burlesque, and
showing how meanly he regarded everything,
even his art wherein he lived and had his
being, when he compared his own exalted ideas
of art and life with the littleness of all his
experiences and performances." Mitchel was
thinking, in all probability, of the ruinous but
very clever postlude to *The Broken-Hearted
Song*, and the interpolation of Yankee dialect
in a lyric raucously beginning,

" O hush such sounds! "

To such spoliations his words apply.   But there
is a vast deal of facetious excellence in Mangan.   Amid less felicitous drollery, the reader
can take pleasure in a snatch of triumphant
parody on Moore, and a recurring chorus which
is a real gold nugget of comic opera : —

> " So spake the stout Haroun-al-Raschid,
>   With his jolly ugly hookah in his hand ! "

Will it be believed that Mangan was a choice
librettist, without his opportunity ?   Were he
earning his living in the same walk to-day, Mr.
W. S. Gilbert might look to his laurels.   Some
of his nonsense runs for all the world like a
Gilbert and Sullivan "topical song," in long
rattling declamatory lines, of wit and anima-
tion all compact.   Behold the exhumed pre-
cursor of *The Mikado!*   The Gilbertian accent
is unmistakably prefigured, in Mangan's humor-
ous hours.   Sundry lines need but to put in an
appearance at the Savoy Theatre, and be wel-
comed at once as long-lost fathers, by all the
six-time A-major *presto e staccato* tribe modern
playgoers know so well : —

> " As backward he staggered
>   With countenance haggard,
>   And feelings as acid as beer after thunder,
>   'Twas plain that the dart which had entered his heart
>   Was rending his physical system asunder ! "

and so on; for there is no dearth of it.   Let us
take *Metempsychosis* as a fair specimen of Mangan's achievement in this direction.   It purports
to derive its parentage from John Frederick
Castelli, "a very select wag," in Klauer-Klat-
towski's *Popular Songs of the Germans.*

METEMPSYCHOSIS

I've studied sundry treatises by spectacled old sages
Anent the capabilities and nature of the soul, and
Its vagabond propensities from even the earliest ages,
As harped on by Spinoza, Plato, Leibnitz, Chubb, and
    Toland.
But of all systems I've yet met or p'raps shall ever
    meet with,
Not one can hold a candle to, (*videlicet*, compete
    with)
The theory of theories Pythagoras proposes,
And called by that profound old snudge (in Greek,)
    metempsychosis.

It seems to me a positive truth, admitting of no modi-
Fication, that the human soul, accustomed to a lodging
Inside a carnal tenement, must, when it quits one
    body,
Instead of sailing to and fro, and profitlessly dodging
About from post to pillar without either pause or pur-
    pose,
Seek out a habitation in some other cozy corpus;

And when, by luck, it pops on one with which its
    habits match, box
Itself therein instanter, like a sentry in a watch-box.

This may be snapped at, sneered at, sneezed at; deuce
    may care for cavils!
Reason is reason.   Credit me, I've met at least one
    myriad
Of instances to prop me up: I've seen upon my
    travels
Foxes who had been lawyers at, no doubt, some former
    period;
Innumerable apes, who, tho' they'd lost their patro-
    nymics,
I recognized immediately as mountebanks and mimics;
And asses, calves et cetera, whose rough bodies gave
    asylum
To certain souls, the property of learned professors
    whilome.

To go on with my catalogue, what will you bet I've
    seen a
Goose, that was reckoned, in her day, a pretty-faced
    young woman?
But more than that.   I knew at once a bloody-lipped
    hyena
To have been a Russian marshal, or an ancient em-
    peror.   (Roman.)
All snakes and vipers, toads and reptiles, crocodiles
    and crawlers,
I set down as court sycophants or hypocritic bawlers;

And there, I may've been right or wrong, but nothing can be truer
Than this, that in a scorpion I beheld a vile reviewer!

So far, we've had no stumbling-block. But now a
puzzling question
Arises. All the afore-named souls were souls of
stunted stature,
Contemptible or cubbish; but Pythag. has no suggestion
Concerning whither transmigrate souls noble in their
nature,
As Homer, Dante, Shakespeare, Schiller! These now,
for example,
What temple can be found for such appropriately
ample?
Where lodge they now? Not, certes, in our present
ninny-hammers
Who mumble rhymes that seem to've been concocted
by their grammars.

Well, then, you see, it comes to this: and after huge
reflection
Here's what I say! A soul that gains, by many trans-
migrations,
The summit, apex, pinnacle, or acme of perfection,
There ends, concludes, and terminates its earthly pere-
grinations;
Then, like an air-balloon, it mounts thro' high Olym-
pus' portals,
And cuts its old connections with mortality and
mortals.

F

And evidence to back me here I don't know any
    stronger
Than that the Truly Great and Good are found on
    earth no longer !

As it is not within the scope of this book to
amass Mangan's comic poetry, we may cull
here perhaps, in passing, three more characteristic samples of it, the last of which, once more,
is a fantasia on the jolly German *Burschenlied*,
which Mangan translated in conjunction with
Gustav Schwab's almost equally good *Bursch's
Departure from College*.   This original epigram
celebrates the author's personal appearance.

> " I, once plump as Shiraz' grape,
>   Am, like Thalbh of thin renown,
> Grown most chasmy, most phantasmy,
>   Yea, most razor-sharp in shape !
> Fact : and if I'm blown thro' town,
>   I'll cut all the sumphs who pass me."

A FAST KEEPER

My friend, Tom Bentley, borrowed from me lately
A score of yellow shiners.   Subsequently
I met the cove, and dunned him rather gently.
Immediately he stood extremely stately,
And swore 'pon honor that he wondered greatly !
We parted coolly.   " Well," (exclaimed I ment'lly,)

" I calculate this isn't acting straightly :
You're what slangwhangers call a scamp, Tom Bent-
     ley ! "
In sooth, I thought his impudence prodigious,
And so I told Jack Spratt a few days after;
But Jack burst into such a fit of laughter !
" Fact is," said he, " poor Tom has turned religious."
I stared, and asked him what it was he meant.
" Why, don't you see ? " quoth Jack. " He keeps the
     Lent."

THE MAKING OF A FRESHMAN

Burschen.
     Very good, very good : he is ripe !
     So let him fill up a pipe,
     So let him fill up a smokified pipe,
          (Ho, ho !
          A smokified pipe.)
     So let him fill up a mighty old pipe.

Fuchs.
     Ugh ! take it away from me quick !
     Ugh, hog-sties ! it makes me so sick,
     Ugh, hog-sties ! it makes me so smokified sick !
          (Ho, ho !
          Dim smokified sick.)
     Ugh, hog-sties ! it makes me so mighty old sick !

Burschen.
     Then let the cub sneak to his den,
     And let him not smoke it again !

No, let him not smoke with us smokified men,
      (Ho, ho!
      Dim smokified men.)
And let him not smoke with us mighty old men.

Fuchs.
    There, now! . . .   I am rid of the spell;
    There, now, I again am all well;
    There, now! I am smokified well:
        (Ho, ho!
        Am smokified well.)
    Hurrah! I again feel mighty old well!

Omnes.
    So grows the Wild Fox a Bursch,
    So grows the Wild Fox a Bursch,
    So grows the Wild Fox a smokified Bursch!
        (Ho, ho!
        A smokified Bursch.)
    So grows the Wild Fox a mighty old Bursch!

For a riotous college-song this passes muster. (Innocent Foxling, never to have smoked
before! Or was there an unholiest substance
in that bowl?)

VIII

Mangan had not been given for nothing his
title to the Erin of song. He atoned to the
venerable tongue he could neither speak nor

understand, by making it articulate in the hearing of the invader. Running into twilight fields of his own, as was his wont, he dedicated exquisite work, albeit a trifle schismatical, to the ancient literature of his country, in the day of its last splendid but brief revival. Several scholars, among them the great Eugene Curry of Mr. Matthew Arnold's admiration, furnished Mangan, toward the end of his life, with literal drafts in English of the many ballads taken down from the lips of the peasants, which he was to render for publisher O'Daly of Anglesea Street and for the Gaelic and Archæological societies; and within these outlines he built up structures not untrue to their first design. Mr. J. H. Ingram, editing Mangan's twelve poems for the third volume of Mr. Alfred H. Miles's collection, *Poets of the Century*, and basing all his facts, if not his judgments, on Mitchel, calls these renditions from the Irish "spiritless." Some persons may think that there is a breathless grandeur in Mangan's chanting of the hymn of Saint Patrick, *At Tarah To-Day*, and that a less "spiritless" thing never came into being. It was with such deep-mouthed apostrophes that he was best fitted to. cope. He was able to try them again in a translation sacred to war, as the other is sacred to Christian peace: *O'Hussey's Ode to The Maguire*: rude

heroic strophes bursting from the heart of the
last hereditary bard of the great sept of Fermanagh, as late as the reign of Charles the First,
while the courtly lyres of England were tinkling a cannon-shot away.   Quite as good as
these, in its province, is the sarcastic rattle of
The Woman of Three Cows.   My Dark Rosaleen
is worth them all, "on a pinnacle apart."   It was
written by a worthy contemporary of Shakespeare, an unknown minstrel of the Tyrconnell chief, Aodh Na Domhnaill (Hugh Roe,
or the Red, O'Donnell), who put upon the
lips of his lord, as addressed to Ireland, the
love-name of "Roisin Dubh," the Black-
Haired Little Rose.   More exact versions of
this symbolic masterpiece have since been
made, but the stormy beauty of Mangan's lines
does away with considerations of law and order.
From an extract such as "Over hills and hollows I have travelled for you, Roisin Dubh!
and crossed Loch Erne in a strong wind; far
would I go to serve my flower; . . . but the
mountains shall be valleys and the rivers flowing backward before I shall let harm befall my
Roisin Dubh," the poet draws the second,
fifth, and last stanzas of his noble seven, the
fifth of these, the passage about "holy delicate
white hands," being a pure gratuity, like a
foam-ball on the stream.

Since *My Dark Rosaleen* is perfect, its genesis cannot be uninteresting. The original literal English of it is to be found in the Egerton MSS. in the British Museum. The song (it was, rather, a group of traditional songs) figures in James Hardiman's *Irish Minstrelsy, or Bardic Remains of Ireland* (1831). Hardiman's translators, Messrs. Dalton, Furlong, Curran, and others, were learned gentlemen of much disinterestedness, giving their leisure to the work, who yet felt it necessary to condone, quite as if they belonged to the eighteenth century, the "barbarity" of the antique phrases, and to foist upon them modern smoothness and circumlocution. *Roisin Dubh* may or may not be, as has been claimed for it also, a personal and passionate old love-song. (To the peasantry of to-day it is that only.) The opening and the close seem to bear out strongly the theory held by most scholars, that it is the allegory of proscribed patriots, who dared not directly address their unhappy country. During this war of the northern clans against Elizabeth, as during the Jacobite insurrections, Ireland was, as the gallant song has it of the MacGregors, "nameless by day." The allusions to Rome and Spain refer to aid promised from both quarters. The unadulterated "prose poem" follows, in full: —

O rosebud, let there not be sorrow on you on account
  of what happened you!
The friars are coming over the sea, and they are
  moving on the ocean;
Your pardon will come from the Pope and from
  Rome in the east,
And spare not the Spanish wine on my Roisin Dubh.

The course is long over which I brought you from
  yesterday to this day.
Over mountains I went with you, and under sails
  across the sea;
The Erne I passed at a bound, though great the flood,
And there was music of strings on each side of me
  and my Roisin Dubh.

You have killed me, my fair one, and may you suffer
  dearly for it!
And my soul within is in love for you, and that
  neither of yesterday nor to-day;
You left me weak and feeble in aspect and in form;
Do not discard me, and I pining for you, my Roisin
  Dubh!

I would walk the dew with you, and the desert of the
  plains,
In hope that I would obtain love from you, or part of
  my desire.
Fragrant little mouth! you have promised me that
  you had love for me:
And she is the flower of Munster, she, my Roisin
  Dubh.

O smooth rose! modest, of the round white breasts,
You are she that left a thousand pains in the very
    centre of my heart.
Fly with me, O first love! and leave the country:
And if I could, would I not make a queen of you,
    my Roisin Dubh?

If I had a plough, I would plough against the hills,
And I would make the gospel in the middle of the
    Mass for my Black Rosebud:
I would give a kiss to the young girl that would give
    her youth to me,
And I would make delights behind the fort with my
    Roisin Dubh.

The Erne shall be in its strong flood, the hills shall
    be uptorn,
And the sea shall have its waves red, and blood shall
    be spilled;
Every mountain-valley and every moor throughout
    Ireland shall be on high,
Some day, before you shall perish, my Roisin Dubh.

No fewer than three times did Mangan try
his hand at this truly bardic fragment. The
first experiment was a happy one: yet our
skilled reviser was not satisfied with it.

Since last night's star, afar, afar,
Heaven saw my speed;

I seemed to fly o'er mountains high
On magic steed.
I dashed thro' Erne!   The world may learn
The cause from love:
For light or sun shone on me none,
But Roisin Dubh.

O Roisin mine, droop not, nor pine;
Look not so dull!
The Pope from Rome shall send thee home
A pardon full;
The priests are near: O do not fear!
From heaven above
They come to thee, they come to free
My Roisin Dubh.

Thee have I loved, for thee have roved
O'er land and sea;
My heart was sore, and evermore
It beat for thee;
I could not weep, I could not sleep,
I could not move!
For night or day I dreamed alway
Of Roisin Dubh.

Thro' Munster land, by shore and strand,
Far could I roam,
If I might get my loved one yet,
And bring her home:

O sweetest flower that blooms in bower,
Or dell, or grove!
Thou lovest me, and I love thee,
My Roisin Dubh.

The sea shall burn, the earth shall mourn,
The skies rain blood,
The world shall rise in dread surprise
And warful mood,
And hill and lake in Eiré shake
And hawk turn dove,
Ere you shall pine, ere you decline,
My Roisin Dubh!

Accordingly, we find a second version by
Mangan in *The Poets and Poetry of Munster*
from which we take the four last verses : —

In years gone by, how you and I seemed glad and
   blest :
My wedded wife, you cheered my life, you warmed
   my breast !
The fairest one the living sun e'er decked with sheen,
The brightest rose that buds or blows, is Dark
   Roisin.

My guiding star of hope you are, all glow and grace,
My blooming love, my spouse above all Adam's
   race :
In deed or thought you cherish naught of low or
   mean ;
The base alone can hate my own, my Dark Roisin.

O never mourn as one forlorn, but bide your hour;
Your friends ere long, combined and strong, will prove
    their power.
From distant Spain will sail a train to change the
    scene
That makes you sad, for one more glad, my Dark
    Roisin.

Till then, adieu, my fond and true, adieu till then!
Tho' now you grieve, still, still believe we'll meet
    again;
I'll yet return with hopes that burn, and broadsword
    keen:
Fear not, nor think you e'er can sink, my Dark
    Roisin!

The theme had taken hold of Mangan's imagination.   Last of all, in 1845 or after, with the
right mood of selection upon him, and with
the warm consciousness at heart of the docility
of the one style he had made his own, the
poet fused together the best in the *Roisin*
ballads, and broke into the inebriating music of
My Dark Rosaleen.

It is, let us say, the most original of them
all.   The manner, too, is all Mangan's; its
noteworthiest feature being the rich recurrence
of words and lines for which *Roisin Dubh* gives
no warrant, and to whose examination we shall
return when we come to speak of Poe.   Be-

tween *My Dark Rosaleen* and the preceding lyrics made from *Roisin Dubh* by the same hand, is a difference: all the difference there can be between things cunningly wrought, and the thing divinely inspired.

Of this translation, and of two or three others from a kindred source, Mr. Maurice Leyne wrote in a supplement to *The Nation*, long ago: "Their beauty can scarcely be exaggerated. To compare with them any actual remains which we have of the Jacobite poetry would be extravagant. They are what an Irish bard might have written if to the deep vague love of country, the longing, the dreaminess, the allegoric expressions of his art, were added all that modern culture can give of distinctness of feeling and sequence of idea. We have other poets who have caught with wonderful fidelity and felicity the Gaelic turns of thought and the structure of the language; but in Mangan the very Gaelic heart seems poured out." Mangan, however, was not always a successful conductor of sounds reaching him obliquely, through the stout persons of Irish scholars. Certain numbers, such as *O'Hussey's Ode*, and *Prince Aldfrid's Itinerary*, are modelled, with the most astonishing closeness, on faithful unrhymed renditions in *The Penny Journal* (1832) and *The University Magazine* (1834). But no

critic can set Mangan's flat and passionless
Eileen Aroon beside the wonderful strain of
Carroll O'Daly, or prefer *The Fair Hills of
Eiré*, *O*, charming as that is, to Sir Samuel
Fergusson's

"A plenteous place is Ireland for hospitable cheer,"

which has the advantage, in this instance, of
greater literalness. And comparison is least
possible between the two native translators,
when it comes to the *Boatman's Hymn*, yet sung,
in vernacular snatches, off the wild western
coast. Not only is the Fergusson version a
hundred-fold more pleasing, but it is, in equal
measure, more Gaelic. It rushes along like
the wind scooping the dusky Kerry sails.

"Bark that bears me thro' foam and squall!
'Tis you in the storm are my castle wall.
Tho' the sea should redden from bottom to top,
From tiller to mast she takes no drop.
On the tide-top, the tide-top,
Wherry *aroon*, my land and store!
On the tide-top, the tide-top,
She is the boat can sail *go leor*."

How does Mangan start off with this finest of
open-air themes?

"O my gallant, gallant bark!
Oft, a many a day, and oft

When the stormy skies above are dark,
And the surges foam aloft,
Dost thou ride
In thy pride
O'er the swelling bosom of the sea;
Tho' lightning flash
And thunder crash,
Still, my royal bark, they daunt not thee.
Yeo-ho, yeo-ho!
The bar is full, the tide runs high.
So! ready hand, and steady eye,
And merrily we go."

And at the close, in the apostrophe to the Atlantic crag (which one poet salutes as

"Whillan ahoy! old heart of stone,"

and the other, *more suo*, as

"Dark Dalán, colossal cliff,")

as well as in the whimsical outcry of the fisher-men terrified at the speed of " Wherry *aroon*," it is easy to decide which translator attains to the sailor-like and singable, and which remains merely literary. I cannot think that Sir Sam-uel Fergusson ever yielded, in power of in-terpretation, to Mangan, in any single case where they chose to handle the same origi-nals. Despite it, we have not from him, nor could we have had, a *Dark Rosaleen*. Mr.

Maurice Leyne, in the illuminating article
quoted a moment ago, speaks of Mangan's
as a typically Irish temperament: "a temperament," according to another sociologist,
"which makes both men and nations feeble
in adversity, and great, gay, and generous in
prosperity." Is he so generic? It is impossible to think of any class or race of Mangans.
Like Swaran in *Ossian*, he "brings his own
dark wing," whereas some readers have asked
for references, antecedents, certificates. Or perhaps, to say that such a one is Celtic, is to put
him back among the indescribables. One Wil-
son, a phrenologist, made in the February of
1835 a professional examination of Mangan's
beautifully-shaped head, with this recorded result. "Constructiveness is hardly developed at
all; on which account he would not have a
genius for mechanism or invention generally,
but he would possess the power of magnifying,
embellishing, and beautifying in the highest degree. A tendency to exaggerate and amplify
would pervade whatever he undertook." Here
we have, disguised as a communication from
the physical sciences, a remarkable bit of literary criticism. The verdict is perfectly true,
though opium had helped to make it so.
Mangan was not least Irish ("Oriental" Irish)
in this, that he loved expansions and dilutions,

and could not forbear yoking quantity with
quality. A hypochondriac too odd to be susceptible of classification, he is

—" like almost anything,
Or a yellow albatross ! "

And eccentricity itself is a purely Celtic property. Strange that his genius is happier on
Saxon than on Celtic ground!

IX

Mangan's chief passion was for the Germans, then in their æsthetic flowering-time ; he
herded by instinct with these contemporaries
best fitted to be his guides and friends. Constant immersion in the strong stream of their
thought (for he read endless German metaphysics as well as German poetry), colored his intellectual life. He knew no stronger influence.
" *Meines Herz Richter*," he calls John Paul.
Mangan's only book published during his lifetime was the *Anthologia Germanica*, which, having run its course in a magazine, was printed
(without its prose passages) at Gavan Duffy's
expense, in 1845. Some of the lyrics included
have a transmitted truthfulness, as of a ray
through clear glass. Even Schiller's great note
is echoed, now and then, with absolute iner-

rancy.   There are few finer illustrations of
aural sensitiveness in a translator than Mangan
gives us in the eleventh and twelfth stanzas
of *Der Gang nach dem Eisenhammer* (*The Message
to the Foundry*).

Da ritt in seines Zornes Wut
Der Graf ins nahe Holz,
Wo ihm in hoher Oefen Glut
Die Eisenstufe schmolz.
Hier nährten früh und spät den Brand
Die Knechte mit geschäft'ger Hand;
Der Funke sprüht, die Bälge blasen,
Als gält' es, Felsen zu verglasen.

Des Wassers und des Feuers Kraft
Verbündet sieht man hier;
Das Mühlrad, von der Flut gerafft,
Umwälzt sich für und für.
Die Werke klappern Nacht und Tag,
Im Lakte pocht der Hämmer Schlag,
Und bildsam von den mächt' gen Streichen,
Muss selbst das Eisen sich erweichen.

At once into a neighboring wood
The Count in frenzy rode,
Wherein an iron foundry stood
Whose furnace redly glowed.
Here, late and early, swinking hands
Fed volumed flame and blazing brands,
While sparkles flew and bellows roared,
And molten ore in billows poured.

Here waves on waves, fires hot and hotter,
In raging strength were found;
Huge mill-wheels, turned by foaming water,
Clanged, clattering, round and round.
Harsh engines brattled night and day;
The thunderous hammer stunned alway
With sledgeblows blended, which descended
Till even the stubborn iron bended.

The Maid of Orleans finds its very self again
in Mangan's English; so does *The Fisher;*
Rückert's enchanting *Das Eine Lied* (*Nature
More than Science*), Uhland's *Lebe wohl, lebe
wohl, mein Lieb,* and *Alexander and the Tree:*
these wed literalness to beauty, in their own
established metre. Half a dozen times, he so
touches the achievement set before him; nay,
rivals it, as he certainly does in the magical
simile about "the piping notes of the coppice
bird," closely inwrought with Kerner's song of
praise to Uhland for his book: a song really as
fresh and rushing in Mangan as in the original,
and far more prodigal of music. Many pages
are simple, spontaneous, choice. But when all
is said, the *Anthologia* is a kaleidoscope, rather
than a mirror. The majority of these German
poems, being what the Irish ones are not, the
children of conventional art, suffer more from
Mangan's swervings and strayings. He treats
his great victims pretty much as Burns, with

every justification, treats the floating Scotch
ballads : he adjusts, he reverses ; into his old
material he infuses a novel substance.   In
scarcely any instance is he content to keep a
poem's given title ; and upon it he can foist
foreign matter, with an almost criminal restlessness.   If he need not confess, with the Sir
E—— B—— L—— of *Bon Gaultier :* —

"I've hawked at Schiller on his lyric throne,
    And given the astonished bard a meaning all my own,"

at least he may well be pardoned for his all-
too-generous doings elsewhere : for Clarence
Mangan seldom detracts from the Muse he pro-
fesses to follow ; his unfaithfulness is in quite
another category.   Having satisfied you with
what exquisite attentiveness he can follow his
exemplars, he hastens to show how variously,
how cunningly, and how effectually he can run
away from them.   The single fact of his having transformed the hard-hearted Kunegund
of *Die Begrüssung auf dem Kynast* (*The Ride
Around the Parapet*), into the Lady Eleanora
von Alleyne, trumpeting her to and fro with
splendid corroborations, is indicative enough of
his habits.   Mangan takes under protest, though
his endeavor is always to make you think him
a great assimilator and economist ; but he is a
prodigal giver.   He hates the niggardly hand,

as much as Horace does, and he cares not a
straw how much of himself he throws away at
his game of setting up a poet in whom he has
no special interest, and who is often his inferior.
This is, indeed, as a severe reviewer named it
at the time, a " vicious system " ; and it cannot
be justified by the undeniable fact that Mangan
imports into his subject an illicit beauty.   The
Germans who had most verbal compression,
who are most set upon a calm statement of
things, are those who suffer most from Mangan's exuberant hullabaloo.   Yet sometimes in
himself, when he is improvising, and does not
feel bound to keep step for step, is a compression very remarkable, and a calm more profound than their own.

The best known, and certainly the loveliest,
of his shorter German translations is Rückert's
ghazel, *Und dann nicht Mehr.*   Even here,
where he keeps, physically, rather close to his
pensive model, he adds metaphor after metaphor, many a lyrical wail, and a heart-stopping
pathos all unwarranted and new ; he seems to
blight and then revivify everything he touches.
Scores of times, as in Wetzel's *Sehnsucht*, itself
very like Mignon's immortal song of the far-off
land and of the spiritual longing to turn thither,
Mangan deliberately transposes and varies his
theme.   He matches Wetzel's graceful eight

lines with twenty-five of his own, melodiously overlapping, and of extraordinary sweetness, in which

"Morn and eve a star invites me,
  One imploring silver star,
  Wooes me, calls me, lures me, lights me,
  To the desert deeps afar,"

with a persistence remote as the "imploring star" itself from good Wetzel's imagination. Still more transformed are the wild and moving measures of *The Last Words of Al Hassan*, which purport to belong to "one Heyden, a name unfamiliar to our ears," and to be found in Wolff's *Hausschatz*, "the repertory of an incredible quantity of middling poetry." Mark the artful depreciation of the German volume, as if to fright a possible speculator in Manganese! If any one hungers for a thorough insight into Mangan's method, he cannot do better than to open the bulky *Hausschatz* (in all of whose editions, however, *Hassan*, by Friedrich August von Heyden, does not figure), and read over the six stanzas of stout commonplace which contain the straightforward remarks of a worsted Bedouin. Not a reference in them does Mangan reproduce, except the profaned Kaaba, the "black-ringleted" unfaithful mistress, the desert wind.

He throws away Heyden's deserted tents, the captive women, the wounded and weary horses, the scattered sheep and shepherd: all the imagery of war and defeat which carry out a pictorial and romantic tradition. What he substitutes is so utterly alien to these that no human being could refer it to Heyden's *Hassan* at all, unless Mangan had chosen to indicate the source of his inspiration. Heyden ends:—

> "Nimm bin dies letze Grüssen.
> Was kam hat kommen müssen:
> Nur Allah's Macht besteht;
> Gelobt sei der Prophet!"

This is worth while being considered as the sub-structure of

> "The wasted moon has a marvellous look
> Amiddle of the starry hordes;
> The heavens, too, shine like a mystic book
> All bright with burning words;
> The mists of the dawn begin to dislimn
> Zahara's castle of sand:
> Farewell, farewell! Mine eyes feel dim,
> They turn to the lampless land,
> 'Llah Hu!
> My heart is weary, mine eyes are dim;
> I will rest in the dark, dark land."

Mangan's *Hassan*, moreover, is richly embroidered with geographical detail. He had a

fine sense for the uses of proper names, and
displayed vague attractions for the region afterwards surveyed by Mr. Matthew Arnold,
whose yellow Oxus and star-lighted Aral Sea
no reader of this generation is likely to forget.
But ἀκριβεία, unerring nicety founded on fore-
thought and research, was not among Mangan's
natural virtues.   He invents neighborhoods
and coasts; he couples cheerfully towns two
thousand miles apart, and even reaches over
into another continent for a gem of a substan-
tive to deck his languorous Asian lines.   But
poetry, after all, is so much finer than gazet-
teers! he seems to insinuate.

The truth is, Clarence Mangan is no translator at all.   He is dominated by his own genuine erratic force, which throve under evil
conditions, and had no clear outlet; and he
cannot contain the ebullition of his natural
speech even in the majestic presence of Goethe.
His mind is not serviceable; he can give an
able and courteous co-operation only when the
demigod chances to agree with his native fire.
The most striking internal evidence that he
had not in him the first instinct of the translator, is that he approaches Heine (whose abrupt
beauty, if indeed it be conveyable at all, Mangan in his trustier mood was curiously well
fitted to convey into English), in order to

appraise him as "darkly diabolical," and to deplore his "melancholy misdirection of glorious faculties." As it was, Mangan wasted on the dreams of anybody else the time he was forbidden to devote to the inspirations of his own brain. It was his misfortune, his punishment also, that with the early loss of enthusiasm, and "that true tranquil perception of the beautiful," which, as he himself feelingly says of an elder writer, "a life led according to the rules of the divine law alone can confer on man," there came an autumnal decadence : a sinking from the exercise of the creative faculty to that of the critical ; a relinquishment of the highest intellectual mood, which was his birthright, for that of the spectator, the sceptic, the jaded philosopher. He recanted his belief in his own powers, and having done that, he held a false but consistent way. The things he accomplished in literature have the look of accidents and commentaries, as he wished ; the pride of his whole shadowed career was to figure in a mask unworthy of him. In such a spirit of evasion he took to his inexplicable trade of translating : accepting a suggestion, and scornfully elaborating it, or ironically referring to the gardens of Ispahan his own roses, whose color seemed too startling for the banks of the Liffey.

X

The question of Mangan's Oriental "translations" is one of keen interest. He is not
known to lovers of poetry, because he played
tricks masterly as any of Chatterton's, and because, unfortunately for the vindication of his
genius, his tricks have never been discovered
and explained, when they were suspected ; and
some who have written of him have left it to
be inferred that he was more of a wiseacre,
and less of an organic force, than he was. His
obliging labor of transposing the Welsh, Da-
nish, Frisian, Swedish, Russian, and Bohemian
(for he solemnly pretends to deal in all of
these) is pure *blague*. If Mangan had had the
polyglot acquirements of his adored Maginn
and of Father Prout, he would have rivalled
their gigantic jokes on the general reader.
Latin and three of the current European
tongues he knew, though not with equal
thoroughness, and he quoted Greek, possibly
at first hand. He had exceptional opportuni-
ties, in the library of Trinity, for linguistic
study, and once went out of his way to bear
witness that our own tongue is nobler than
them all ; but it seems plain that he was no
better versed in the eldest literatures than in
Gaelic. He was not, of course, absolutely

ignorant of their nature. In an elegy on Sarsfield, put into English, Mangan singled out two lines of primitive vehemence touching the slain Jacobite general, Jerome; and after giving the original Irish in a footnote, he adds: " This is one of those peculiarly powerful forms of expression to which I find no parallel except in the Arabic language." So that he would, presumably, have us believe he knew what Arabic was made of, even if he could not parse it. In this same spirit, he once gravely contradicted the dean of Orientalists, Sir William Jones. And again, in the course of a contemptuous review in *The Dublin University Magazine* for March, 1838, he breaks off with — " Enough of so ungracious a theme." (The theme is Hammer-Purgstall's *Turkish Poetry*.) " We must see whether it be not practicable to exhibit the Ottoman Muse in apparel somewhat more attractive than that which decorates her here! " The Schlegels, Herder, Rückert, and others whom Mangan read, were full of Oriental influences, direct or indirect. He was a voracious student of De Sacy and Galland, of *Fundgruben des Orients*, and of d'Herbelot's *Oriental Catalogue*. During the earlier half of the century, the eyes of scholars were turned often to the East. By 1830 there was enough of it reflected in German letters, enough even in

the spurious bulbuls of *Lalla Rookh*, to supply
a man of nimble apprehension like Mangan,

—" sagacious of his quarry from afar,"

with his personal visions.   He expressly states
somewhere that he dislikes the Orientals for
their mysticism.   Meanwhile, on a fine mystical principle, he approximates them, he has
sympathies with them.   He has all the sense
of awe and horror, the joy in action and the
memory of action, the bright fatalism, of a
Mussulman.   Whenever he puts on a turban,
natural to him as was the himation to Keats,
mischief is afoot.   He did not wear it " for
the grandeur of the thing," like a greater poet,
poor Collins, who, in his last days, confessed
to the Wartons his suspicion that his *Oriental
Eclogues* were, rather, his Irish Eclogues.
" Translation's so feasible ! " Mangan exclaims
in a jolly passage wherein he blames other
bards who do not dedicate themselves, for the
hungry public's sake, to that excellent diver-
sion.   Lamb himself had no more fun out of
Ritson and John Scott the Quaker, than Mangan has out of his poems by Selber, with notes
by Dr. Berri Abel Hummer.   The nomenclat-
ure of some of his puppets is quite too daring.
Berri Abel, Ben Daood, and Bham-Booz-eel
are bad enough, but Baugtrauter is notorious.

He declared continually that his " translations "
were not rigidly exact, or he refused altogether
to gratify the curiosity of his audience. " It is
the course that liberal feeling dictates," he says,
with a strict humor worthy of Newman, " to let
them suppose what they like." And all the
time he is enriching them and cheating himself,
adorning the annals of reversed forgery, and
cutting off from the circulation of his mother-
tongue some of its most original accents. He
produced several Ottoman " proverbs," in the
September of 1837, which are the everyday
saws of our western civilization served with
spice. Reduced to their lowest terms, these
mystical mouthings grin at one like a bottled
imp. " Speech is Silver, but Silence is
Golden," they say ; " Enough is as good as a
Feast " ; " The Pot calls the Kettle Black " ;
" A Bird in the Hand is Worth Two in the
Bush " ! Mangan took tremendous delight in
throwing dust in devoted eyes. It is within
reason that in his roaring stanzas dedicated *To
the Ingleeze Khafir, Djaun Bool Djenkinzun*,
the dear and dunderheaded gentleman addressed might miss the point altogether. It
would not be so conceivable that he hood-
winked also the Trinity Fellows at his elbow,
were it not for two considerations. In the
first place, nobody was especially well ac-

quainted with him; he was intangible. As none could affirm with authority whether he had but one coat in his wardrobe, or where and how he kept his distressing relatives; so none could track his elusive mental habits, and say, " This knowledge, and not that, has he acquired." Again, specialists do not grow on every bush, even in Trinity. The names of authors whom he cited, Mehisi, Kemal-Oomi, Baba Khodjee, Selim-il-Anagh, Mustafa Reezah, Burhan-ed-Deen, Mohammed Ben Osman, Ben Ali Nakkash (may their tribe decrease !) were not illuminating; neither were the mottoes in good Arabic, but somewhat irrelevant to their purpose, with which he prefaced his apocrypha. He attributes one strain to a sixteenth-century Zirbayeh, another to Lameejah, a third to a phonetic nightingale called Waheedi. He abstracts from a manuscript in possession of " the queen of Transoxiana " one of the loveliest of his songs, and fathers it upon Al Makeenah, a fighting bard of his fancy. Once he was brought to task for concealing himself under the cloak of Hafiz, whereupon he replied that any critic could discern that the verses were only Hafiz ! His custom was to leave Hafiz alone, with Saadi and Omar, these being persons somewhat familiar to the general. The poets he courts are more preciously private to himself than ever Cyril Tourneur was, years ago, to the elect. Some of their names stand out memorably bright, and only just beneath those of the splendid phantom Mirza Schaffy, and the Haji-Abdu el-Yezdi, who had some reality so long as Sir Richard Burton lived. The attention of a competent Orientalist may never have been drawn to specifications which would at once throw the unwary off the trail ; but it is likely that they passed with modest minor scholars who would have suspected anybody of this roguery sooner than innocent bespectacled Mangan.

It is as a son of the Prophet that he claims his full applause. *Al Hassan* is more than equalled by *The Wail and Warning of the Three Khalendeers* (which Thackeray would have relished had he known it), by *The Time of the Barmecides*, the vehement *Howling Song of Al Mohara*, and others, drawn, like these, from the impossible Persian, and many of which are only to be found scattered up and down the capital-lettered yellow pages of extinct provincial journals.

It is more than likely that his taste for Eastern poetry, gratified under such ironic conditions, was in Mangan a reaction from the little he knew of the bardic antiquities of his own Ireland ; for he appears to have been much at-

tracted to Vallencey's most tenable theory that
the Milesians were the lost tribe of Israel. The
all-but-identity of the typical Turkish wail : —

" Wulla-hu, wulwulla-hu ! "

with the more melodious Gaelic

" Ullu, ullalu ! "

fascinated him; and he used both rather too
freely.   Working on Shane O'Golain's *Lament*
in 1848 he took fire, at three o'clock of a Fri-
day morning, and resolved to give as good as
he got.   " I will shortly send you," he writes
to his patron, " a funeral wail from the Turkish,
on the decease of one of the Sultans.   The
spirit of the composition closely resembles what
we meet with in similar Irish poems."   (Marry
come up! so it must, slyest of Mangans.)   This
was probably the *Elegy for Sulieman the Magnificent*, a fairly unimpressive production.   With
his genius for analogies, the " translator " found
ancient Irish, at second-hand, as Oriental as
need be.   Adjurations, apostrophes, superla-
tives, monotones, reiterations, vague but bold
colors, belonged, as outstanding features, to
both languages; and to all these characteris-
tics his own habits of speech and thought were
congenial.

What Matthew Arnold said of the Celtic

literature in general, may apply to Mangan's
share in it. "It is not great poetical work;
but it is poetry, with the air of greatness invest-
ing it." His Eastern fictions, like most of his
Western ones, deal usually with a mood· of
reminiscence and regret, and they have the arch
and poignant pathos in which English song is
not rich. The mournful echo of days gone by,
the light tingeing a present cloud from the absent sun, are everywhere in Mangan's world.
He looks back forever, not with moping, but
with a certain shrewd sense of triumph and
heartiness. He embraces the tragical to-day,
like Pascal's crushed and thinking reed of
mankind, *parce qu'il sait qu'il meurt, et l'avan-
tage que l'univers a sur lui: l'univers n'en sait
rien.* He delivers a lament as if it were a
cheer; in his strange temperament they blend
in one. It is clear to posterity that this looking back on rosy hours is a sham, a poet's
fantasy. What idyllic yesterday cradled and
reared so ill-adventured a soul? Out of his
imagination his "rich Bagdad" never existed;
though it be cherished there as only the solitary and disregarded intelligence can cherish its
ideal, he is lord of it yet, and can bid it vanish, at one imperious gesture of relinquishment.
Down tumbles Bagdad! The crash thereof is
in the public ears; and who will refuse to be-

H

lieve that there was a Clarence Mangan who
knew something of the blessed Orient, something, too, of felicity, even though it passed?

XI

With his provoking banter, in April of 1840,
he calls attention, in a magazine, to *The Time of
the Barmecides*, a composition of his own, which
he had given to the same pages just a year
before, and which he had bettered infinitely,
meanwhile, by a few discreet touches. Starting off with a motto (obviously of his own
manufacture), that

" There runs thro' all the dells of Time
No stream like Youth again,"

he proceeds to explain the second appearance
of his favored lyric. " It was published some
months back, but in such suspicious company
that it probably remained unread, except by
the very few persons who have always believed
us too honorable to attempt imposing on or
mystifying the public. We now, therefore,
take the liberty of reintroducing the poem to
general notice, embellished with improvements,
merely premising that if any lady or gentleman wishes to have a copy of the original (or,

indeed, of any originals of our oversettings),
we are quite ready to come forward and treat:
terms cash, except to young ladies." With
talk of such vain and transparent nonsense,
Mangan attempts to parry his rightful praise.
He would have us think that to his laborious
searching and transcribing, "with the help," as
he says, of "punch and patience," we are in-
debted for the existence of his finest work.
But the punch is direct from Castaly's well,
and the patience covers the rapturous drudgery
known to all true art. What held him back
from acknowledging his own homespun glories
was a trait both of shyness and of perversity.
He must have been conscious that his rhythms
were nothing short of innovations. Nearly
everything which bears his name has a voluptu-
ous dance-measure which no one had written
before: a beauty so novel and compelling,
that it is remarkable it has lacked recognition.
With characteristic shrinking, Mangan sealed
his charter of merit to supposititious ancients
and aliens. Perspicacious readers are besought
to consider it less likely that in one poet was
a voice of such individuality that it breaks
forth through a hundred disguises, than that
bards resident through the ages in the four
zones, Jew and Gentile,

"Bold Plutarch, Neptune, and Nicodemus,"

are the co-heirs of the self-same astonishing style. Wits were at work on him, even as on a rebus, long before he died. Some anonymous writer, aware of a new sound when he heard it, addressed to him an apostrophe not idle, since it shows that the sagacious race of mousers abides always and everywhere, and that, according to a metaphysical truism made famous by President Lincoln's homely adaptation of it, no one person can deceive all:—

"Various and curious are thy strains, O Clarence
    Mangan,
Rhyming and chiming in a very odd way;
Rhyming and chiming! and the like of them no
    man can
Easily find in a long summer's day."

Mangan's shibboleth is the refrain. The refrain is characteristic, in some shape or other, of all old poetry. It belongs to Judea and Greece, no less than to northern France, to the England of the Percy Reliques, and the Persianized Germany of Mangan's study. After a long lapse, it had its first full modern use in *The Ancient Mariner*, and in the peculiar cadence of all Coleridge's stops and keys. The fact that at divers periods, fashions of thoughts and speech infect the air, is a vindication of many laurelled heads; for it is a theory which pinches

nobody.   Almost on the same morning, within
twenty years of Coleridge's retirement to High-
gate, Mrs. Browning, Mangan, and Edgar Allan
Poe were involuntarily conspiring to fix and
perpetuate a poetic accident, destined to its
subtlest and not wholly unforeseen collateral
development in Rossetti.   Among these, Mrs.
Browning invented and foreshadowed much,
but with a light hand.   Poe's ringing of /the
word-changes is, on the other hand, so bold,
that any successor who approximates his manner is sure now of smiling detection and dis-
couragement.   Whatever recalls

> " Come, let the burial rite be read,
>   The funeral song be sung!
> An anthem for the queenliest dead
>   That ever died so young;
> A dirge for her, the doubly dead,
>   In that she died so young,"

is all very fine, we say, but it will not do;
the thing was done to perfection once: we
must let Poe reign in his own kingdom.   Let
us have a care lest we are letting Poe reign in
Mangan's kingdom.   The unmistakable mark
of Poe's maturer poetry, the employment of
sonorous successive lines which cunningly fall
short of exact duplication, belong also to Mangan, in the same degree.   There is this passage

of his, for instance, in the reverie of the way-
farer beside the river Mourne, who longs for
everlasting rest delayed, and who hears, in answer, a prophetic voice from the martyred tree
in the saw-mill : —

> " ' For this grieve not; thou knowest what thanks
> The weary-souled and the meek owe
> To Death ! '   I awoke, and heard four planks
> Fall down with a saddening echo,
> I heard four planks
> Fall down with a hollow echo ! "

And one verse out of the powerful many which
bear the burden of " Karaman ! " will serve to
illustrate the point yet more clearly : —

> " I was mild as milk till then,
> I was soft as silk till then ;
> Now my breast is like a den,
> Karaman !
> Foul with blood and bones of men,
> Karaman !
> With blood and bones of slaughtered men,
> Karaman, O Karaman ! "

Were it not for the imperfect rhyme in the
Saw-Mill stanza, any critic would attribute all
the lines cited to Poe, both for manner, and
for perfect mastery of ghastly detail.

It happens that the Muse over in Dublin
has the advantage of priority.   Poe's maiden

work has not the lovely tautology which has since been associated with his name. Judging by the pains which he took to dissect the rainbow of his genius in his *Philosophy of Composition*, he would have us assured that *The Raven* was his earliest experiment in the values of that saying-over or singing-over which, like a looped ribbon, flutters about the close of so many of his posthumous verses. Moreover, *The Raven* was "only that and nothing more." Poe's own thrilling tale of *Ligeia*, dating from 1838, provided every one of the "properties" essential to the effect of *The Raven*, and even the same psychological situation. It is not inconceivable that the prose was converted into poetry, exclusively for the purpose of trying a rash harmonic experiment on an approved instrument. At any rate, the element in the great lyric which was not already in *Ligeia*, is precisely this haunting iteration of sweet sounds. *The Raven* was first published anonymously in the January of 1845. It spread like wildfire in America, and reached London the next year. In a letter to Poe, dated April, 1846, Miss Elizabeth Barrett Barrett says: "Your *Raven* has produced a sensation, a 'fit of horror,' here in England. Some of my friends are taken by the fear of it, and some by the music." The English parodies of it, which would certify

that it was popular and familiar, began in
1853. *Ulalume* appeared in *Colton's Review*,
in 1847; and it may be considered as the
perfect blossom of Poe's acquired tendencies.
Lenore, first intoned as *A Pæan* (1831), came
out in Mr. James Russell Lowell's journal, *The
Pioneer*, in 1843. It is instructive to observe
that it has not, there, a single touch of the
repetitions which now give it such memorable
glamour; the repetitions were superadded later
and on second thought. Now Mangan, from
1839 and 1840 on, bestowed on almost everything he wrote the curious involved diction in
question. Two poems of his in particular,
which have mere extrinsic value, may therefore
yield up their opening stanzas as arch-speci-
mens. *The Winniger Winehouse*, we are told,
is "slightly improved from Hoffmann of Fall-
ersleben." *The Kiosk of Moostanzar-Billah* has
no history.

> " Hurrah for the Winniger Winehouse,
>   The sanded Winniger Winehouse !
> Eighteen of us meet in a circle, and treat
> Each other all day at the Winehouse.
> As thinking but doubles men's troubles,
> 'Tis shirked in the emerald parlor;
> Tho' banks be broken and war lour,
> We've eyes alone for such bubbles

As wink on our cups in the Winehouse,
Our golden cups in the Winehouse,
(As poets would feign !) but 'tis glasses we drain
In the sanded Winniger Winehouse ! "

————

" The pall of the sunset fell
Vermilioning earth and water;
The bulbul's melody broke from the dell,
A song to the rose, the summer's daughter!
The lulling music of Tigris' flow
Was blended with echoes from many a mosque
As the muezzin chanted the *Allah-el-illah*:
Yet my heart in that hour was low,
For I stood in a ruined Kiosk:
O my heart in that hour was low
For I stood in the ruined Kiosk
Of the Caliph Moostanzar-Billah;
I mused alone in the ruined Kiosk
Of the mighty Moostanzar-Billah."

The same emphatic notes occur in *The Three Talismans*, *The Wayfaring Tree*, *The Saw-Mill*, and *The Karamanian Exile;* in *The Last Words of Al Hassan*, and in the very different and very beautiful *Time of the Barmecides;* in *The Wail and Warning of the Three Khalendeers*, and in *My Dark Rosaleen;* and something not far from them in *Night is Nearing*, *Twenty Golden Years ago*, *The Time ere the Roses were Blowing*,

and *The Howling Song*.   Indeed, it is difficult
to quote from him at all and not detect the accent associated forever with Poe.   Under cover
of his spurious Orientalism, Mangan allowed
himself much autobiographical utterance; and
he found it convenient, as an Oriental middle-
man, to introduce, and to fully develop, without suspicion from outsiders, his ornate original
da capo.   Indeed, one sometimes feels quite
certain that he was a practising Mussulman
only for the sake of it.   In *The Dervish and
the Vizier*, Mangan is his own superexcellent
parodist: here he breaks into a ridiculous ex-
aggeration of the refrain, in a comic narrative
of great gusto.   Having once mastered his invention, Mangan, in the end, came near being
mastered by it.   He imported a sort of stam-
mering into many of his renderings from foreign
languages, to the conceivable amazement of
dead authors; and the catch-word of a stanza
was often multiplied until it attained the nu-
merical importance of Mozart's triumphant
Amens.   No one will deny that the *Schwertlied*
itself gains by this vandalism.   Poe, in this re-
spect, is merely Manganesque.   In *The Dublin
University Magazine*, during the years when
Poe was attaining his zenith of success, figure
successive specimens of the unchanged art of
the man who had the start of him by at least

five years; for *The Barmecides* was in print in
1839, and *The Karamanian Exile*, a finished
model of its kind, was contemporary with the
as yet cisatlantic *Raven*, and the predecessor of
Ulalume, Lenore, Eulalie, For Annie, and the
rest. Coleridge's is too great a name by which ·
to measure, and Mrs. Browning is an influence
apart, when one comes to scrutinize the neck-
and-neck achievements of Mangan and Poe.

Mr. Joseph Skipsey openly implies that Poe
fell across Mangan's experimental measures
during his own editorial and journalistic career.
The proposition might have more weight,
coming from a more cautious pen; yet it is a
practicable guess, did one care to entertain it.
The American's thrift and hardihood, his
known accomplishment of buccaneering, benefi-
cent as it chanced to be in the application,
helped him to adopt and bring into notice any
reform perishing in obscure hands. Thus he
supplemented the octosyllabic cadences of *Lady
Geraldine's Courtship* in ·

" The silken, sad, uncertain rustling of each purple
    curtain,"

with a patrician aggressiveness never to be con-
founded with common theft. On the other
side, no arraignment of this sort can be brought
against poor chivalrous Mangan which would

not be a chronological absurdity.   Coleridge
the forerunner might have pushed his verbal
practice farther ; but he lacked the sensational-
ism which is a noble ingredient if used spar-
ingly and in season, and of which Mangan and
Poe, beyond all doubt, were possessed.   Now,
it is not to be forgotten that one of these two
lived and died, as it were, in a hole ; that at
no time was he in the current of events, or so
placed, withdrawn in the violet shadow of the
Wicklow Hills, that he could and would scan
even the near English horizon.   It was the
business of the other to sit in a watch-tower,

> "Where Helicon breaks down
> In cliff to the sea."

Poe, if it may be said respectfully, was what the
Gypsies call a *jinney-mengro :* one-who-knows-
what - is - up - and - cannot - be - gulled.   Under
circumstances comparatively kind, from an offi-
cial chair, and with the bravery which is half
the battle, he bequeathed to the soil of English literature a hitherto exotic beauty.   It is
unnecessary to ask whether he learned his lyric
latitude of phrase from *The Dublin University
Magazine.*   But Clarence Mangan, shrinking
like the Thane before the supernatural " All
hail hereafter ! " is the true founder, neverthe-

less, of the most picturesque feature in modern verse.

While Poe links himself for good with his immediate predecessors in *The Haunted Palace*, *The City by the Sea*, and the opening of *Al Aaraaf*, and so falls gracefully into his dynastic place, Mangan has wayward secondary leanings, sometimes to the whimsical, affectionate temper of Béranger, sometimes to the bare strength of the Elizabethans themselves, as in his lines where Fate

"Tolls the disastrous bell of all our years,"

a line as unlike as possible to

"Helen, thy beauty is to me
Like those Nicean barks of yore."

He is addicted to compound words; and in such mongrel usages as "youthhood," "gloom-somely," and "aptliest," he makes straight for the pitfalls dug for the radiant intelligence of Mrs. Browning. Poe is too "dainty, airy, amber-bright," for sophomoric blunders, for wretched puns, for breathless haste, for dactyls maimed and scarred in the wars. He never makes Mangan's lunges; his every cæsural pause is fixed by conclave of the Muses. And there is over all his entrancing work an air of

incomparable self-attentiveness, a touch of satisfied completion, as of a *coquette bien chaussée,
bien gantée.* The other's charm is less urban :

> " A winning wave, deserving note,
> In the tempestuous petticoat."

The two Celts had much, very much, in common ; Poe's Attic taste, sprung from his fortunate training, is responsible for most of the
difference. To affirm of him, as has often
been done, that he worshipped beauty with his
whole soul ; that he loved the occult sciences,
the phrenologists, and the old mystics ; that his
existence was but an affecting struggle with the
adversaries of darkness ; even that he was of a
frail physique, his forehead high and pale, the
lower part of his face sensitive and dejected ; —
this is to describe Mangan equally well. They
had kindred dreams ; they were haunted by the
same loathing of the " dishonor of the grave " ;
they died, under almost identical circumstances
of pain and mystery, in the same year. Their
respective sense of humor was unevenly appor-
tioned. In point of achievement, too, or of the
forces which make achievement possible, they
are hardly to be compared. Poe was ever the
artist ; his imagination was not only sumptu-
ous, but steadfast ; his utterances were fewer,
and had finality. In the moral contrast, it is

the Irish poet who gains. Poe, with his manifold gifts (if we may pervert the terms of Lamb's
theological thesis *not* "defended or oppugned,
or both, at Leipsic or Göttingen") was "of the
highest order of the seraphim illuminati who
sneer." He nursed grudges and hungered for
homage; he was seldom so happy as in a thriv-
ing quarrel. Mangan was a pattern of sweet
gratitude and deference, and left his art to
prosper or perish, as Heaven should please.

In 1803, the year of Mangan's birth, Mrs.
Hemans printed her first verses, and Moore,
already a popular young minstrel, was commis-
sioned to be Admiralty Registrar at Bermuda.
The *Lyrical Ballads* had sunk, softly as a snow-
flake, into the earth one twelvemonth before.
Mangan's early youth was the flowering-time
of Keats, Shelley, and Byron; and he was
writing for penny journals while the new minor
notes, Hood's, Praed's, Moore's, were filling
the air. He died, not companionless, with
Emily Brontë, Hartley Coleridge, and Thomas
Lovell Beddoes, in 1849: three spirits of lavish promise, defrauded and unfulfilled like his
own, yet happier than he, inasmuch as they
have had since many liegemen and remember-
ers. Let him come forward at last in a quieter
hour, with his own whimsical misgiving man-

ner, or with questions pathetically irrelevant, as
one whom the fairies had led astray : —

> "O sayest thou the soul shall climb
> The magic mount she trod of old,
> Ere childhood's time?"

He has been, for a half-century, wandering
on the dark marge of Lethe.   It will not do,
as yet, to startle him with gross applause.
Otherwise, his gratified editor would like to
repeat, introducing Clarence Mangan, the gallant words with which Schumann once began a
review of the young Chopin: "Hats off, gentlemen : a Genius!"

My Dark Rosaleen

And Other Translations from the Gaelic

MY DARK ROSALEEN [1] (1)

O my Dark Rosaleen,
Do not sigh, do not weep!
The priests are on the ocean green,
They march along the deep.
There's wine from the royal Pope
Upon the ocean green;
And Spanish ale shall give you hope,
My Dark Rosaleen!
My own Rosaleen!
Shall glad your heart, shall give you hope,
Shall give you health, and help, and hope,
My Dark Rosaleen!

Over hills and thro' dales,
Have I roamed for your sake;
All yesterday I sailed with sails
On river and on lake.
The Erne at its highest flood
I dashed across unseen,

[1] This impassioned song, entitled, in the original, *Roisin Dubb*, or The Black-Haired Little Rose, was written in the reign of Elizabeth by one of the poets of the celebrated Tyrconnellian chieftain, Hugh the Red O'Donnell. It purports to be an allegorical address from Hugh to Ireland on the subject of his love and struggles for her, and his resolve to raise her again to the glorious position she held as a nation, before the irruption of the Saxon and Norman spoilers.

[All the notes at the bottom of the page in this book are Mangan's own. Figures in parentheses refer to the Editor's notes at the end of the book.]

For there was lightning in my blood,
My Dark Rosaleen!
My own Rosaleen!
O there was lightning in my blood,
Red lightning lightened thro' my blood,
My Dark Rosaleen!

All day long, in unrest,
To and fro, do I move.
The very soul within my breast
Is wasted for you, love!
The heart in my bosom faints
To think of you, my queen,
My life of life, my saint of saints,
My Dark Rosaleen!
My own Rosaleen!
To hear your sweet and sad complaints,
My life, my love, my saint of saints,
My Dark Rosaleen!

Woe and pain, pain and woe,
Are my lot, night and noon,
To see your bright face clouded so,
Like to the mournful moon.
But yet will I rear your throne
Again in golden sheen;
'Tis you shall reign, shall reign alone,
My Dark Rosaleen!
My own Rosaleen!
'Tis you shall have the golden throne,
'Tis you shall reign, and reign alone,
My Dark Rosaleen!

Over dews, over sands,
Will I fly for your weal :
Your holy delicate white hands
Shall girdle me with steel.
At home in your emerald bowers,
From morning's dawn till e'en,
You'll pray for me, my flower of flowers,
My Dark Rosaleen !
My fond Rosaleen !
You'll think of me thro' daylight hours,
My virgin flower, my flower of flowers,
My Dark Rosaleen !

I could scale the blue air,
I could plough the high hills,
O I could kneel all night in prayer,
To heal your many ills !
And one beamy smile from you
Would float like light between
My toils and me, my own, my true,
My Dark Rosaleen !
My fond Rosaleen !
Would give me life and soul anew,
A second life, a soul anew,
My Dark Rosaleen !

O the Erne shall run red
With redundance of blood,
The earth shall rock beneath our tread,
And flames wrap hill and wood,
And gun-peal and slogan-cry
Wake many a glen serene,

Ere you shall fade, ere you shall die,
My Dark Rosaleen!
My own Rosaleen!
The Judgment Hour must first be nigh,
Ere you can fade, ere you can die,
My Dark Rosaleen!

PRINCE ALDFRID'S ITINERARY
THROUGH IRELAND[1]

I found in Innisfail the fair,
In Ireland, while in exile there,
Women of worth, both grave and gay men,
Many clerics and many laymen.

I travelled its fruitful provinces round,
And in every one of the five I found,
Alike in church and in palace hall,
Abundant apparel, and food for all.

Gold and silver I found in money;
Plenty of wheat and plenty of honey;
I found God's people rich in pity,
Found many a feast, and many a city.

I also found in Armagh the splendid,
Meekness, wisdom, and prudence blended,

---

[1] Amongst the Anglo-Saxon students resorting to Ireland was Prince Aldfrid, afterwards King of the Northumbrian Saxons. His having been educated there about the year 684 is corroborated by Venerable Bede in his *Life of S. Cutbbert*. The original poem of which this is a translation, attributed to Aldfrid, is still extant in the Irish language.

Fasting, as Christ hath recommended,
And noble councillors untranscended.

I found in each great church moreo'er,
Whether on island or on shore,
Piety, learning, fond affection,
Holy welcome and kind protection.

I found the good lay monks and brothers
Ever beseeching help for others,
And, in their keeping, the Holy Word
Pure as it came from Jesus the Lord.

I found in Munster unfettered of any,
Kings, and queens, and poets a many,
Poets well-skilled in music and measure;
Prosperous doings, mirth and pleasure.

I found in Connaught the just, redundance
Of riches, milk in lavish abundance;
Hospitality, vigor, fame,
In Cruachan's [1] land of heroic name.

I found in the country of Connall [2] the glorious,
Bravest heroes ever victorious;
Fair-complexioned men and warlike,
Ireland's lights, the high, the starlike!

I found in Ulster from hill to glen,
Hardy warriors, resolute men;

[1] Cruachan, or Croghan, was the name of the royal palace of Connaught.
[2] Tyrconnell, the present Donegal.

Beauty that bloomed when youth was gone,
And strength transmitted from sire to son.

I found in the noble district of Boyle,
(*MS. here illegible.*)
Brehons, Erenachs,[1] weapons bright,
And horsemen bold and sudden in fight.

I found in Leinster the smooth and sleek,
From Dublin to Slewmargy's [2] peak,
Flourishing pastures, valor, health,
Long-living worthies, commerce, wealth.

I found, besides, from Ara to Glea,
In the broad rich country of Ossorie,
Sweet fruits, good laws for all and each,
Great chess-players, men of truthful speech.

I found in Meath's fair principality
Virtue, vigor, and hospitality;
Candor, joyfulness, bravery, purity,
Ireland's bulwark and security.

I found strict morals in age and youth,
I found historians recording truth;
The things I sing of in verse unsmooth,
I found them all.   I have written sooth.[3]

[1] Brehon, a law judge ; Erenach, a ruler, an archdeacon.
[2] Slewmargy, a mountain in the Queen's County, near the river Barrow.
[3] "Bede assures us that the Irish were a harmless and friendly people.
To them many of the Angles had been accustomed to resort in search of
knowledge, and on all occasions had been received and supported gratuitously.
Aldfrid lived in spontaneous exile among the Scots (Irish) through his desire of knowledge, and was called to the throne of Northumbria after the
decease of his brother Egfrid in 685." — *Lingard's England*, vol. i. chap. 3.

KINKORA[1]

(MAC-LIAG)

O where, Kinkora! is Brian the Great,
And where is the beauty that once was thine?
O where are the princes and nobles that sate
At the feast in thy halls, and drank the red wine?
Where, O Kinkora?

O where, Kinkora! are thy valorous lords?
O whither, thou hospitable! are they gone?
O where are the Dalcassians of the golden swords?[2]
And where are the warriors Brian led on?
Where, O Kinkora?

And where is Morrough, the descendant of kings,
The defeater of a hundred, the daringly brave,
Who set but slight store by jewels and rings,
Who swam down the torrent and laughed at its wave?
Where, O Kinkora?

And where is Donogh, King Brian's worthy son?
And where is Conaing, the beautiful chief?

[1] This poem is ascribed to Mac-Liag, the secretary of Brian Boruimha, who fell at the battle of Clontarf, in 1014; and the subject of it is a lamentation for the fallen condition of Kinkora, the palace of that monarch, consequent on his death. The decease of Mac-Liag is recorded in the "*Annals of the Four Masters*," as having taken place in 1015. A great number of his poems are still in existence, but none of them has obtained a popularity so widely extended as his *Lament*. The palace of Kinkora, which was situated on the banks of the Shannon, near Killaloe, is now a heap of ruins.

[2] *Colg n-or*, or the swords *of Gold*, i.e. of the *Gold-bilted* Swords.

And Kian and Corc? Alas! they are gone:
They have left me this night alone with my grief!
Left me, Kinkora!

And where are the chiefs with whom Brian went forth?
The sons never-vanquished of Evin the brave,
The great King of Osnacht, renowned for his worth,
And the hosts of Baskinn from the western wave?
Where, O Kinkora?

O where is Duvlann of the swift-footed steeds?
And where is Kian who was son of Molloy?
And where is King Lonergan, the fame of whose deeds
In the red battle-field no time can destroy?
Where, O Kinkora?

And where is that youth of majestic height,
The faith-keeping Prince of the Scots? Even he,
As wide as his fame was, as great as was his might,
Was tributary, Kinkora, to thee!
Thee, O Kinkora!

They are gone, those heroes of royal birth
Who plundered no churches, and broke no trust;
'Tis weary for me to be living on earth
When they, O Kinkora, lie low in the dust.
Low, O Kinkora!

O never again will princes appear,
To rival the Dalcassians [1] of the cleaving swords;

---

[1] The Dalcassians were Brian's body-guard.

I can never dream of meeting afar or anear,
In the east or the west, such heroes and lords!
Never, Kinkora!

O dear are the images my memory calls up
Of Brian Boru! how he never would miss
To give me at the banquet, the first bright cup.
Ah! why did he heap on me honor like this?
Why, O Kinkora?

I am Mac-Liag, and my home is on the lake:
Thither often, to that palace whose beauty is fled,
Came Brian to ask me, and I went for his sake. —
O my grief! that I should live, and Brian be dead!
Dead, O Kinkora!

ST. PATRICK'S HYMN BEFORE TARA[1]

At Tara to-day, in this awful hour,
I call on the Holy Trinity!
Glory to Him who reigneth in power,
The God of the elements, Father, and Son,
And Paraclete Spirit, which Three are the One,
The ever-existing Divinity!

[1] The original Irish of this hymn was published by Dr. Petrie, in vol.
xviii., "Transactions of the Royal Irish Academy." It is in the Bearla
Feine, the most ancient dialect of the Irish, the same in which the Brehon
laws were written. It was printed from the *Liber Hymnorum*, preserved
in the Library of Trinity College, Dublin, a manuscript, which, as Dr.
Petrie proves by the authority of Usher and others, must be nearly twelve
hundred and fifty years old.

At Tara to-day I call on the Lord,
On Christ, the Omnipotent Word,
Who came to redeem from death and sin
Our fallen race;
And I put and I place
The virtue that lieth and liveth in
His Incarnation lowly,
His Baptism pure and holy,
His Life of toil, and tears, and affliction,
His dolorous Death, his Crucifixion,
His Burial, sacred and sad and lone,
His Resurrection to life again,
His glorious Ascension to Heaven's high throne,
And, lastly, his future dread
And terrible Coming to judge all men,
Both the living and dead; —

At Tara to-day I put and I place
The virtue that dwells in the Seraphim's love,
And the virtue and grace
That are in the obedience
And unshaken allegiance
Of all the Archangels and Angels above,
And in the hope of the Resurrection
To everlasting reward and election,
And in the prayers of the Fathers of old,
And in the truths the Prophets foretold,
And in the Apostles' manifold preachings,
And in the Confessors' faith and teachings,
And in the purity ever dwelling
Within the immaculate Virgin's breast,

And in the actions bright and excelling
Of all good men, the just and the blest ; —

At Tara to-day, in this fateful hour,
I place all Heaven with its power,
And the sun with its brightness,
And the snow with its whiteness,
And fire with all the strength it hath,
And lightning with its rapid wrath,
And the winds with their swiftness along their path,
And the sea with its deepness,
And the rocks with their steepness,
And the earth with its starkness [1] ; —
All these I place,
By God's almighty help and grace,
Between myself and the Powers of Darkness !

At Tara to-day
May God be my stay !
May the strength of God now nerve me !
May the power of God preserve me !
May God the Almighty be near me !
May God the Almighty espy me !
May God the Almighty hear me !
May God give me eloquent speech !
May the arm of God protect me !
May the wisdom of God direct me !
May God give me power to teach and to preach !
May the shield of God defend me !

[1] Properly, "strength," "firmness," from the Anglo-Saxon *stark*, "strong, stiff."

May the host of God attend me,
And ward me,
And guard me
Against the wiles of demons and devils,
Against the temptations of vices and evils,
Against the bad passions and wrathful will
Of the reckless mind and the wicked heart;
Against every man who designs me ill,
Whether leagued with others or plotting apart!

In this hour of hours,
I place all those powers
Between myself and every foe
Who threatens my body and soul
With danger or dole,
To protect me against the evils that flow
From lying soothsayers' incantations,
From the gloomy laws of the Gentile nations,
From heresy's hateful innovations,
From idolatry's rites and invocations;
Be those my defenders,
My guards against every ban,
And spells of smiths, and Druids, and women;
In fine, against every knowledge that renders
The light Heaven sends us dim in
The spirit and soul of man!

May Christ, I pray,
Protect me to-day
Against poison and fire,
Against drowning and wounding,

That so, in His grace abounding,
I may earn the preacher's hire!

Christ, as a light,
Illumine and guide me!
Christ as a shield, o'ershadow and cover me!
Christ be under me! Christ be over me!
Christ be beside me
On left hand and right!
Christ be before me, behind me, about me!
Christ this day be within and without me!

Christ, the lowly and meek,
Christ, the All-Powerful, be
In the heart of each to whom I speak,
In the mouth of each who speaks to me!
In all who draw near me,
Or see me or hear me!

At Tara to-day, in this awful hour,
I call on the Holy Trinity!
Glory to Him who reigneth in power,
The God of the Elements, Father, and Son,
And Paraclete Spirit, which Three are the One,
The ever-existing Divinity!

Salvation dwells with the Lord,
With Christ, the Omnipotent Word:
From generation to generation
Grant us, O Lord, thy grace and salvation!

O'DALY'S KEEN FOR O'NEILL (2)

O mourn, Erin, mourn!
He is lost, he is dead,
By whom thy proudest flag was borne,
Thy bravest heroes led:
The night-winds are uttering
Their orisons of woe,
The raven flaps his darkling wing
O'er the grave of Owen Roe,
Of him who should have been thy King,
The noble Owen Roe.

Alas, hapless land,
It is ever thus with thee;
The eternal destinies withstand
Thy struggle to be free.
One after one thy champions fall,
Thy valiant men lie low,
And now sleeps under shroud and pall
The gallant Owen Roe,
The worthiest warrior of them all,
The princely Owen Roe!

Where was sword, where was soul
Like to his below the skies?
Ah, many a century must roll
Ere such a chief shall rise!
I saw him in the battle's shock:
Tremendous was his blow:
As smites the sledge the anvil block,
His blade smote the foe.

He was a tower; a human rock
Was mighty Owen Roe.

Woe to us! Guilt and wrong
Triumph, while, to our grief,
We raise the *keen*, the funeral song
Above our fallen chief.
The proud usurper sways with power,
He rules in state and show,
While we lament our fallen tower,
Our leader, Owen Roe;
While we, like slaves, bow down and cower,
And weep for Owen Roe.

But the high will of Heaven
Be fulfilled evermore!
What tho' it leaveth us bereaven
And stricken to the core,
Amid our groans, amid our tears,
We still feel and know
That we shall meet in after years
The sainted Owen Roe:
In after years, in brighter spheres,
Our glorious Owen Roe!

THE FAIR HILLS OF EIRÉ, O

(DONOGH MAC CON-MARA) (3)

Take a blessing from my heart to the land of my
    birth,
And the fair hills of Eiré, O!

K

And to all that yet survive of Eibhear's tribe on earth,
On the fair hills of Eiré, O !
In that land so delightful the wild thrush's lay,
Seems to pour a lament forth for Eiré's decay.
Alas, alas, why pine I a thousand miles away
From the fair hills of Eiré, O !

The soil is rich and soft, the air is mild and bland,
Of the fair hills of Eiré, O !
Her barest rock is greener to me than this rude land;
O the fair hills of Eiré, O !
Her woods are tall and straight, grove rising over
        grove;
Trees flourish in her glens below and on her heights
        above;
Ah, in heart and in soul I shall ever, ever love
The fair hills of Eiré, O !

A noble tribe, moreover, are the now hapless Gael,
On the fair hills of Eiré, O !
A tribe in battle's hour unused to shrink or fail
On the fair hills of Eiré, O !
For this is my lament in bitterness outpoured
To see them slain or scattered by the Saxon sword:
O woe of woes to see a foreign spoiler horde
On the fair hills of Eiré, O !

Broad and tall rise the *cruachs* in the golden morning
        glow
On the fair hills of Eiré, O !
O'er her smooth grass for ever sweet cream and honey
        flow
On the fair hills of Eiré, O !

Oh, I long, I am pining, again to behold
The land that belongs to the brave Gael of old.
Far dearer to my heart than a gift of gems or gold
Are the fair hills of Eiré, O !

The dewdrops lie bright mid the grass and yellow
    corn
On the fair hills of Eiré, O !
The sweet-scented apples blush redly in the morn
On the fair hills of Eiré, O !
The water-cress and sorrel fill the vales below,
The streamlets are hushed till the evening breezes
    blow,
While the waves of the Suir, noble river ! ever flow
Neath the fair hills of Eiré, O !

A fruitful clime is Eiré's, through valley, meadow,
    plain,
And the fair hills of Eiré, O !
The very bread of life is in the yellow grain
On the fair hills of Eiré, O !
Far dearer unto me than the tones music yields
Is the lowing of the kine and the calves in her fields,
In the sunlight that shone long ago on the shields
Of the Gaels, on the fair hills of Eiré, O !

THE GERALDINE'S DAUGHTER (4)

(EGAN O'RAHILLY)

A beauty all stainless, a pearl of a maiden
Has plunged me in trouble, and wounded my heart.

With sorrow and gloom is my soul overladen,
An anguish is there, that will never depart.
I could voyage to Egypt across the deep water,
Nor care about bidding dear Eiré farewell,
So I only might gaze on the Geraldine's daughter,
And sit by her side in some green pleasant dell!

Her curling locks wave round her figure of lightness,
All dazzling and long, like the purest of gold;
Her blue eyes resemble twin stars in their brightness,
And her brow is like marble or wax to behold.
The radiance of heaven illumines her features
Where the snows and the rose have erected their
        throne;
It would seem that the sun had forgotten all
        creatures,
To shine on the Geraldine's daughter alone.

Her bosom is swan-white, her waist smooth and
        slender,
Her speech is like music, so sweet and so free.
The feelings that glow in her noble heart lend her
A mien and a majesty lovely to see.
Her lips, red as berries, but riper than any,
Would kiss away even a sorrow like mine!
No wonder such heroes and noblemen many
Should cross the blue ocean to kneel at her shrine.

She is sprung from the Geraldine race, the great
        Grecians,
Niece of Mileadh's sons of the Valorous Bands,

Those heroes, the seed of the olden Phœnicians,
Though now trodden down, without fame, without
    lands;
Of her ancestors flourished the Barrys and Poers,
To the Lords of Bunratty she too is allied,
And not a proud noble near Cashel's high towers
But is kin to this maiden, the Geraldine's pride.

Of Saxon or Gael there is none to excel in
Her wisdom, her features, her figure, this fair;
In all she surpasses the far-famous Helen,
Whose beauty drove thousands to death and despair.
Whoe'er could but gaze on her aspect so noble
Would feel from thenceforward all anguish depart;
Yet for me 'tis, alas, my worst woe and my trouble
That her image must always abide in my heart!

A LAMENTATION FOR THE DEATH OF SIR MAURICE FITZGERALD, KNIGHT OF KERRY, WHO WAS KILLED IN FLANDERS, IN 1642

(PIERCE FERRITER)

There was lifted up one voice of woe,
One lament of more than mortal grief,
Through the wide south to and fro,
For a fallen chief.
In the dead of night that cry thrilled thro' me;
I looked out upon the midnight air.

Mine own soul was all as gloomy,
As I knelt in prayer.

O'er Loch Gur, that night, once, twice, yea, thrice,
Passed a wail of anguish for the brave,
That half curdled into ice
Its moon-mirroring wave.
Then uprose a many-toned wild hymn in
Choral swell from Ogra's dark ravine,
And Mogeely's phantom women [1]
Mourned the Geraldine!

Far on Carah Mona's emerald plains
Shrieks and sighs were blended many hours,
And Fermoy in fitful strains
Answered from her towers.
Youghal, Kinalmeaky, Imokilly,
Mourned in concert, and their piercing *keen*
Woke to wondering life the stilly
Glens of Inchiquin.

From Loughmoe to yellow Dunanore
There was fear; the traders of Tralee
Gathered up their golden store,
And prepared to flee;
For in ship and hall, from night till morning
Showed the first faint beamings of the sun,
All the foreigners heard the warning
Of the dreaded one!

[1] Banshees.

" This," they spake, " portendeth death to us,
If we fly not swiftly from our fate."
Self-conceited idiots, thus
Ravingly to prate !
Not for base-born higgling Saxon trucksters
Ring laments like these by shore and sea ;
Not for churls with souls of hucksters
Waileth our banshee !

For the high Milesian race alone
Ever flows the music of her woe;
For slain heir to bygone throne,
And for chief laid low !
Hark ! . . . Again, methinks, I hear her weeping
Yonder.   Is she near me now, as then ?
Or was but the night-wind sweeping
Down the hollow glen ?

ELLEN BAWN (5)

(TRADITIONAL)

Ellen Bawn, O Ellen Bawn, you darling, darling
    dear, you,
Sit awhile beside me here ; I'll die unless I'm near
    you !
'Tis for you I'd swim the Suir and breast the Shan-
    non's waters ;
For, Ellen dear, you've not your peer in Galway's
    blooming daughters !

Had I Limerick's gems and gold at will to meet and
  measure,
Were Loughrea's abundance mine, and all Por-
  tumna's treasure,
These might lure me, might ensure me many and
  many a new love,
But ah! no bribe could pay your tribe for one like
  you, my true love!

Blessings be on Connaught! That's the place for
  sport and raking;
Blessings, too, my love, on you, a-sleeping and
  awaking!
I'd have met you, dearest Ellen, when the sun went
  under,
But, woe! the flooding Shannon broke across my
  path in thunder.

Ellen! I'd give all the deer in Limerick's parks and
  arbors,
Aye, and all the ships that rode last year in Munster
  harbors,
Could I blot from time the hour I first became your
  lover;
For O! you've given my heart a wound it never can
  recover!

Were to God that in the sod my corpse to-night were
  lying,
And the wild birds wheeling o'er it, and the winds
  a-sighing!

Since your cruel mother and your kindred choose to
    sever
Two hearts that Love would blend in one for ever
    and for ever.

O'HUSSEY'S ODE TO THE MAGUIRE[1] (6)

Where is my chief, my master, this bleak night,
    mavrone?
O cold, cold, miserably cold is this bleak night for
    Hugh!
Its showery, arrowy, speary sleet pierceth one thro'
    and thro',

[1] O'Hussey, the last hereditary bard of the great sept of Maguire, of
Fermanagh, who flourished about 1630, possessed a fine genius. He com-
menced his vocation when quite a youth, by a poem celebrating the escape
of the famous Hugh Roe O'Donnell from Dublin Castle, in 1591, into
which he had been treacherously betrayed. The noble ode which O'Hussey
addressed to Hugh Maguire, when that chief had gone on a dangerous expedition, in the depth of an unusually severe winter, is as interesting an example
of the devoted affection of the bard to his chief, and as vivid a picture of
intense desolation, as could be well conceived. Mr. Fergusson, in a fine
piece of criticism on this poem, remarks : "There is a vivid vigor in these
descriptions, and a savage power in the antithetical climax, which claim a
character almost approaching to sublimity. Nothing can be more graphic,
yet more diversified, than his images of unmitigated horror : nothing more
grandly startling than his heroic conception of the glow of glory triumphant
over frozen toil. We have never read this poem without recurring, and
that by no unworthy association, to Napoleon in his Russian campaign.
Yet, perhaps, O'Hussey has conjured up a picture of more inclement desolation, in his rude idea of northern horrors, than could be legitimately employed
by a poet of the present day, when the romance of geographical obscurity
no longer permits us to imagine the Phlegrean regions of endless storm,
where the snows of Hæmus fall mingled with the lightnings of Etna, amid
Bistonian wilds or Hyrcanian forests." — *Dublin University Magazine,*
vol. iv.

Pierceth one to the very bone.
Rolls real thunder? Or was that red livid light
Only a meteor? I scarce know; but through the
    midnight dim
The pitiless ice-wind streams. Except the hate that
    persecutes him,
Nothing hath crueler venomy might.

An awful, a tremendous night is this, meseems!
The flood-gates of the rivers of heaven, I think, have
    been burst wide;
Down from the overchargèd clouds, like to headlong
    ocean's tide,
Descends gray rain in roaring streams.

Tho' he were even a wolf ranging the round green
    woods,
Tho' he were even a pleasant salmon in the un-
    chainable sea,
Tho' he were a wild mountain eagle, he could scarce
    bear, he,
This sharp sore sleet, these howling floods.

O mournful is my soul this night for Hugh Maguire!
Darkly as in a dream he strays. Before him and
    behind
Triumphs the tyrannous anger of the wounding wind,
The wounding wind that burns as fire.

It is my bitter grief, it cuts me to the heart
That in the country of Clan Darry this should be his
    fate!

O woe is me, where is he? Wandering, houseless,
    desolate,
Alone, without or guide or chart!

Medreams I see just now his face, the strawberry-
    bright,
Uplifted to the blackened heavens, while the tempest-
    uous winds
Blow fiercely over and round him, and the smiting
    sleet-shower blinds
The hero of Galang to-night!

Large, large affliction unto me and mine it is
That one of his majestic bearing, his fair stately form,
Should thus be tortured and o'erborne; that this un-
    sparing storm
Should wreak its wrath on head like his!

That his great hand, so oft the avenger of the op-
    pressed,
Should this chill churlish night, perchance, be para-
    lyzed by frost;
While through some icicle-hung thicket, as one lorn
    and lost,
He walks and wanders without rest.

The tempest-driven torrent deluges the mead,
It overflows the low banks of the rivulets and ponds;
The lawns and pasture-grounds lie locked in icy
    bonds,
So that the cattle cannot feed.

The pale-bright margins of the streams are seen by
    none;
Rushes and sweeps along the untamable flood on
    every side;
It penetrates and fills the cottagers' dwellings far and
    wide:
Water and land are blent in one.

Through some dark woods, 'mid bones of monsters,
    Hugh now strays,
As he confronts the storm with anguished heart, but
    manly brow.
O what a sword-wound to that tender heart of his,
    were now
A backward glance at peaceful days!

But other thoughts are his, thoughts that can still in-
    spire
With joy and an onward-bounding hope the bosom of
    Mac-Nee:
Thoughts of his warriors charging like bright billows
    of the sea,
Borne on the wind's wings, flashing fire!

And tho' frost glaze to-night the clear dew of his
    eyes,
And white ice-gauntlets glove his noble fine fair fin-
    gers o'er,
A warm dress is to him that lightning-garb he ever
    wore,
The lightning of the soul, not skies.

AVRAN [1]

Hugh marched forth to fight : I grieved to see him so
   depart.
And lo ! to-night he wanders frozen, rain-drenched,
   sad, betrayed ;
But the memory of the lime-white mansions his right
   hand hath laid
In ashes, warms the hero's heart !

A LAMENT FOR THE PRINCES OF TY-
RONE AND TYRCONNELL, BURIED IN
SAN PIETRO MONTORIO AT ROME [2]

(OWEN ROE MAC AN BHAIRD)

O woman of the piercing wail, (7)
Who mournest o'er yon mound of clay
With sigh and groan,
Would God thou wert among the Gael !
Thou wouldst not then from day to day
Weep thus alone.

[1] A concluding stanza, generally intended as a recapitulation of the entire
poem.
[2] This is an elegy on the death of the princes of Tyrone and Tyrconnell,
who, having fled with others from Ireland in the year 1607, and afterwards
dying in Rome, were interred on St. Peter's Hill in one grave.   The poem
is the production of The O'Donnell's bard, Owen Roe Mac an Bhaird, or
Ward, who accompanied the family in their exile ; it is addressed to Nuala,
The O'Donnell's sister, who was also one of the fugitives.   As the circumstances connected with the flight of the northern earls, which led to
the subsequent confiscation of the six Ulster counties by James I. may not
be immediately in the recollection of many of our readers, it may be proper
briefly to state that it was caused by the discovery of a letter directed to Sir

'Twere long before around a grave
In green Tyrconnell, one could find
This loneliness;
Near where Beann-Boirche's banners wave,
Such grief as thine could ne'er have pined
Companionless.

William Ussher, Clerk of the Council, dropped in the council-chamber
on the seventh of May, and which accused the northern chieftains generally of a conspiracy to overthrow the government. This charge is now
totally disbelieved. As an illustration of the poem, and as an interesting
piece in itself of hitherto unpublished literature, we extract the account of
the flight as recorded in the *Annals of the Four Masters* and translated by
Mr. O'Donovan : "Maguire (Cuconnaught), and Donogh, son of Mahon,
who was son of the Bishop O'Brien, sailed in a ship to Ireland, and put in
at the harbor of Swilly. They then took with them from Ireland the earl
O'Neill (Hugh, son of Ferdoragh) and the Earl O'Donnell (Rory, son of
Hugh, who was son of Magnus) and many others of the nobles of the
province of Ulster. These are the persons who went with O'Neill,
namely : his Countess Catherina, daughter of Magennis, and her three
sons, Hugh, the Baron, John, and Brian; Art Oge, son of Cormac, who
was son of the Baron; Ferdoragh, son of Con, who was son of O'Neill;
Hugh Oge, son of Brian, who was son of Art O'Neill; and many others
of his most intimate friends. These were they who went with the Earl
O'Donnell, namely : Caffer, his brother, with his sister Nuala; Hugh, the
Earl's child, wanting three weeks of being one year old; Rose, daughter of
O'Doherty and wife of Caffer, with her son Hugh, aged two years and
three months; his (Rory's) brother's son Donnell Oge, son of Donnell;
Naghtan, son of Calvach, who was son of Donogh Cairbreach O'Donnell;
and many others of his intimate friends. They embarked on the festival of
the Holy Cross in autumn. This was a distinguished company; and it is
certain that the sea has not borne and the wind has not wafted, in modern
times, a number of persons in one ship more eminent, illustrious, or noble
in point of genealogy, heroic deeds, valor, feats of arms, and brave achievements than they. Would that God had but permitted them to remain in
their patrimonial inheritances until the children should arrive at the age of
manhood ! Woe to the heart that meditated, woe to the mind that conceived, woe to the council that recommended the project of this expedition,
without knowing whether they should, to the end of their lives, be able to
return to their native principalities or patrimonies." The Earl of Tyrone was
the illustrious Hugh O'Neill, the Irish leader in the wars against Elizabeth.

Beside the wave in Donegal,
In Antrim's glens, or fair Dromore,
Or Killillee,
Or where the sunny waters fall
At Assaroe, near Erna shore,
This could not be.
On Derry's plains, in rich Drumclieff,
Throughout Armagh the Great, renowned
In olden years,
No day could pass but woman's grief
Would rain upon the burial-ground
Fresh floods of tears!

O no!—From Shannon, Boyne, and Suir,
From high Dunluce's castle-walls,
From Lissadill,
Would flock alike both rich and poor:
One wail would rise from Cruachan's halls
To Tara hill;
And some would come from Barrow-side,
And many a maid would leave her home
On Leitrim's plains,
And by melodious Banna's tide,
And by the Mourne and Erne, to come
And swell thy strains!

Oh, horses' hoofs would trample down
The mount whereon the martyr-saint [1]

---

[1] St. Peter. This passage is not exactly a blunder, though at first it may seem one : the poet supposes the grave itself transferred to Ireland, and he naturally includes in the transference the whole of the immediate locality around the grave.

Was crucified;
From glen and hill, from plain and town,
One loud lament, one thrilling plaint,
Would echo wide.
There would not soon be found, I ween,
One foot of ground among those bands
For museful thought,
So many shriekers of the *keen* [1]
Would cry aloud, and clap their hands,
All woe-distraught!

Two princes of the line of Conn
Sleep in their cells of clay beside
O'Donnell Roe:
Three royal youths, alas! are gone,
Who lived for Erin's weal, but died
For Erin's woe.
Ah, could the men of Ireland read
The names these noteless burial-stones
Display to view,
Their wounded hearts afresh would bleed,
Their tears gush forth again, their groans
Resound anew!

The youths whose relics moulder here
Were sprung from Hugh, high prince and lord
Of Aileach's lands;
Thy noble brothers, justly dear,
Thy nephew, long to be deplored
By Ulster's bands.

---

[1] *Caoine*, the funeral-wail, pronounced *Keen.*

Theirs were not souls wherein dull time
Could domicile decay, or house
Decrepitude!
They passed from earth ere manhood's prime,
Ere years had power to dim their brows,
Or chill their blood.

And who can marvel o'er thy grief,
Or who can blame thy flowing tears,
That knows their source?
O'Donnell, Dunnasava's chief,
Cut off amid his vernal years,
Lies here a corse
Beside his brother Cathbar, whom
Tyrconnell of the Helmets mourns
In deep despair:
For valor, truth, and comely bloom,
For all that greatens and adorns,
A peerless pair.

Oh, had these twain, and he, the third,
The Lord of Mourne, O'Niall's son
(Their mate in death,
A prince in look, in deed and word),
Had these three heroes yielded on
The field their breath,
Oh, had they fallen on Criffan's plain,
There would not be a town nor clan
From shore to sea,
But would with shrieks bewail the slain,
Or chant aloud the exulting *rann*[1]
Of jubilee!

[1] Song.

L

When high the shout of battle rose,
On fields where freedom's torch still burned
Thro' Erin's gloom,
If one, if barely one of those
Were slain, all Ulster would have mourned
The hero's doom!
If at Athboy, where hosts of brave
Ulidian horsemen sank beneath
The shock of spears,
Young Hugh O'Niall had found a grave,
Long must the north have wept his death,
With heart-wrung tears!

If on the day of Ballachmyre
The Lord of Mourne had met, thus young,
A warrior's fate,
In vain would such as thou desire
To mourn, alone, the champion sprung
From Niall the Great!
No marvel this: for all the dead,
Heaped on the field, pile over pile,
At Mullach-brack,
Were scarce an *eric*[1] for his head,
If Death had stayed his footsteps, while
On victory's track!

If on the Day of Hostages
The fruit had from the parent bough
Been rudely torn,
In sight of Munster's bands, Mac-Nee's,

[1] A compensation or fine.

Such blow the blood of Conn, I trow,
Could ill have borne.
If on the day of Balloch-boy,
Some arm had laid, by foul surprise,
The chieftain low,
Even our victorious shout of joy
Would soon give place to rueful cries
And groans of woe!

If on the day the Saxon host
Were forced to fly, a day so great
For Ashanee,[1]
The chief had been untimely lost,
Our conquering troops should moderate
Their mirthful glee.
There would not lack on Lifford's day,
From Galway, from the glens of Boyle,
From Limerick towers,
A marshalled file, a long array
Of mourners to bedew the soil
With tears in showers!

If on the day a sterner fate
Compelled his flight from Athenry,
His blood had flowed,
What numbers all disconsolate
Would come unasked, and share with thee
Affliction's load!
If Derry's crimson field had seen
His life-blood offered up, though 'twere

1 Ballyshannon.

On victory's shrine,
A thousand cries would swell the *keen*,
A thousand voices of despair
Would echo thine!

Oh, had the fierce Dalcassian swarm
That bloody night on Fergus' banks,
But slain our chief
When rose his camp in wild alarm,
How would the triumph of his ranks   ?
Be dashed with grief!
How would the troops of Murbach mourn
If on the Curlew Mountains' day
Which England rued,
Some Saxon hand had left them lorn,
By shedding there, amid the fray,
Their prince's blood!

Red would have been our warrior's eyes
Had Roderick found on Sligo's field
A gory grave;
No northern chief would soon arise
So sage to guide, so strong to shield,
So swift to save.
Long would Leith-Cuinn[1] have wept if Hugh
Had met the death he oft had dealt
Among the foe;
But, had our Roderick fallen too,
All Erin must, alas, have felt
The deadly blow.

[1] Leith-Cuinn, northern half of Ireland.   Leith-Moga, southern half.

What do I say? Ah, woe is me!
Already we bewail in vain
Their fatal fall!
And Erin, once the great and free,
Now vainly mourns her breakless chain,
And iron thrall.
Then, daughter of O'Donnell, dry
Thine overflowing eyes, and turn
Thy heart aside,
For Adam's race is born to die,
And sternly the sepulchral urn
Mocks human pride.

Look not, nor sigh, for earthly throne,
Nor place thy trust in arm of clay,
But on thy knees
Uplift thy soul to God alone,
For all things go their destined way
As He decrees.
Embrace the faithful crucifix,
And seek the path of pain and prayer
Thy Saviour trod;
Nor let thy spirit intermix
With earthly hope, with worldly care,
Its groans to God!

And Thou, O mighty Lord! whose ways
Are far above our feeble minds
To understand,
Sustain us in these doleful days,
And render light the chain that binds
Our fallen land!

Look down upon our dreary state,
And thro' the ages that may still
Roll sadly on,
Watch thou o'er hapless Erin's fate,
And shield at least from darker ill
The blood of Conn !

A LOVE SONG (8)

(TRADITIONAL)

Lonely from my home I come,
To cast myself upon your tomb
And to weep.
Lonely from my lonesome home,
My lonesome house of grief and gloom,
While I keep
Vigil often all night long,
For your dear, dear sake,
Praying many a prayer, so wrong,
That my heart would break !

Gladly, O my blighted flower,
Sweet apple of my bosom's tree !
Would I now
Stretch me in your dark death-bower
Beside your corpse, and lovingly
Kiss your brow.
But we'll meet ere many a day
Never more to part,
For even now I feel the clay
Gathering round my heart.

In my soul doth darkness dwell,
And thro' its dreary winding caves
Ever flows,
Ever flows with moaning swell,
One ebbless flood of many waves
Which are woes.
Death, love, has me in his lures;
But that grieves not me,
So my ghost may meet with yours
On yon moon-loved lea.

When the neighbors near my cot
Believe me sunk in slumber deep,
I arise
(For, oh, 'tis a weary lot,
This watching aye, and wooing sleep
With hot eyes);
I arise, and seek your grave,
And pour forth my tears,
While the winds that nightly rave
Whistle in mine ears.

Often turns my memory back
To that dear evening in the dell,
When we twain
Sheltered by the sloe-bush black,
Sat, laughed, and talked, while thick sleet fell,
And cold rain.
Thanks to God! no guilty leaven
Dashed our childish mirth:
You rejoice for this in Heaven,
I not less on earth!

Love! the priests feel wroth with me,
To find I shrine your image still
In my breast,
Since you are gone eternally,
And your fair frame lies in the chill
Grave at rest;
But true love outlives the shroud,
Knows nor check nor change,
And beyond time's world of cloud
Still must reign and range.

Well may now your kindred mourn
The threats, the wiles, the cruel arts,
Long they tried
On the child they left forlorn!
They broke the tenderest heart of hearts,
And she died.
Curse upon the love of show!
Curse on pride and greed!
They would wed you " high "—and woe!
Here behold their meed.

A LULLABY

(OWEN ROE O'SULLIVAN) (9)

O hushaby, baby!   Why weepest thou?
The diadem yet shall adorn thy brow,
And the jewels thy sires had, long agone,
In the regal ages of Eoghan and Conn,
Shall all be thine.
O hushaby, hushaby, child of mine!

My sorrow, my woe, to see thy tears,
Pierce into my heart like spears.

I'll give thee that glorious apple of gold
The three fair goddesses sought of old,
I'll give thee the diamond sceptre of Pan,
And the rod with which Moses, that holiest man,
Wrought marvels divine:
O hushaby, hushaby, child of mine!

I'll give thee that courser, fleet on the plains,
That courser with golden saddle and reins,
Which Falvey rode, the mariner-lord,
When the blood of the Danes at Cashel-na-Nord
Flowed like to dark wine:
O hushaby, hushaby, child of mine!

I'll give thee the dazzling sword was worn
By Brian on Cluan-tarava's morn,
And the bow of Murrough, whose shaft shot gleams
That lightened as when the arrowy beams
Of the noon-sun shine:
O hushaby, hushaby, child of mine!

And the hound that was wont to speed amain
From Cashel's rock to Bunratty's plain,
And the eagle from gloomy Aherlow,
And the hawk of Skellig; all these I'll bestow
On thee and thy line:
O hushaby, hushaby, child of mine!

And the golden fleece that Jason bore
To Hellas' hero-peopled shore.

And the steed that Cuchullin bought of yore
With cloak and necklet and golden store
And meadows and kine:
O hushaby, hushaby, child of mine!

And Connal's unpierceable shirt of mail,
And the shield of Nish, the prince of the Gael;
These twain for thee, my babe, shall I win,
With the flashing spears of Achilles and Finn,
Each high as a pine:
O hushaby, hushaby, child of mine!

And the swords of Diarmuid and fierce Fingal,
The slayers on heath and (alas!) in hall;
And the charmed helmet that Oscar wore
When he left Mac Treoin to welter in gore,
Subdued and supine:
O hushaby, hushaby, child of mine!

And the jewel wherewith Queen Eofa proved
The valor and faith of the hero she loved;
The magic jewel that nerved his arm
To work his enemies deadly harm
On plain and on brine:
O hushaby, hushaby, child of mine!

And the wondrous cloak renowned in song,
The enchanted cloak of the dark Dubh-long,
By whose powerful aid he battled amid
The thick of his foes, unseen and hid.
This, too, shall be thine:
O hushaby, hushaby, child of mine!

The last, not least, of thy weapons, my son,
Shall be the glittering glaive of O'Dunn,
The gift from Ænghus' powerful hands,
The hewer-down of the Fenian bands
With edge so fine!
O hushaby, hushaby, child of mine!

And a princess too, transcending all
Who have held the hearts of men in thrall,
Transcending Helen of history,
Thy bride in thy palmier years shall be;
Thy bride heroine:
O hushaby, hushaby, child of mine!

Even Hebe, who fills the nectar up
For Love, in his luminous crystal cup,
Shall pour thee out a wine in thy dreams,
As bright as thy poet-father's themes
When inspired by the Nine.
O hushaby, hushaby, child of mine!

And silken robes, and sweet soft cates
Shall thou wear and eat, beyond thy mates.
Ah, see, here comes thy mother, Moirin!
She, too, has the soul of an Irish queen:
She scorns to repine!
Then hushaby, hushaby, child of mine!
My sorrow, my woe, to see thy tears,
Pierce into my heart like spears.

THE EXPEDITION AND DEATH OF
KING DATHY (10)

King Dathy assembled his Druids and Sages,
And thus he spake to them : "Druids and Sages!
What of King Dathy?
What is revealed in destiny's pages
Of him or his?   Hath he
Aught for the future to dread or to dree?
Good to rejoice in, or evil to flee?
Is he a foe of the Gall
Fitted to conquer, or fated to fall?"

And Beirdra the Druid made answer as thus:
(A priest of a hundred years was he.)
"Dathy! thy fate is not hidden from us!
Hear it thro' me!
Thou shalt work thine own will:
Thou shalt slay, thou shalt prey,
And be conqueror still!
Thee the earth shall not harm!
Thee we charter and charm
From all evil and ill;
Thee the laurel shall crown!
Thee the wave shall not drown!
Thee the chain shall not bind!
Thee the spear shall not find!
Thee the sword shall not slay!
Thee the shaft shall not pierce!
Thou, therefore, be fearless and fierce
And sail with thy warriors away
To the lands of the Gall,

There to slaughter and sway,
And be victor o'er all!"

So Dathy he sailed away, away
Over the deep resounding sea;
Sailed with his hosts in armor gray
Over the deep resounding sea,
Many a night and many a day;
And many an islet conquered he,
He and his hosts in armor gray.
And the billow drowned him not,
And the fetter bound him not,
And the blue spear found him not,
And the red sword slew him not,
And the swift shaft knew him not,
And the foe o'erthrew him not.
Till one bright morn, at the base
Of the Alps, in rich Ausonia's regions,
His men stood marshalled face to face
With the mighty Roman legions.
Noble foes!
Christian and heathen stood there among those,
Resolute all to overcome,
Or die for the eagles of ancient Rome!

When, behold! from a temple anear
Came forth an aged priest-like man
Of a countenance meek and clear;
Who, turning to Eiré's Ceann,[1]
Spake him as thus: "King Dathy, hear!

---

[1] *Ceann,* head, king.

Thee would I warn!
Retreat, retire : repent in time
The invader's crime.
Or better for thee thou hadst never been born!"
But Dathy replied : "False Nazarene!
Dost thou, then, menace Dathy, thou?
And dreamest thou that he will bow
To one unknown, to one so mean,
So powerless as a priest must be?
He scorns alike thy threats and thee!
On, on, my men, to victory!"

And, with loud shouts for Eiré's King,
The Irish rush to meet the foe,
And falchions clash and bucklers ring, —
When, lo!
Lo! a mighty earthquake shock!
And the cleft plains reel and rock;
Clouds of darkness pall the skies;
Thunder crashes,
Lightning flashes,
And in an instant Dathy lies
On the earth, a mass of blackened ashes!
Then, mournfully and dolefully,
The Irish warriors sailed away
Over the deep resounding sea,
Till, wearily and mournfully,
They anchored in Eblana's Bay.
Thus the Seanachies [1] and Sages
Tell this tale of long-gone ages.

---

[1] *Seanachies,* historians.

THE WOMAN OF THREE COWS[1]

(TRADITIONAL)

O woman of three cows, agragh! don't let your
tongue thus rattle:
O don't be saucy, don't be stiff, because you may
have cattle.
I've seen (and here's my hand to you, I only say
what's true!)
A many a one with twice your stock not half so
proud as you.

Good luck to you, don't scorn the poor, and don't
be their despiser,
For worldly wealth soon melts away, and cheats the
very miser.
And death soon strips the proudest wreath from
haughty human brows:
Then don't be stiff, and don't be proud, good
woman of three cows!

See where Momonia's heroes lie, proud Owen
More's descendants!
'Tis they that won the glorious name and had the
grand attendants:

[1] This ballad, which is of homely cast, was intended as a rebuke to the
saucy pride of a woman in humble life who assumed airs of consequence,
being the owner of three cows. Its author's name is unknown, but its age
can be determined from the language, as belonging to the early part of the
seventeenth century. That it was formerly very popular in Munster may be
concluded from the fact that the phrase " Easy, O woman of three cows ! "
has become a saying in that province on any occasion upon which it is desirable to lower the pretensions of a boastful or consequential person.

If they were forced to bow to fate, as every mortal
bows,
Can you be proud, can you be stiff, my woman of
three cows?

The brave sons of the Lord of Clare, they left the
land to mourning,
Mavrone![1] for they were banished, with no hope of
their returning:
Who knows in what abodes of want those youths
were driven to house?
Yet you can give yourself these airs, O woman of
three cows!

O think of Donnell of the Ships, the chief whom
nothing daunted!
See how he fell in distant Spain, unchronicled,
unchanted.
He sleeps, the great O'Sullivan, whom thunder
cannot rouse:
Then ask yourself, should you be proud, good
woman of three cows!

O'Ruark, Maguire, those souls of fire whose names
are shrined in story,
Think how their high achievements once made Erin's
greatest glory;
Yet now their bones lie mouldering under weeds and
cypress boughs,
And so, for all your pride, will yours, O woman of
three cows!

[1] My grief.

The O'Carrolls, also, famed when fame was only for
the boldest,
Rest in forgotten sepulchres with Erin's best and
oldest;
Yet who so great as they of yore in battle and
carouse?
Just think of that, and hide your head, good woman
of three cows.

Your neighbor's poor, and you, it seems, are big
with vain ideas,
Because, inagh,[1] you've got three cows; one more, I
see, than she has!
That tongue of yours wags more, at times, than
charity allows:
But if you're strong, be merciful, great woman of
three cows!

Avran

Now there you go: you still, of course, keep up your
scornful bearing;
And I'm too poor to hinder you. But, by the cloak
I'm wearing,
If I had but four cows myself, even though you
were my spouse,
I'd thwack you well to cure your pride, my woman
of three cows!

[1] Forsooth.

M

A FAREWELL TO PATRICK SARSFIELD, LORD LUCAN (11)

(TRADITIONAL)

Farewell, O Patrick Sarsfield : may luck be on your
    path !
Your camp is broken up; your work is marred for
    years.
But you go to kindle into flame the King of France's
    wrath,
Though you leave sick Eiré in tears.
(*Och, ochone !*)

May the white sun and moon rain glory on your
    head,
All hero as you are, and holy man of God !
To you the Saxons owe a many an hour of dread
In the land you have often trod.
(*Och, ochone !*)

The Son of Mary guard you, and bless you to the
    end !
'Tis altered is the time when your legions were astir.
When at Cullen you were hailed as a conqueror and
    friend,
And you crossed Narrow-water, near Birr.
(*Och, ochone !*)

I'll journey to the north, over mount, moor, and
    wave :
'Twas there I first beheld, drawn up in file and line,

The brilliant Irish hosts; they were bravest of the
    brave,
But, alas, they scorned to combine.
(*Och, ochone !*)

I saw the royal Boyne, when his billows flashed with
    blood;
I fought at Graine Og, where a thousand horsemen
    fell;
On the dark empurpled plain of Aughrim, too, I
    stood,
On the plain by Tuberdonny's well.
(*Och, ochone !*)

To the heroes of Limerick, the city of the fights,
Be my best blessing borne on the wings of the air!
We had card-playing there o'er our camp-fires at
    night,
And the Word of Life too, and prayer.
(*Och, ochone !*)

But for you, Londonderry, may plague smite and
    slay
Your people, may ruin desolate you stone by stone!
Thro' you there's many a gallant youth lies coffinless
    to-day,
With the winds for mourners alone.
(*Och, ochone !*)

I clomb the high hill on a fair summer noon,
And saw the Saxons muster, clad in armor blinding-
    bright:

Oh, rage withheld my hand, or gunsman and dragoon
Should have supped with Satan that night!
(*Och, ochone!*)

How many a noble soldier, how many a cavalier
Careered along this road, seven fleeting weeks ago,
With silver-hilted sword, with matchlock and with
      spear,
Who now, *mavrone!* lieth low.
(*Och, ochone!*)

All hail to thee, Ben Edir![1] but ah, on thy brow
I see a limping soldier, who battled and who bled
Last year in the cause of the Stuart, though now
The worthy is begging his bread.
(*Och, ochone!*)

And Diarmuid, O Diarmuid! he perished in the
      strife;
His head it was spiked upon a halbert high;
His colors they were trampled; he had no chance of
      life
If the Lord God Himself stood by!
(*Och, ochone!*)

But most, O my woe! I lament and lament
For the ten valiant heroes who dwell nigh the Nore,
And my three blessed brothers; they left me, and
      they went
To the wars, and returned no more.
(*Och, ochone!*)

---

[1] Ben Edir : the beautiful Hill of Howth, near Dublin.

On the bridge of the Boyne was our first overthrow;
By Slaney the next, for we battled without rest;
The third was at Aughrim.   O Eiré, thy woe
Is a sword in my bleeding breast.
(*Och, ochone!*)

Oh, the roof above our heads, it was barbarously fired,
While the black Orange guns blazed and bellowed
        around!
And as volley followed volley, Colonel Mitchel[1] in-
        quired,
Whither Lucan still stood his ground?
(*Och, ochone!*)

But O'Kelly still remains, to defy, and to toil.
He has memories that hell won't permit him to
        forget,
And a sword that will make the blue blood flow like oil
Upon many an Aughrim yet!
(*Och, ochone!*)

And I never shall believe that my fatherland can fall,
With the Burkes,[2] and the Decies, and the son of
        royal James,
And Talbot the captain, and Sarsfield above all,
The beloved of damsels and dames.
(*Och, ochone!*)

---

[1] Colonel Mitchelburne, the Governor of Derry, in the Williamite service.
[2] The five of the De Burgo or Burke family who were loyal to James II.:
Lords Clanrickard, Brittas, Bophin, Castleconnell, and Galway.   "The
son of royal James" is the famous James Fitz James, Duke of Berwick,
subsequently Marshal, Duke, and Peer of France.

THE RUINS OF DONEGAL CASTLE (12)

(TRADITIONAL)

O mournful, O forsaken pile
What desolation dost thou dree!
How tarnished is the beauty that was thine erewhile,
Thou mansion of chaste melody.

Demolished lie thy towers and halls;
A dark, unsightly earthen mound
Defaces the pure whiteness of thy shining walls,
And solitude doth gird thee round.

Fair fort, thine hour has come at length,
Thine older glory has gone by.
Lo, far beyond thy noble battlements of strength
Thy corner-stones all scattered lie.

Where now, O rival of the gold
Emania, be thy wine-cups all?
Alas, for these thou now hast nothing but the cold,
Cold stream that from the heavens doth fall!

Thy clay-choked gateways none can trace
Thou fortress of the once bright doors;
The limestones of thy summit now bestrew thy base,
Bestrew the outside of thy floors;

Above thy shattered window-sills
The music that to-day breaks forth
Is but the music of the wild winds of the hills,
The wild winds of the stormy north.

What spell o'er came thee, mighty fort,
What fatal fit of slumber strange,
O palace of the wine, O many-gated court !
That thou shouldst undergo this change ?

Thou wert, O bright-walled, beaming one
Thou cradle of high deeds and bold !
The Tara of assemblies to the sons of Conn,
Clan Connell's council-hall of old ;

Thou wert a new Emania, thou,
A northern Cruachan in thy might,
A dome like that which stands by Boyne's broad
        water now,
Thou Erin's Rome of all delight !

In thee were Ulster's tributes stored,
And lavished like the flowers in May.
And into thee were Connaught's thousand treasures
        poured,
Deserted tho' thou art to-day !

How often from thy turrets high,
Thy purple turrets, have we seen
Long lines of glittering ships, when summer-time
        drew nigh,
With masts and sails of snow-white sheen !

How often seen when gazing round
From thy tall towers, the hunting trains
The blood-enlivening chase, the horseman and the
        hound,
Thou fastness of a hundred plains !

How often to thy banquet bright
We have seen the strong-armed Gaels repair,
And when the feast was over, once again unite
For battle, in thy basscourt fair!

Alas for thee, thou fort forlorn;
Alas for thy low, lost estate:
It is my woe of woes, this melancholy morn
To see thee left thus desolate.

O there hath come of Connell's race
A many and many a gallant chief
Who, if he saw thee now, thou of the once glad
        face,
Could not dissemble his deep grief.

Could Manus of the lofty soul
Behold thee as this day thou art,
Thou of the regal towers! what bitter, bitter dole
What agony would rend his heart!

Could Hugh MacHugh's imaginings
Portray for him the rueful plight,
What anguish, O thou palace of the northern kings!
Were his, thro' many a sleepless night.

Could even the mighty prince whose choice
'Twas to o'erthrow thee, could Hugh Roe
But view thee now, methinks, he would not much
        rejoice
That he had laid thy turrets low.

Oh, who could dream that one like him,
One sprung of such a line as his,
Thou of the embellished walls! would be the man to
dim
Thy glories by a deed like this?

From Hugh O'Donnell, thine own brave
And far-famed sovereign, came the blow;
By him, thou lonesome castle o'er the Esky's wave!
By him was wrought thine overthrow.

Yet not because he wished thee ill,
Left he thee thus bereaven and void:
The prince of the victorious tribe of Dalach still
Loved thee, yea, thee whom he destroyed.

He brought upon thee all this woe,
Thou of the fair-proportioned walls!
Lest thou shouldst ever yield a shelter to the foe,
Shouldst house the black ferocious Galls;

Shouldst yet become, in saddest truth,
A *Dun-na-Gall*,[1] the stranger's own:
For this cause only, stronghold of the Gaelic youth!
Lie thy majestic towers o'erthrown.

It is a drear, a dismal sight,
This of thy ruin and decay,
Now that our kings, and bards, and men of mark of
might,
Are nameless exiles far away.

[1] Fort of the Foreigner.

Yet better thou shouldst fall, meseems,
By thine own king of many thrones,
Than that the truculent Galls should rear around thy
    streams
Dry mounds, and circles of great stones.

As doth in many a desperate case
The surgeon by the malady,
So hath, O shield and bulwark of great Coffey's race!
Thy royal master done by thee.

The surgeon, if he be but wise,
Examines till he learns and sees
Where lies the fountain of his patient's health, where
    lies
The germ and root of his disease;

Then cuts away the gangrened part,
That so the sounder may be freed
Ere the disease hath power to reach the sufferer's
    heart,
And so bring death without remead.

Now thou hast held the patient's place
And thy disease hath been the foe;
So he, thy surgeon, O proud house of Dalach's race!
Who should he be if not Hugh Roe?

But he, thus fated to destroy
Thy shining walls, will yet restore
And raise thee up anew in beauty and in joy,
So that thou shalt not sorrow more.

By God's help, he who wrought thy fall
Will reinstate thee yet in pride;
Thy variegated halls shall be rebuilded all,
Thy lofty courts, thy chambers wide.

Yes, thou shalt live again, and see
Thy youth renewed; thou shalt outshine
Thy former self by far, and Hugh shall reign in thee,
The Tyrconnellian's king, and thine.

SANCTA OPERA DOMINI.

(JOHN MURPHY)

Holy are the works of Mary's blessed Son,
Holy are His mercies unto every one.
Holy is the sun that lighteth heaven;
Holy is the weather, morn and even;
Holy is the wind that woos the flowers;
Holy are the gentle April showers;
Holy is the summer's cheering glow;
Holy is the rain God sends below.
Holy are all in His abodes of love,
Holy is every Heaven of His above,
Holy is the sun and every star:
Holy is He who sends their light afar. .
Holy are the winds that fall and rise;
Holy are the waters and the skies;
Holy is all outspread beneath His eye.
Holy are the birds He formed to fly;
Holy are the hazel woodlands green;
Holy are the vineyards in their sheen:

Holy are the fruits they bear and bring,
Holy is the earth wherefrom they spring.
Holy is the ever-circling Heaven;
Holy is every thought to Jesus given;
Holy is all that He hath made, and sees,
Holy are all His ways and His decrees.
Holy are the ocean strands and floods;
Holy are the dark umbrageous woods;
Holy are the herbs and plants and flowers;
Holy is all creation with her powers;
Holy are the earth's four-corner bosoms;
Holy are the mossy rocks and blossoms.
Holy is fire that giveth light and cheer;
Holy is all that I have written here.
Holy is the sea's voice, calm or hoarse,
Holy are the streamlets in their course;
Holy are the healthy moorlands bare,
Holy are the fishes, and the air.
Holy are the Counsel and the Will,
Holy are God's works, and most pure from ill.
Holy are His laws, His faith and troth;
Holy are His wrath and patience both.
Holy is Heaven with its nine Orders bright,
Holy is Jesus, its great Lord and light :
Holy is Heaven, above all holiness,
Holy is the King the angels bless.
Holy are the saints in Heaven that be;
Holy is the adorable Trinity :
Holy are all high Heaven's works and words,
Holy is love, the saints' love and the Lords'!

KATHALEEN NY–HOULAHAN [1] (13)

(TRADITIONAL)

Long they pine in weary woe, the nobles of our land,
Long they wander to and fro, proscribed, alas! and
    banned;
Feastless, houseless, altarless, they bear the exile's
    brand;
But their hope is in the coming-to of Kathaleen Ny-
    Houlahan!

Think her not a ghastly hag too hideous to be seen,
Call her not unseemly names, our matchless
    Kathaleen!
Young she is, and fair she is, and would be crowned
    a queen,
Were the king's son at home here with Kathaleen
    Ny-Houlahan!

Sweet and mild would look her face, O none so sweet
    and mild,
Could she crush the foes by whom her beauty is
    reviled;
Woollen plaids would grace herself, and robes of silk
    her child,
If the king's son were living here with Kathaleen
    Ny-Houlahan!

Sore disgrace it is to see the arbitress of thrones
Vassal to a *Saxoneen* of cold and sapless bones!

[1] *Anglice*, Catherine O'Holohan, a name by which Ireland was alle-
gorically known.

Bitter anguish wrings our souls; with heavy sighs
    and groans
We wait the young deliverer of Kathaleen Ny-
    Houlahan!

Let us pray to Him who holds life's issues in His
    hands,
Him who formed the mighty globe, with all its
    thousand lands;
Girdling them with seas and mountains, rivers deep,
    and strands,
To cast a look of pity upon Kathaleen Ny-Houlahan!

He who over sands and waves led Israel along,
He who fed with heavenly bread that chosen tribe
    and throng,
He who stood by Moses when his foes were fierce
    and strong, —
May He show forth His might in saving Kathaleen
    Ny-Houlahan!

WELCOME TO THE PRINCE

(WILLIAM HEFFERNAN) (14)

Lift up the drooping head,
Meehal Dubh Mac-Giolla Kierin![1]
Her blood yet boundeth red
Through the myriad veins of Erin.
No, no, she is not dead
Meehal Dubh Mac-Giolla Kierin!

[1] Dark Michael M'Gilla Kerin, Prince of Ossory.

Lo! she redeems
The lost years of bygone ages:
New glory beams
Henceforth on her history's pages!
Her long penitential night of sorrow
Yields at length before the reddening morrow!
You heard the thunder-shout,
Meehal Dubh Mac-Giolla Kierin!
Saw the lightning streaming out
O'er the purple hills of Erin!
And bide you yet in doubt,
Meehal Dubh Mac-Giolla Kierin?
O doubt no more!
Through Ulidia's voiceful valleys,
On Shannon's shore,
Freedom's burning spirit rallies.
Earth and Heaven unite in sign and omen [1]
Bodeful of the downfall of our foemen.

Thurot commands the North,
Meehal Dubh Mac-Giolla Kierin!
Louth sends her heroes forth
To hew down the foes of Erin!
Swords gleam in field and *gorth*,[2]
Meehal Dubh Mac-Giolla Kierin!
Up, up, my friend!
There's a glorious goal before us;

---

[1] This is an allusion to that well-known atmospherical phenomenon of the "cloud armies," which is said to have been so common about this period in Scotland.
[2] *Gorth* literally means Garden.

Here will we blend
Speech and soul in this grand chorus:
" By the Heaven that gives us one more token,
We will die, or see our shackles broken!"

Charles leaves the Grampian Hills,
Meehal Dubh Mac-Giolla Kierin!
Charles, whose appeal yet thrills
Like a clarion-blast, through Erin.
Charles, he whose image fills
Thy soul, too, Mac-Giolla Kierin!
Ten thousand strong,
His clans move in brilliant order,
Sure that ere long
He will march them o'er the border,
While the dark-haired daughters of the Highlands
Crown with wreaths the Monarch of three islands.

Fill, then, the ale-cup high,
Meehal Dubh Mac-Giolla Kierin!
Fill! the bright hour is nigh
That shall give her own to Erin.
Those who so sadly sigh,
Even as you, Mac-Giolla Kierin,
Henceforth shall sing.
Hark!   O'er heathery hill and dell come
Shouts for the King!
Welcome, our deliverer, welcome!
Thousands this glad night, ere turning bedward,
Will with us drink " Victory to Charles Edward!"

THE SONG OF GLADNESS

(WILLIAM HEFFERNAN)

It was on a balmy evening, as June was departing fast,
That alone, and meditating in grief on the times a-past,
I wandered through the gloomsome shades
Of bosky Aherlow,
A wilderness of glens and glades.
When suddenly, a thrilling strain of song
Broke forth upon the air in one incessant flow,
Sweeter it seemed to me, (both voice and word,)
Than harmony of the harp, or carol of the bird,
For it foretold fair Freedom's triumph, and the doom
  of Wrong.

The celestial hymns and anthems, that far o'er the
    sounding sea
Come to Erin from the temples of bright-bosomed
    Italy;
The music which from hill and rath
The playful fairy race
Pour on the wandering warrior's path,
Bewildering him with wonder and delight,
Or the cuckoo's full note from some green sunless
    place,
Some sunken thicket in a stilly wood,
Had less than that rich melody made mine Irish blood
Bound in its veins for ecstasy, or given my soul new
    might!

N

And while so I stood and listened, behold, thousand
    swarms of bees,
All arrayed in gay gold armor, shone red through the
    dusky trees!
I felt a boding in my soul,
A truthful boding too,
That Erin's days of gloom and dole
Will soon be but remembered as a dream,
And the olden glory show eclipséd by the new.
Where will the Usurper[1] then be?   Banished far!
Where his vile hireling henchmen?   Slaughtered all
    in war!
For blood shall rill down every hill, and blacken
    every stream.

I am Heffernan of Shronehill: my land mourns in
    thraldom long;
And I see but one sad sight here, the weak trampled
    by the strong.
Yet if to-morrow, underneath
A burial stone I lay,
Clasped in the skeleton arms of death,
And if a pilgrim wind again should waft
Over my noteless grave the song I heard to-day,
I would spring up revivified, reborn,
A living soul again, as on my birthday morn,
Ay! even though coffined, over-earthed, tombed-in,
    and epitaphed!

[1] George I.

THE DREAM OF JOHN MAC DONNELL

(JOHN MAC DONNELL, USUALLY CALLED MAC DONNELL CLARAGH)

I lay in unrest. Old thoughts of pain,
That I struggled in vain to smother,
Like midnight spectres haunted my brain ;
Dark fantasies chased each other ;
When, lo ! a figure — who might it be ?
A tall fair figure stood near me !
Who might it be ?   An unreal Banshee,
Or an angel sent to cheer me ?

Though years have rolled since then, yet now
My memory thrillingly lingers
On her awful charm, her waxen brow,
Her pale translucent fingers,
Her eyes that mirrored a wonder-world,
Her mien of unearthly mildness,
And her waving raven tresses that curled
To the ground in beautiful wildness.

" Whence comest thou, spirit ? " I asked, methought,
" Thou art not one of the banished ? "
Alas, for me, she answered nought,
But rose aloft and evanished ;
And a radiance, like to a glory, beamed
In the light she left behind her.
Long time I wept, and at last, medreamed,
I left my shieling to find her. (15)

And first I turned to the thunderous north,
To Gruagach's mansion kingly;
Untouching the earth, I then sped forth
To Inver-lough, and the shingly
And shining strand of the fishful Erne,
And thence to Cruachan the golden,
Of whose resplendent palace ye learn
So many a marvel olden.

I saw the Mourna's billows flow;
I passed the walls of Shenady,
And stood in the hero-thronged Ardroe,
Embosked amid greenwoods shady;
And visited that proud pile that stands
Above the Boyne's broad waters,
Where Ænghus dwells with his warrior-bands
And the fairest of Ulster's daughters.

To the halls of Mac Lir, to Creevroe's height,
To Tara, the glory of Erin,
To the fairy palace that glances bright
On the peak of the blue Cnocfeerin,
I vainly hied. I went west and east;
I travelled seaward and shoreward;
But thus was I greeted at field and at feast:
" Thy way lies onward and forward ! "

At last I reached, I wist not how,
The royal towers of Ival,
Which under the cliff's gigantic brow
Still rise without a rival.

And here were Thomond's chieftains all
With armor and swords and lances,
And here sweet music filled the hall,
And damsels charmed with dances.

And here, at length, on a silver throne
Half-seated, half-reclining,
With forehead white as the marble stone,
And garments starrily shining,
And features beyond a poet's pen,
The sweetest, saddest features,
Appeared before me once again
The fairest of living creatures!

"Draw near, O mortal!" she said with a sigh,
"And hear my mournful story.
The guardian spirit of Erin am I,
But dimmed is mine ancient glory.
My priests are banished, my warriors wear
No longer victory's garland,
And my child, my son, my beloved heir,
Is an exile in a far land."

I heard no more, I saw no more;
The bonds of slumber were broken:
And palace and hero, and river and shore
Had vanished and left no token.
Dissolved was the spell that had bound my will
And my fancy thus, for a season.
But a sorrow therefore hangs over me still
Despite the teachings of reason.

THE SORROWS OF INNISFAIL

(GEOFFREY KEATING) (16)

Through the long drear night I lie awake, for the
   sorrows of Innisfail.
My bleeding heart is ready to break; I cannot but
   weep and wail.
O shame and grief and wonder! her sons crouch
   lowly under
The footstool of the paltriest foe
That ever yet hath wrought them woe.

How long, O Mother of light and song, how long
   will they fail to see
That men must be bold, no less than strong, if they
   truly will to be free?
They sit but in silent sadness, while wrongs that
   should rouse them to madness,
Wrongs that might wake the very dead,
Are piled on thy devoted head!

Thy castles, thy towers, thy palaces proud, thy stately
   mansions all,
Are held by the knaves who crossed the waves to
   lord it in Brian's hall.
Britannia, alas! is portress in Cobhthach's golden
   fortress,
And Ulster's and Momonia's lands
Are in the robber stranger's hands.

The tribe of Eoghan is worn with woe; the O'Donnell reigns no more;
O'Niall's remains lie mouldering low, on Italy's far-off shore;
And the youths of the pleasant valley are scattered, and cannot rally,
While foreign despotism unfurls
A flag 'mid hordes of base-born churls.

The chieftains of Naas were valorous lords, but their valor was crushed by craft:
They fell beneath envy's butcherly dagger, and calumny's poisoned shaft.
A few of their mighty legions yet languish in alien regions,
But most of them, the frank, the free,
Were slain through Saxon perfidy.

Ah, lived the princes of Ainy's plains, and the heroes of green Domgole,
And the chiefs of the Mauige, we still might hope to baffle our doom and dole.
Well then might the dastards shiver who herd by the blue Bride river!
But ah, those great and glorious men
Shall draw no glaive on earth again!

All-powerful God! look down on the tribes who mourn throughout the land,
And raise them some deliverer up, of a strong and smiting hand.

Oh! suffer them not to perish, the race Thou wert
    wont to cherish,
But soon avenge their fathers' graves,
And burst the bonds that keep them slaves!

LEATHER AWAY WITH THE WATTLE, O! (17)

(THOMAS COTTER)

Last night, while stars did glisten
By a hillside near the cove,
I sat awhile to listen
The sweet bird's pleasant lays of love.
A damsel tall of stature
With golden tresses long and low,
Which, (loveliest sight in Nature!)
Down to the bright green grass did flow,
And breast as fair as snow in air,
Without compare for beauteous show,
Stood near, and sang me sweetly:
"Come, Leather Away with the Wattle, O!"

Her eyebrows dark and slender
Were each bended like a bow;
Her eyes beamed love as tender
As only poets feel and know;
Her face where rose and lily
Were both portrayed in brightest glow,
Her mien so mild and stilly,
All made my full heart overflow!

A tale she told of that Prince bold
Whose crown of gold the Gael doth hold.
I hearkened, all-delighted,
To " Leather Away with the Wattle, O ! "

I asked this lovely creature
Was she Helen famed of yore,
(So like she seemed in feature !)
Whose name will live forevermore;
Or Dierdre, meekest, fairest,
Whom Uisneach's sons wrought direful woe;
Or Cearnaid, richest, rarest,
Who first made mills on water go;
Or Meadhbh the young, of ringlets long ?
So sweet her song along did flow,
Her song so rich and charming
Of " Leather Away with the Wattle, O ! "

And thus in tones unbroken,
While sweet music filled her eye,
In accents blandly spoken
The damsel warbled this reply :
" Albeit I know and blame not
Your marvellous poetic lore,
You know mine ancient name not,
Tho' once renowned from shore to shore;
I am Innis famed, of Heroes named,
Forsaken, lost in pain and woe,
But waiting for a chorus
To ' Leather Away with the Wattle, O ! '

They died in war, for ages,
The brave sons of Art and Eoghan,

Mute are the bards and sages,
And ah, the priests are sad and lone.
But Charles, despising danger,
Shall soon ascend green Eiré's throne,
And drive the Saxon stranger
Afar from hence to seek his own.
Then, full of soul and freed from dole,
Without control the wine shall flow,
And we will sing in chorus:
'Come, Leather Away with the Wattle, O!'"

LAMENT FOR BANBA [1]

(EGAN O'RAHILLY)

O my land, O my love!
What a woe, and how deep,
Is thy death to my long-mourning soul!
God alone, God above,
Can awake thee from sleep,
Can release thee from bondage and dole!
(Alas, alas, and alas,
For the once proud people of Banba!)

As a tree in its prime,
Which the axe layeth low,
Didst thou fall, O unfortunate land!
Not by time, nor thy crime,
Came the shock and the blow:
They were given by a false felon hand!

[1] Banba (*Banva*) was one of the most ancient names given by the Bards
to Ireland.

(Alas, alas, and alas,
For the once proud people of Banba !)

O my grief of all griefs
Is to see how thy throne
Is usurped, whilst thyself art in thrall !
Other lands have their chiefs,
Have their kings; thou alone
Art a wife, yet a widow withal.
(Alas, alas, and alas,
For the once proud people of Banba !)

· The high house of O'Niall
Is gone down to the dust,
The O'Brien is clanless and banned;
And the steel, the red steel,
May no more be the trust
Of the faithful and brave in the land.
(Alas, alas, and alas,
For the once proud people of Banba !)

True, alas ! wrong and wrath
Were of old all too rife.
Deeds were done which no good man admires.
And perchance Heaven hath
Chastened us for the strife
And the blood-shedding ways of our sires !
(Alas, alas, and alas,
For the once proud people of Banba !)

But, no more ! This our doom,
While our hearts yet are warm,

Let us not over-weakly deplore;
For the hour soon may loom
When the Lord's mighty hand
Shall be raised for our rescue once more!
And our grief shall be turned into joy
For the still proud people of Banba!

THE DAWNING OF THE DAY[1]

· (o'DORAN)

'Twas a balmy summer morning,
Warm and early,
Such as only June bestows;
Everywhere, the earth adorning,
Dews lay pearly
In the lily-bell and rose.
Up from each green leafy bosk and hollow
Rose the blackbird's pleasant lay.
And the soft cuckoo was sure to follow.
'Twas the dawning of the day!

Through the perfumed air the golden
Bees flew round me;
Bright fish dazzled from the sea;
Till medreamt some faëry olden

---

[1] The following song, translated from the Irish of O'Doran, refers to a singular atmospherical phenomenon said to be sometimes observed at Black-rock, near Dundalk, at daybreak, by the fishermen of that locality.   Many similar narratives are to be met with in the poetry of almost all countries; but O'Doran has endeavored to give the legend a political coloring, of which, I apprehend, readers in general will hardly deem it susceptible.

World-spell bound me
In a trance of witchery!
Steeds pranced round anon with stateliest housings,
Bearing riders pranked in rich array,
Like flushed revellers after wine-carousings:
'Twas the dawning of the day!

Then a strain of song was chanted,
And the lightly
Floating sea-nymphs drew anear.
Then again the shore seemed haunted
By hosts brightly
Clad, and wielding shield and spear!
Then came battle-shouts, an onward rushing,
Swords, and chariots, and a phantom fray.
Then all vanished. The warm skies were blushing
In the dawning of the day!

Cities girt with glorious gardens,
(Whose immortal
Habitants, in robes of light,
Stood, methought, as angel-wardens
Nigh each portal,)
Now arose to daze my sight.
Eden spread around, revived and blooming;
When . . . lo! as I gazed, all passed away.
I saw but black rocks and billows looming
In the dim chill dawn of day.

DIRGE FOR THE O'SULLIVAN BEARE (18)

In Ivera there is darkness,
(Darkness, darkness;)
In Ivera there is darkness.
And the laughing dancer's tread,
And joyous music, and the voice of song
Are heard no more; the day it weareth long,
For O'Sullivan lies dead,
Dead in stiffest starkness,
(Stiffest starkness!)

O the false, false traitor Scully,
(Scully, Scully!)
O the false, false traitor Scully!
He who should have helped his chief,
He basely sold him, basely sold the good
Great man to whom he owed his life and blood.
Perfidy beyond belief!
God requite him fully,
(Well and fully.)

O may all earth's blackest evils,
(Evils, evils,)
O may all earth's blackest evils
Haunt him on life's briary path!
May sickness waste him to and thro' the bone!
And when he stands before God's judgment throne,
May that just God, in His wrath,
Give him up to devils,
(Up to devils!)

Never will we, O no, never,
(Never, never,)
Never will we, O no, never
Pardon him who thus could sell
His generous chief to death and foul disgrace!
May heaven's fair light grow black upon his face!
May the burning marl of hell
Be his bed for ever,
(And for ever!)

Didst thou fall by sword and slaughter,
(Slaughter, slaughter.)
Had they slain thee in fair slaughter,
Tho' thy corpse were one red wound,
I would not weep: but ah, the woe to kill,
To rack, to butcher thee; and, ghastlier still,
Drag thee, like a fish harpooned,
Thro' the blood-streaked water,
(Thro' the water!)

And thy headless trunk was buried,
(Buried, buried,)
And thy headless trunk was buried
Distant from thy fathers' graves;
In no green spot of holy Christian ground
They laid thee, 'neath no consecrated mound.
To a pit, by ruffian slaves,
Wert thou darkly hurried,
(Darkly hurried.)

And they spiked thy head so gory,
(Gory, gory,)

Yes! they spiked thy head so gory,
As thine were a felon's end,
High, high above the jail.   Tempest and rain
Alone shall wave those long black locks again,
Lightning only ever lend
Those dimmed eyes a glory,
(Lend a glory.)

There is keening, there is weeping,
(Weeping, weeping.)
There is keening, there is weeping
Thro' the once glad haunts of song;
Ivera's broken heart is bleeding now;
Funeral gloom has darkened every brow,
, And the chill day waxeth long,
For our chief lies sleeping,
(Ever sleeping.)

O thou ocean of blue billows!
(Billows, billows,)
O thou ocean of blue billows!
From Cork harbor to Bearhaven
A curse this blessed night lies on thy flood.
For with its wave is blent the pure heart-blood
Of that chief whose head, whose raven
Locks, the storm-wind pillows.
(Storm-wind pillows!)

Translations, Chiefly from the German

THE MAID OF ORLEANS

(SCHILLER)

At thee the mocker[1] sneers in cold derision,
Thro' thee he seeks to desecrate and dim
Glory for which he hath no soul nor vision,
For God and angel are but sounds with him.
He makes the jewels of the heart his booty,
And scoffs at man's belief and woman's beauty.

Yet thou, a lowly shepherdess, descended
Not from a kingly but a godly race,
Art crowned by Poesy : amid the splendid
Of Heaven's high stars she builds thy dwelling-
    place,
Garlands thy temples with a wreath of glory,
And swathes thy memory in eternal story.

The base of this weak world exult at seeing
The fair defaced, the lofty in the dust;
Yet grieve not : there are godlike hearts in being
Which worship still the beautiful and just.
Let Momus and his mummers please the crowd!
Of nobleness alone a noble mind is proud.

---

[1] Voltaire.

THE FISHERMAN

(GOETHE)

The waters rush, the waters roll; a fisherman sits
    angling by.
He gazes o'er their glancing floor with sleepy brow
    and listless eye;
And while he looks and while he lolls, the flood is
    moved as by a storm
And slowly from its heaving depth ascends a humid
    woman's form.

She sings, she speaks: " Why lure, why wile, with
    human craft, with human snare
My little brood, my helpless brood, to perish in this
    fiery air ?
Ah, couldst thou guess the dreamy bliss we feel
    below the purple sea,
Thou wouldst forsake the earth and all, to dwell
    beneath with them and me.

The moon, the sun, their travel done, come down to
    sleep in ocean caves;
They reascend their glorious thrones with doubled
    beauty from the waves.
Ah, sure the blue ethereal dew, the shining heaven
    these waters show,
Nay, e'en thine own reflected face, must draw thee,
    win thee, down below."

The waters rush, the waters roll; about his naked
  feet they move.
An aching longing fills his soul, as when we look on
  her we love.
She sings to him, she speaks to him : alas, he feels
  that all is o'er;
She drags him down; his senses swim: the fisherman is seen no more.

MIGNON'S SONG

(GOETHE)

O dost thou know the clime where citron fruits are
  blooming fair ?
The gold-hued orange burns amid the dusky greenery
  there ;
From skies of speckless blue are wafted airlets warm
  and soft ;
There sleepy myrtles grow; there trees of laurel
  stand aloft.
That bright land dost thou know ?
Thither with thee, my love, I long to go.

And dost thou know the pile, with roof on colon-
  nades reclining ?
The broad saloon is bright, the chambers there are
  darkly shining ;
And alabaster forms look down upon me pityingly :
" Alas, unhappy child, what ill the world has done to
  thee ! "

That dwelling dost thou know?
Thither, protector mine, with thee I'll go.

Knowest thou the mountain's brow?   Its pathway
    clouds and shadows cover:
Amid the darkling mist, the mule pursues his blind
    way over.
The dragon and his brood lurk in a thousand cavern-
    hollows;
The rent rock topples down; the headlong sweep of
    water follows.
That mountain dost thou know?
Thither our way lies.   Father! let us go.

NATURE MORE THAN SCIENCE

(RÜCKERT)

I have a thousand thousand lays,
Compact of myriad myriad words,
And so can sing a million ways,
Can play at pleasure on the chords
Of tunèd harp or heart;
Yet is there one sweet song
For which in vain I pine and long;
I cannot reach that song, with all my minstrel-art!

A shepherd sits within a dell
O'ercanopied from rain and heat:
A shallow but pellucid well
Doth ever bubble at his feet.

His pipe is but a leaf,
Yet there, above that stream,
He plays and plays, as in a dream,
One air, that steals away the senses like a thief.

A simple air, it seems in truth,
And who begins will end it soon;
Yet, when that hidden shepherd youth
So pours it in the ear of noon,
Tears flow from those anear.
All songs of yours and mine
Condensed in one, were less divine
Than that sweet air to sing, that sweet, sweet air to
    hear!

'Twas yesternoon he played it last:
The hummings of a hundred bees
Were in mine ears; yet, as I passed,
I heard him through the myrtle trees.
Stretched all along he lay
Mid foliage half-decayed;
His lambs were feeding while he played;
And sleepily wore on the stilly summer-day. (19)

THE DYING FLOWER

(RÜCKERT)

" Drop not, poor flower! There's hope for thee.
The spring again will breathe and burn,
And glory robe the kingly tree
Whose life is in the sun's return;

And once again its buds will chime
Their peal of joy from viewless bells,
Though all the long dark winter-time
They mourned within their dreary cells."

" Alas, no kingly tree am I,
No marvel of a thousand years :
I cannot dream a winter by,
And wake with song when spring appears !
At best, my life is kin to death ;
My little all of being flows
From summer's kiss, from summer's breath,
And sleeps in summer's grave of snows."

" Yet, grieve not ! Summer may depart,
And beauty seek a brighter home :
But thou that bearest in thy heart
The germ of many a life to come,
Mayst lightly reck of autumn's storms ;
Whate'er thy individual doom
Thine essence, blent with other forms,
Will still shine out in radiant bloom."

" Yes : moons will wane ; and bluer skies
Breathe blessing forth for flower and tree.
I know that while the unit dies,
The myriad live immortally ;
But shall my soul survive in them ?
Shall I be all I was before ?
Vain dream ! I wither, soul and stem :
I die, and know my place no more.

The sun may lavish life on them ;
His light, in summer morns and eves,
May color every dewy gem
That sparkles on their tender leaves ;
But this will not avail the dead :
The glory of his wondrous face
Who now rains lustre on my head,
Can only mock my burial-place.

And woe to me, fond foolish one,
To tempt an all-consuming ray,
To think a flower could love a sun,
Nor feel her soul dissolve away !
O could I be what once I was
How should I shun his fatal beam !
Wrapt in myself, my life should pass
But as a still dark painless dream.

But vainly in my bitterness
I speak the language of despair :
In life, in death, I still must bless
The sun, the light, the cradling air.
Mine early love to them I gave,
And now that yon bright orb on high
Illumines but a wider grave,
For them I breathe my final sigh.

How often soared my soul aloft
In balmy bliss too deep to speak,
When Zephyr came, and kissed with soft
Sweet incense-breath my blushing cheek,

When beauteous bees and butterflies
Flew round me in the summer beam,
Or when some virgin's glorious eyes
Bent o'er me like a dazzling dream!

Ah, yes!   I know myself a birth
Of that all-wise Almighty Love
Which made the flower to bloom on earth,
And sun and stars to burn above;
And if, like them, I fade and fail,
If I but share the common doom,
Let no lament of mine bewail
My dark descent to Hades' gloom.

Farewell, thou lamp of this green globe!
Thy light is on my dying face,
Thy glory tints my faded robe,
And clasps me in a death-embrace.
Farewell, thou balsam-dropping spring!
Farewell, ye skies that beam and weep!
Unhoping, and unmurmuring,
I bow my head and sink to sleep."

GONE IN THE WIND

(RÜCKERT)

Solomon, where is thy throne?   It is gone in the wind.
Babylon, where is thy might?   It is gone in the wind.
Like the swift shadows of noon, like the dreams of
      the blind,
Vanish the glories and pomps of the earth in the wind.

Man, canst thou build upon aught in the pride of thy
    mind?
Wisdom will teach thee that nothing can tarry behind :
Tho' there be thousand bright actions embalmed and
    enshrined,
Myriads and millions of brighter are snow in the wind.

Solomon, where is thy throne?   It is gone in the wind.
Babylon, where is thy might?   It is gone in the wind.
All that the genius of man hath achieved or designed
Waits but its hour to be dealt with as dust by the
    wind.

Say, what is pleasure?   A phantom, a mask undefined;
Science?   An almond, whereof we can pierce but the
    rind;
Honor and affluence?   *Firmans* that Fortune hath
    signed,
Only to glitter and pass on the wings of the wind.

Solomon, where is thy throne?   It is gone in the
    wind.
Babylon, where is thy might?   It is gone in the
    wind.
Who is the fortunate?   He who in anguish hath
    pined!
He shall rejoice when his relics are dust in the wind.

Mortal, be careful with what thy best hopes are en-
    twined;
Woe to the miners for Truth, where the lampless
    have mined!

Woe to the seekers on earth for what none ever find:
They and their trust shall be scattered like leaves on
the wind.

Solomon, where is thy throne?   It is gone in the
wind.
Babylon, where is thy might?   It is gone in the
wind.
Happy in death are they only whose hearts have
consigned
All earth's affections and longings and cares to the
wind.

Pity thou, reader, the madness of poor humankind
Raving of knowledge; (and Satan so busy to blind!)
Raving of glory, like me; for the garlands I bind,
Garlands of song, are but gathered, and strewn in the
wind.

Solomon, where is thy throne?   It is gone in the
wind.
Babylon, where is thy might?   It is gone in the
wind.
I, Abul-Namez, must rest; for my fire is declined,
And I hear voices from Hades like bells on the wind.

THE GLAIVE SONG

(THEODOR KÖRNER[1])

" Glaive that lightenest by my side,
What may mean thy bright sheen ?
Glaive that lightenest by my side,
Wouldst thou woo me as a bride,
To the red battle-ground,
Hurrah!
Where the thunders of the cannon resound?
Hurrah!
Where the thunders of the cannon resound ?"

" Gallant master, valiant knight!
I rejoice in thy voice!
Gallant master, valiant knight!
I so shine, so lighten bright,

---

[1] "Körner, as most of my readers are aware, was one of the most enthu-
siastic and heroic of those young German patriots who so nobly rose up in
the year 1813, to protect the liberties of their fatherland against foreign
aggression. He was gifted with both genius and courage of a high degree;
and the character of his short life, which terminated at the early age of
twenty-two, is faithfully symbolized by the lyre and sword which stand
crossed upon his tomb at Babelow, in Mecklenburgh-Schwerin. The following song, which he is said to have written a few hours before his death
on the battle-plain of Gadebusch, in August, 1813, has long held rank
among the young Germanists as their Marseillaise; but no translation of it
worth looking at, so far as I am aware, has as yet appeared in English, and
perhaps I may not have succeeded better than others in my attempt to trans-
pose the spirit of it into that language. To be thoroughly understood and
felt it should be heard in the Burschensaal at Jena, where the students sing it
in chorus, crossing their swords with each other at the recurrence of each
'Hurrah!'" It is needless to add that Mangan never so heard it.

I, thy bride and thy glaive,
Hurrah!
Because wedded to a hero so brave,
Hurrah!
Because wedded to a hero so brave!"

"True! my joyous brilliant steel,
I am brave, am no slave;
True! my joyous brilliant steel!
And to-day, for woe or weal,
Here I plight thee my troth,
Hurrah!
It is victory or death for us both!
Hurrah!
It is victory or death for us both!"

"O thy bride delights to hear
That glad shout thus rung out!
O thy bride delights to hear
That proud peal so clarion-clear!
When, O when dawns the day,
Hurrah!
When thou bearest thy beloved away,
Hurrah!
When thou bearest thy beloved away?"

"When the drums beat loud to arms
Then is born that bright morn!
When the drums beat loud to arms,
When the thrilling bugle warms
The quick blood in all veins;
Hurrah!

Then I bear thee to the red battle-plains,
Hurrah !
Then I bear thee to the red battle-plains ! ''

" O that glorious day of days,
May its noon shine out soon,
Shine out soon with blood-red rays !
O that glorious day of days !
May it dawn and expire,
Hurrah !
Amid trumpet-blasts and thunder and fire,
Hurrah !
Amid trumpet-blasts and thunder and fire ! ''

" Why so restless, bride of mine ?
Why just now startedst thou ?
Why so restless, bride of mine,
In that iron room of thine ?
Thou art restless and wild,
Hurrah !
Thou art wild in thy delight as a child,
Hurrah !
Thou art wild in thy delight as a child ! ''

" Wild I am in my delight —
Wild and glad, wild and mad !
Wild I am in my delight —
Thirsting, burning for the fight,
When the glaive and the gun,
Hurrah !
Blend the lightning and the earthquake in one,
Hurrah !
Blend the lightning and the earthquake in one ! ''

" Quiet thee, my hope, my heart :
Bear the gloom of thy room !
Quiet thee, my hope, my heart :
Bide a season where thou art.
Thou shalt soon be released,
Hurrah !
And shalt banquet at the great battle-feast,
Hurrah !
And shalt banquet at the great battle-feast ! "

" I must forth !   O let us rove,
Hand in hand, o'er the land.
I must forth !   I burn to rove
Through the gardens of my love,
Where the roses, blood-red,
Hurrah !
Bloom in brilliantest array o'er the dead,
Hurrah !
Bloom in brilliantest array o'er the dead ! "

" As thou wilt, then, faithful one !
South or north, we'll go forth !
As thou wilt, then, faithful one.
Let us follow fortune on
Over hill, dell, and heath,
Hurrah !
Till I deck thee with my first laurel-wreath,
Hurrah !
Till I deck thee with my first laurel-wreath ! "

" O joy ! joy !   Lead on, O lead !
Now are we truly free.

O joy! joy!   Lead on, O lead!
Onward, forward, will we speed
To the broad nuptial-plain,
Hurrah!
Where we'll wed amid the tempest and red rain,
Hurrah!
Where we'll wed amid the tempest and red rain!"

So spake out, in joy and pride,
On their way to the fray,
So spake out, in joy and pride
One young bridegroom and his bride.
Up, then, youth of the land!
Hurrah!
Up, and proffer your beloved the hand!
Hurrah!
Up and proffer your beloved the hand.

Let her not hang down her head,
Her, your bride, by your side!
Let her not hang down her head,
By your side, as one half-dead:
Let her feel your embrace,
Hurrah!
Let her glory shed its rays on your face,
Hurrah!
Let her glory shed its rays on your face!

Press her bright mouth unto yours!
Cold it seems, but its beams
Are the brave man's warmest lures.
Press her bright mouth unto yours!

P

She should not be denied,
Hurrah!
Cursed is he who basely turns from the bride,
Hurrah!
Cursed is he who basely turns from the bride.

Brothers, look! The morning breaks.
Up, arise! for time flies:
Brothers, look! The morning breaks,
The sky reddens, the earth shakes.
Are you true men and good?
Hurrah!
Then be foremost at the Bridal of Blood!
Hurrah!
Stand up foremost at the Bridal of Blood!

ALEXANDER THE GREAT AND THE TREE

(DE LA MOTTE FOUQUÉ)

The sun is warm, the air is bland,
The heavens wear that stainless blue
Which only in an orient land
The eye of man may view;
And lo! around, and all abroad
A glittering host, a mighty horde;
And at their head a demigod
Who slays with lightning sword.

The bright noon burns, but idly now
Those warriors rest by vale and hill,

And shadows on their leader's brow
Seem ominous of ill.
Spell-bound, he stands beside a tree;
And well he may, for, through its leaves
Unstirred by wind, come brokenly
Moans, as of one that grieves.

How strange! he thought: life is a boon
Given and resumed; but how, and when?
E'en now, I asked myself how soon
I should go home again;
How soon I might again behold
My mourning mother's tearful face,
How soon my kindred might enfold
Me in their dear embrace!

There was an Indian magian there,
And, stepping forth, he bent his knee.
" O King!" he said, " be wise: beware
This too prophetic tree."
" Ha!" cried the King, " thou knowest, then, seer,
What yon strange oracle reveals?"
" Alas!" the magian said, "I hear
Deep words like thunder-peals.

I hear the groans of more than man,
Hear tones that warn, denounce, beseech;
Hear, woe is me! how darkly ran
That strain of thrilling speech.
' O King,' it spake, ' all-trampling King,
Thou leadest legions from afar,
But battle droops his clotted wing, (20)
Night menaces thy star!

Fond visions of thy boyhood's years
Dawn like dim light upon thy soul;
Thou seest again thy mother's tears
Which love could not control.
Ah, thy career in sooth is run,
Ah, thou indeed returnest home;
The mother waits to clasp her son
Low in her gloomful dome!

Yet go rejoicing: he who reigns
O'er earth alone, leaves worlds unscanned;
Life binds the spirit as with chains:
Seek thou the phantom-land!
Leave conquest all it looks for here;
Leave willing slaves a bloody throne;
Thine henceforth is another sphere:
Death's realm, the dark unknown!'"

The magian ceased.   The leaves were hushed,
But wailings broke from all around;
Until the chief, whose red blood flushed
His cheek with hotter bound,
Spake in the tones of one with whom
Fear never yet had been a guest:
" And when doth Fate achieve my doom ?
And where shall be my rest ? "

" O noble heart ! " the magian said,
And tears unbidden filled his eyes,
" We should not weep for thee; the dead
Change but their home and skies;
The moon shall beam, the myrtles bloom
For thee no more; yet, sorrow not!

The immortal pomp of Hades' gloom
Best consecrates thy lot.

In June, in June, in laughing June,
And where the dells show deepest green,
Pavilioned overhead at noon
With gold and silver sheen,
These be for thee the place, the time.
Trust not thy heart, trust not thine eyes:
Beyond the mount thy warm hopes climb
The land of darkness lies!"

Unblenching at the fateful words,
The hero turned around in haste.
"On, on!" he cried, "ye million swords:
Your course, like mine, is traced.
Let me but close life's narrow span
Where weapons clash and banners wave!
I would not live to mourn that man
But conquers for a grave."

STREW THE WAY WITH FLOWERS

(HÖLTY)

O strew the way with rosy flowers,
And dupe with smiles thy grief and gloom!
For tarnished leaves and songless hours
Await thee in the tomb.
Lo, in the brilliant festal hall
How lightly youth and beauty tread!

Yet, gaze again : the grass is tall
Above their charnel bed.

In blaze of noon the jewelled bride
Before the altar plights her faith :
Ere weep the skies of eventide
Her eyes are dulled in death.
Then sigh no more.   If life be brief,
So are its woes ; and why repine ?
Pavilioned by the linden leaf,
We'll quaff the chaliced wine.

Wild music from the nightingale
Comes floating on the loaded breeze,
To mingle in the bowery vale
With hum of summer bees ;
Then taste the joys that God bestows,
The beaded wine, the faithful kiss !
For while the tide of pleasure flows,
Death bares his black abyss.

In vain the zephyr's breath perfumes
The house of death ; in vain its tones
Shall mourn at midnight round the tombs
Where sleep our blackening bones.
The star-bright bowl is broken there,
The witchery of the lute is o'er,
And, wreck of wrecks ! there lie the fair
Whose beauty wins no more.

THE ERL-KING'S DAUGHTER (21)

(HERDER)

Sir Olf rode fast toward Thurlston's walls
To meet his bride in his father's halls.

He saw blue lights flit over the graves;
The elves came forth from their forest caves.

They dance anear on the glossy strand,
And the erl-king's daughter held out her hand.

" Oh, welcome, Sir Olf! to our jubilee:
Step into the circle, and dance with me."

" I dare not dance, I dare not stay:
To-morrow will be my nuptial day!"

" Two golden spurs will I give to thee;
And I pray thee, Sir Olf, to tarry with me."

" I dare not tarry, I dare not delay:
To-morrow is fixed for my nuptial day!"

" Will give thee a shirt so white and fine
Was bleached yestreen in the new moonshine."

" I dare not hearken to elf nor fay!
To-morrow is fixed for my nuptial day."

" A measure of gold I will give unto thee;
And I pray thee, Sir Olf, to dance with me."

" The measure of gold will I carry away,
But I dare not dance, and I dare not stay."

" *Then, since thou wilt go, even go with a blight !*
A true-lover's token I leave thee, sir knight."

She lightly struck with her wand on his heart,
And he swooned and swooned from the deadly smart;

She lifted him up on his coal-black steed:
" *Now hie thee away with a fatal speed!* "

Then shone the moon, and howled the wolf,
And the sheen and the howl awoke Sir Olf.

He rode over mead, he rode over moor;
He rode till he rode to his own house door.

Within sat, white as the marble, his bride;
But his gray-haired mother stood watching outside.

" My son, my son, thou art haggard and wan!
Thy brow is the brow of a dying man."

" And haggard and wan I well may be,
For the erl-king's daughter hath wounded me."

" I pray thee, my son, dismount, and bide.
There is mist on the eyes of thy pining bride."

" O mother! I should but drop dead from my steed.
I will wander abroad for the strength I need."

"And what shall I tell thy bride, my son,
When the morning dawns, and the tiring is done?"

"Oh, tell my bride that I rode to the wood
With my hounds in leash, and my hawk in hood."

When morning dawned with crimson and gray,
The bride came forth in her wedding array.

They poured out mead, they poured out wine:
"Now, where is thy son, O gold-mother mine?"

"My son, gold-daughter, rode into the wood,
With his hounds in leash, and his hawk in hood."

Then the bride grew sick with an ominous dread:
"Ah, woe is me! for Sir Olf is dead."

She drooped like a lily that feels the blast;
She drooped, and drooped, till she died; at last

They rest in the charnel side by side,
The stricken Sir Olf and his faithful bride.

But the erl-king's daughter dances still
Where the moonlight sleeps on the frosted hill.

THE GRAVE, THE GRAVE

(MAHLMANN)

Blest are the dormant
In death : they repose
From bondage and torment,
From passions and woes,
From the yoke of the world and the snares of the
    traitor.
The grave, the grave is the true liberator !

Griefs chase one another
Around the earth's dome ;
In the arms of the mother
Alone is our home.
Woo pleasure, ye triflers !   The thoughtful are wiser :
The grave, the grave is their one tranquillizer !

Is the good man unfriended
On life's ocean-path,
Where storms have expended
Their turbulent wrath ?
Are his labors requited by slander and rancor ?
The grave, the grave is his sure bower-anchor !

To gaze on the faces
Of lost ones anew,
To lock in embraces
The loved and the true,
Were a rapture to make even Paradise brighter.
The grave, the grave is the great reuniter !

Crown the corpse then with laurels,
The conqueror's wreath,
Make joyous with carols
The chamber of death,
And welcome the victor with cymbal and psalter:
The grave, the grave is the only exalter!

A SONG

(CONRAD WETZEL)

When the roses blow,
Man looks out for brighter hours;
When the roses glow,
Hope relights her lampless bowers.
Much that seemed, in winter gloom,
Dark with heavy woe,
Wears a gladsome hue and bloom
When the roses blow,
When the roses blow;
Wears a gladsome hue and bloom
When the roses blow!

When the roses blow,
Love that slept shall wake anew;
Merrier blood shall flow
Through the springald's veins of blue.
And if sorrow wrang the heart,
Even that shall go:
Pain and mourning must depart
When the roses blow,
When the roses blow;

Pain and mourning must depart
When the roses blow !

When the roses blow, (22)
Look to heaven, my fainting soul :
There, in stainless show,
Spreads the veil that hides thy goal.
Not while winter breathes his blight,
Burst thy bonds below :
Let the earth look proud and bright,
Let the roses blow,
Let the roses blow.
O let earth look proud and bright,
Let the roses blow !

TO LUDWIG UHLAND ON THE LAST
VOLUME OF HIS POEMS (23)

(JUSTINUS KERNER)

As a headlong stream that winter had bound,
When spring re-showers her beams on the plains
Breaks loose with a fierce impatient sound
From its icy chains :

As a tree, despoiled by the axe of the north
Of his leaves of green, and fruits of gold,
New leaves, new fruits, afresh puts forth,
As bright as the old :

As riotous wine, whose fiery strength
By the walls of the flask was prisoned long,

Out-gushes in purple pride at length,
A bubbling song :

As the pealing of some vast organ floats
On the air to the ear of him who has heard,
In many long days, but the piping notes
Of the coppice bird :

So rushes, Uhland ! so streams and rolls
The flood of thy song, a flood of fire !
So thrills thro' the depths of all hearts and souls
The might of thy lyre !

` THE POET'S CONSOLATION (24)

(JUSTINUS KERNER)

What tho' no maiden's tears ever be shed
O'er my clay bed,
Yet will the generous night never refuse
To weep its dews.

And tho' no friendly hand garland the cross
Above my moss,
Still will the dear, dear moon tenderly shine
Down on that sign.

And if the saunterer-by songlessly pass
Thro' the long grass,
There will the noontide bee pleasantly hum, .
And warm winds come.

Yes, you at least, ye dells, meadows, and streams,
Stars and moonbeams,
Will think on him whose weak meritless lays
Teemed with your praise!

THE LOVE–ADIEU

(UHLAND)

Fare thee well, fare thee well, my dove!
Thou and I must sever;
One fond kiss, one fond kiss of love,
Ere we part for ever:

And one rosé, one red rose, Marie,
Choose me from the bowers;
But no fruit, ah! no fruit for me,
Naught but fragile flowers.

A DRINKING–SONG

(ALOYS SCHREIBER)

Look, look! this wine is German.
Therefore streams it full and flowing,
Therefore beams it bold and glowing;
Therefore, like a thirsty merman,
Quaff the brilliant cup divine:
Brother, this is German wine!

Fill, fill a bumper goblet!
Fill it high, and toast our olden

Fatherland, and them, the golden
Maids and men who aye ennoble it.
Fill the purple cup divine :
Brother, this is German wine !

Drink, drink to ancient usage :
May their memory greenly flourish,
Who of yore were first to nourish
Flesh and soul with this, and grew sage,
Quaffing such immortal wine.
Drink the Fathers of the vine !

Toast, toast the resurrection
Of our country from her torpor !
We have spurned the French usurper ;
Freedom binds us and affection,
Me with thee, and mine with thine :
Toast our triumph here in wine !

German worth and German wine,
German speech and German manners,
Be the motto on our banners !
None can tremble, none can pine,
While he drinks of German wine.

SWABIAN POPULAR SONG

Where are they, the belovèd,
The gladsome, all ?
Where are they, the belovèd,
The gladsome, all ?

They left the festal hearth and hall.
They pine afar from us in alien climes.
O, who shall bring them back to us once more?
Who shall restore
Life's fairy floral times?
Restore
Life's fairy floral times?

Where are they, the belovèd,
The gallant, all?
Where are they, the belovèd,
The gallant, all?
At freedom's thrilling clarion-call
They went forth in the pride of youthhood's powers.
O, who shall give them back to us once more?
Who shall restore
Long-buried hearts and hours?
Restore
Long-buried hearts and hours?

Where are they, the belovèd,
The gifted, all?
Where are they, the belovèd,
The gifted, all?
They would not yield their souls the thrall
Of gold, nor sell the glory of their lays.
O, who shall give them back to us once more?
Who shall restore
The bright young songful days?
Restore
The bright young songful days?

God only can restore us
The lost ones all,
But God He will restore us
The lost ones all!
What tho' the future's shadows fall
Dark o'er their fate, seen darker through our tears,
Our God will give them back to us once more.
He can restore
The vanished golden years;
Restore
The vanished golden years!

HOLINESS TO THE LORD

(OTTO RUNGE)

There blooms a beautiful Flower, it blooms in a far-
off land;
Its life has a mystic meaning for few to understand.
Its leaves illumine the valley, its odor scents the
wood;
And if evil men come near it, they grow for the
moment good.

When the winds are tranced in slumber, the rays of
this luminous Flower
Shed glory more than earthly o'er lake and hill and
bower;
The hut, the hall, the palace, yea, earth's forsakenest
sod,
Shine out in the wondrous lustre that fills the heaven
of God.

Q

Three Kings came once to a hostel wherein lay the
    Flower so rare :
A star shone over its roof, and they knelt adoring there.
Whenever thou seest a damsel whose young eyes
    dazzle and win,
O pray that her heart may cherish this Flower of
    Flowers within !

THE RIDE AROUND THE PARAPET (25)

(RÜCKERT)

She said : " I was not born to mope at home in lone-
    liness,"
The Lady Eleanora von Alleyne.
She said : " I was not born to mope at home in lone-
    liness.
When the heart is throbbing sorest, there is balsam in
    the forest,
There is balsam in the forest for its pain,"
Said the Lady Eleanora,
Said the Lady Eleanora von Alleyne.

She doffed her silks and pearls, and donned instead
    her hunting-gear,
The Lady Eleanora von Alleyne.
She doffed her silks and pearls, and donned instead
    her hunting-gear,
And, till summer-time was over, as a huntress and a rover
Did she couch upon the mountain and the plain,
She, the Lady Eleanora,
Noble Lady Eleanora von Alleyne.

Returning home again, she viewed with scorn the
    tournaments,
The Lady Eleanora von Alleyne.
Returning home again, she viewed with scorn the
    tournaments ;
She saw the morions cloven, and the crowning chap-
    lets woven,
And the sight awakened only the disdain
Of the Lady Eleanora,
Of the Lady Eleanora von Alleyne.

" My feeling towards man is one of utter scornful-
    ness,"
Said Lady Eleanora von Alleyne.
" My feeling towards man is one of utter scornful-
    ness ;
And he that would o'ercome it, let him ride around
    the summit
Of my battlemented castle by the Maine ! "
Said the Lady Eleanora,
Said the Lady Eleanora von Alleyne.

So came a knight anon to ride around the parapet
For Lady Eleanora von Alleyne.
So came a knight anon to ride around the parapet :
Man and horse were hurled together o'er the crags
    that beetled nether.
Said the lady, " There, I fancy, they'll remain ! "
Said the Lady Eleanora,
Queenly Lady Eleanora von Alleyne !

Then came another knight to ride around the parapet
For Lady Eleanora von Alleyne.
Then came another knight to ride around the parapet.
Man and horse fell down, asunder, o'er the crags that
    beetled under.
Said the lady, " They'll not leap the leap again! "
Said the Lady Eleanora,
Lovely Lady Eleanora von Alleyne.

Came other knights anon to ride around the parapet
For Lady Eleanora von Alleyne.
Came other knights anon to ride around the parapet;
Till six and thirty corses of both mangled men and
    horses
Had been sacrificèd victims at the fane
Of the Lady Eleanora,
Stately Lady Eleanora von Alleyne!

That woeful year was by, and Ritter none came after-
    wards
To Lady Eleanora von Alleyne.
That woeful year was by, and Ritter none came after-
    wards;
The castle's lonely basscourt looked a wild o'er-grown-
    ·   with-grass court;
'Twas abandoned by the Ritters and their train
To the Lady Eleanora,
Haughty Lady Eleanora von Alleyne!

She clomb the silent wall, she gazed around her sovran-
    like,
The Lady Eleanora von Alleyne!

She clomb the silent wall, she gazed around her sovran-
   like.
"And wherefore have departed all the brave, the lion-
   hearted,
Who have left me here to play the castellaine?"
Said the Lady Eleanora,
Said the Lady Eleanora von Alleyne.

"And is it fled for aye, the palmy time of chivalry?"
Cried Lady Eleanora von Alleyne.
"And is it fled for aye, the palmy time of chivalry?
Shame light upon the cravens! May their corpses
   gorge the ravens,
Since they tremble thus to wear a woman's chain,"
Said the Lady Eleanora,
Said the Lady Eleanora von Alleyne.

The story reached, at Gratz, the gallant Margrave
   Gondibert
Of Lady Eleanora von Alleyne.
The story reached, at Gratz, the gallant Margrave
   Gondibert.
Quoth he: "I trow the woman must be more or less
   than human;
She is worth a little peaceable campaign,
Is the Lady Eleanora,
Is the Lady Eleanora von Alleyne!"

He trained a horse to pace round narrow stones laid
   merlon-wise,
For Lady Eleanora von Alleyne.

He trained a horse to pace round narrow stones laid
    merlon-wise.
" Good gray! do thou thy duty; and this rocky-
    bosomed beauty
Shall be taught that all the vauntings are in vain
Of the Lady Eleanora,
Of the Lady Eleanora von Alleyne."

He left his castle-halls, he came to Lady Eleanor's,
The Lady Eleanora von Alleyne.
He left his castle-halls, he came to Lady Eleanor's.
"O lady best and fairest, here am I! and, if thou
    carest,
I will gallop round the parapet amain,
Noble Lady Eleanora,
Noble Lady Eleanora von Alleyne!"

She saw him spring to horse, that gallant Margrave
    Gondibert,
The Lady Eleanora von Alleyne.
She saw him spring to horse, that gallant Margrave
    Gondibert.
"O bitter, bitter sorrow! I shall weep for this
    to-morrow;
It were better that in battle he were slain,"
Said the Lady Eleanora,
Said the Lady Eleanora von Alleyne.

Then rode he round and round the battlemented
    parapet,
For Lady Eleanora von Alleyne.

Then rode he round and round the battlemented
 parapet :
The lady wept and trembled, and her paly face
 resembled,
As she looked away, a lily wet with rain ;
Hapless Lady Eleanora,
Hapless Lady Eleanora von Alleyne !

So rode he round and round the battlemented parapet,
For Lady Eleanora von Alleyne ;
So rode he round and round the battlemented parapet.
" Accursed be my ambition !   He but rideth to perdi-
 tion,
He but rideth to perdition without rein ! "
Wept the Lady Eleanora,
Wept the Lady Eleanora von Alleyne.

Yet rode he round and round the battlemented parapet,
For Lady Eleanora von Alleyne.
Yet rode he round and round the battlemented parapet.
Meanwhile her terror shook her, yea, her breath well
 nigh forsook her ;
Fire was burning in the bosom and the brain
Of the Lady Eleanora,
Of the Lady Eleanora von Alleyne !

Then rode he round and off the battlemented parapet,
To Lady Eleanora von Alleyne.
Then rode he round and off the battlemented parapet !
" Now blest be God for ever !   This is marvellous !
 I never

Cherished hope of laying eyes on thee again ! "
Cried the Lady Eleanora,
Joyous Lady Eleanora von Alleyne.

" The man of men thou art, for thou hast fairly con-
        quered me,
The Lady Eleanora von Alleyne !
The man of men thou art, for thou hast fairly con-
        quered me :
I greet thee as my lover, and, ere many days be
        over,
Thou shalt wed me and be lord of my domain ! "
Said the Lady Eleanora,
Said the Lady Eleanora von Alleyne.

Then bowed the graceful knight, the gallant Mar-
        grave Gondibert,
To Lady Eleanora von Alleyne.
Then bowed that graceful knight, the gallant Mar-
        grave Gondibert,
And thus he answered coldly : " There be many who
        as boldly
Will adventure an achievement they disdain
For the Lady Eleanora,
For the Lady Eleanora von Alleyne.

Mayest bide until they come, O stately Lady
        Eleanor !
O Lady Eleanora von Alleyne !
Mayest bide until they come, O stately Lady Elea-
        nor !

And thou and they may marry; but, for me, I must
    not tarry :
I have won a wife already out of Spain,
Virgin Lady Eleanora,
Virgin Lady Eleanora von Alleyne ! "

Thereon he rode away, the gallant Margrave Gondi-
    bert,
From Lady Eleanora von Alleyne.
Thereon he rode away, the gallant Margrave Gondi-
    bert,
And long in shame and anguish did that haughty lady
    languish,
Did she languish without pity for her pain,
She, the Lady Eleanora,
She, the Lady Eleanora von Alleyne !

And year went after year, and still in barren maiden-
    hood
Lived Lady Eleanora von Alleyne.
And wrinkled eld crept on, and still her lot was
    maidenhood.
And, woe ! her end was tragic : she was changed, at
    length, by magic,
To-an ugly wooden image, they maintain !
She, the Lady Eleanora,
She, the Lady Eleanora von Alleyne.

And now, before the gate, in sight of all, transmog-
    rified,
Stands Lady Eleanora von Alleyne.
Before her castle-gate, in sight of all, transmogrified !

And he that won't salute her must be fined in foam-
ing pewter,
If a boor; but, if a burgher, in champagne,
For the Lady Eleanora,
Wooden Lady Eleanora von Alleyne!

MY HOME (26)

(CONRAD WETZEL)

Morn and eve a star invites me,
One imploring silver star,
Woos me, calls me, lures me, lights me
To the desert deeps afar,
To a lovely orient land,
Where the sun at morning early
Rises fresh, and young, and glowing;
Where the air is light and bland,
And the falling raindrops pearly:
Therefore am I going, going
Home to this my lovely land,
Where the sun at morning early
Rises fresh, and young, and glowing;
Where the airs are light and bland,
And the rain is warm and pearly:
All unheeding, all unknowing,
I am speeding, I am going,
Going home to my, to my land,
To my only lonely island
In the desert deeps afar;
Yet unknowing, and undreaming

Why I go, or how, or whither,
Save that one imploring star,
Ever-burning, ever-beaming,
Woos me, lures me, lights me thither.

THE FAIRIES' PASSAGE (27)

(KOPISCH)

Tap, tap, rap, rap! " Get up, gaffer Ferryman."
" Eh!   Who is there?"   The clock strikes three.
" Get up, do, gaffer!   You are the very man
We have been long, long, longing to see."
The ferryman rises, growling and grumbling,
And goes fum-fumbling, and stumbling, and tumbling
Over the wares on his way to the door.
But he sees no more
Than he saw before,
Till a voice is heard : " O Ferryman dear!
Here we are waiting, all of us, here.
We are a wee, wee colony, we ;
Some two hundred in all, or three.
Ferry us over the river Lee
Ere dawn of day,
And we will pay
The most we may
In our own wee way!"

" Who are you?   Whence came you?
What place are you going to?"

" Oh, we have dwelt over-long in this land :
The people get cross, and are growing so knowing,
    too !
Nothing at all but they now understand.
We are daily vanishing under the thunder
Of some huge engine or iron wonder;
That iron, ah ! it has entered our souls."
" Your souls ? O gholes,
You queer little drolls,
Do you mean——? " " Good gaffer, do aid us
        with speed,
For our time, like our stature, is short indeed !
And a very long way we have to go :
Eight or ten thousand miles or so,
Hither and thither, and to and fro,
With our pots and pans
And little gold cans;
But our light caravans
Run swifter than man's."

" Well, well, you may come," said the ferryman
        affably :
" Patrick, turn out, and get ready the barge."
Then again to the little folk: " Tho' you seem
        laughably
Small, I don't mind, if your coppers be large."
Oh, dear ! what a rushing, what pushing, what
        crushing,
(The watermen making vain efforts at hushing
The hubbub the while,) there followed these words !
What clapping of boards,
What strapping of cords,

What stowing away of children and wives,
And platters, and mugs, and spoons, and knives !
Till all had safely got into the boat,
And the ferryman, clad in his tip-top coat,
And his wee little fairies were safely afloat.
Then ding, ding, ding,
And kling, kling, kling,
How the coppers did ring
In the tin pitcherling !

Off, then, went the boat, at first very pleasantly,
Smoothly, and so forth; but after a while
It swayed and it swagged this and that way, and
    presently
Chest after chest, and pile after pile,
Of the little folk's goods began tossing and rolling,
And pitching like fun, beyond fairy controlling.
O Mab ! if the hubbub were great before,
It was now some two or three million times more.
Crash ! went the wee crocks and the clocks; and the
    locks
Of each little wee box were stove in by hard knocks;
And then there were oaths, and prayers, and cries :
" Take care ! " — " See there ! " — " Oh, dear, my
    eyes ! "
" I am killed ! " — " I am drowned ! " — with groans
    and sighs,
Till to land they drew.
" Yeo-ho ! Pull to !
Tiller-rope, thro' and thro' ! "
And all's right anew.

" Now jump upon shore, ye queer little oddities.
(Eh, what is this ? . . . Where are they, at all ?
Where are they, and where are their tiny commodi-
    ties ?
Well, as I live ! " . . .)   He looks blank as a wall,
Poor ferryman !   Round him and round him he
    gazes,
But only gets deeplier lost in the mazes
Of utter bewilderment.   All, all are gone,
And he stands alone,
Like a statue of stone,
In a doldrum of wonder.   He turns to steer,
And a tinkling laugh salutes his ear,
With other odd sounds : " Ha, ha, ha, ha !
Fol lol ! zidzizzle ! quee quee ! bah ! bah !
Fizzigigiggidy ! pshee ! sha sha ! "
" O ye thieves, ye thieves, ye rascally thieves ! "
The good man cries.   He turns to his pitcher,
And there, alas, to his horror perceives
That the little folk's mode of making him richer
Has been to pay him with withered leaves !

THE LAST WORDS OF AL–HASSAN (28)

(FRIEDRICH AUGUST VON HEYDEN)

Farewell for ever to all I love,
To river and rock, farewell ;
To Zoumlah's gloomful cypress-grove,
And Shaarmal's tulipy dell !

To Deenween-Kullaha's light blue bay,
And Oreb's lonely strand!
My race is run; I am called away:
I go to the lampless land.
'Llah Hu!
I am called away from the light of day
To my tent in the dark dark land;

I have seen the standard of Ali stained
With the blood of the brave and free,
And the Kaaba's venerable stone profaned
By the truculent Wahabee.
O Allah, for the light of another sun,
With my Bazra sword in hand!
But I rave in vain; my course is run:
I go to the lampless land.
'Llah Hu!
My course is run, my goal is won,
I go to the dark dark land!

Yet, why should I live a day, an hour?
The friends I valued lie low;
My sisters dance in the halls of the Giaour,
My brethren fight for the foe.
None stood by the banner this arm unfurled
Save Kharada's mountain-band!
'Tis well that I leave so base a world,
Tho' to dwell in the lampless land.
'Llah Hu!
'Tis well that I leave so false a world,
Tho' to dwell in the dark dark land!

Even she, my loved and lost Ameen,
The moon-white pearl of my soul,
Could pawn her peace for the show and sheen
Of silken Istambol.
How little did I bode what a year would see
When we parted at Sarmarcand;
My bride in the harem of the Osmanlee,
Myself in the lampless land.
'Llah Hu!
My bride in the harem of the Osmanlee,
Myself in the dark dark land!

We weep for the noble who perish young,
Like flowers before their bloom;
The great-souled few, who, unseen and unsung,
Go down to the charnel's gloom;
But, written on the brow of each, if man
Could read it and understand,
Is the changeless decree of Heaven's divan:
We are born for the lampless land!
'Llah Hu!
By the dread firman of Heaven's divan,
All are born for the dark dark land!

The wasted moon has a marvellous look
Amiddle of the starry hordes;
The heavens, too, shine like a mystic book
All bright with burning words.
The mists of the dawn begin to dislimn
Zahara's castles of sand.
Farewell! farewell!   Mine eyes feel dim:
They turn to the lampless land.

'Llah Hu!
My heart is weary, mine eyes are dim,
I would rest in the dark dark land!

AND THEN NO MORE

(RÜCKERT)

I saw her once, one little while, and then no more:
'Twas Eden's light on earth awhile, and then no more.
Amid the throng, she passed along the meadow-floor:
Spring seemed to smile on earth awhile, and then no
    more.
But whence she came, which way she went, what
    garb she wore,
I noted not; I gazed awhile, and then no more.

I saw her once, one little while, and then no more:
'Twas Paradise on earth awhile, and then no more:
Ah! what avail my vigils pale, my magic lore?
She shone before mine eyes awhile, and then no more.
The shallop of my peace is wrecked on Beauty's shore;
Near Hope's fair isle it rode awhile, and then no more!

I saw her once, one little while, and then no more:
Earth looked like Heaven a little while, and then no
    more.
Her presence thrilled and lightened to its inner core,
My desert breast, a little while, and then no more.
So may, perchance, a meteor glance at midnight
    o'er
Some ruined pile a little while, and then no more.

R

I saw her once, one little while, and then no more.
The earth was Peri-land awhile, and then no more.
O might I see but once again, as once before,
Through chance or wile, that shape awhile, and then
        no more !
Death soon would heal my griefs : this heart, now sad
        and sore,
Would beat anew a little while, and then no more !

MOTHER AND SON

(HANDRIC TZVELK)

" Hie to the wood, and seek thy sister,
Son for ever gay !
Hie to the wood, and tell thy sister
She bring home her mother's breast-knot,
Son for ever gay."

" Wandering in the wood I missed her,
Golden mother gray !
In the wood I lost and missed her.
Where she bides I guess and guess not,
Golden mother gray."

" Fare to the mill and seek thy brother,
Son for ever gay !
Fetch him home to his mourning mother.
See, the eve gets dark and darker,
Son for ever gay."

" Mother now he hath found another,
Golden mother gray,
Even the holy Virgin Mother!
Stark as death he lies; none starker,
Golden mother gray."

" Hence, and find thy staffless father,
Son for ever gay!
Green herbs went he forth to gather
Mid the dews of morning early,
Son for ever gay."

" Vainly might I seek my father,
Golden mother gray!
Heavenly herbs he now doth gather
Where the dews shine bright and pearly,
Golden mother gray."

" When shall I again behold them,
Son for ever gay?
When again shall I behold them,
Ah, when fold them to my bosom,
Son for ever gay?"

" To thy bosom shall thou fold them,
Golden mother gray!
Thou shalt once again behold them
When the blighted tree shall blossom,
Golden mother gray."

" When shall blossom tree that's blighted,
Son for ever gay?
When can blossom tree that's blighted?

Blighted tree may naught and none raise,
Son for ever gay."

"When the morn shall first be lighted,
Golden mother gray!
When the morn shall first be lighted
In the west, by western sun-rays,
Golden mother gray."

"When shall dawn that wondrous morning,
Son for ever gay?
When shall break that wondrous morning?
When be seen the western sunrise,
Son for ever gay?"

"When the Archangel's trump gives warning,
Golden mother gray!
When the Judgment peal gives warning;
When the dead shall every one rise,
Golden mother gray."

TWO SONNETS FROM VINCENZO DA FILICAJA

I

Where is thine arm, Italia? why shouldst thou
Fight with the stranger's?   Fierce alike to me
Seem thy defender and thine enemy:
Both were thy vassals once, tho' victors now. (29)
Thus dost thou guard the wreath that bound thy brow,
The wreck of perished empire?   When to thee
Virtue and valor pledged their fealty

Was this thy glorious promise, this thy vow?
Go, then : reject thine ancient worth, and wed
Degenerate sloth ; mid blood, and groans, and cries,
Sleep on, all heedless of the loud alarms,
Sleep, vile adulteress ! From thy guilty bed
Too soon the avenging sword shall bid thee rise,
Or pierce thee, slumbering in thy minion's arms.

II

Here on the spot where stately cities rose,
No stone is left, to mark in letters rude
Where earth did her tremendous jaws unclose,
Where Syracuse, or where Catania stood.
Along the silent margin of the flood
I seek, but cannot find ye ! Naught appears
Save the deep-settled gloom of solitude,
That checks my step, and fills mine eyes with tears.

O Thou whose mighty arm the blow hath dealt,
Whose justice gave the judgment ! shall not I
Adore that power which I have seen and felt ?
Rise from the depths of darkness where ye lie,
Ye ghosts of buried cities ; rise, and be
A sad memorial to futurity.

THE MARINER'S BRIDE

(LUIS DE CAMOENS)

Look, mother ! the mariner's rowing
His galley adown the tide ;
I'll go where the mariner's going,
And be the mariner's bride !

I saw him one day through the wicket,
I opened the gate and we met;
As a bird in the fowler's net,
Was I caught in my own green thicket.
O mother, my tears are flowing,
I've lost my maidenly pride :
I'll go if the mariner's going,
And be the mariner's bride !

This Love the tyrant evinces,
Alas ! an omnipotent might ;
He darkens the mind like night,
He treads on the necks of princes !
O mother, my bosom is glowing !
I'll go, whatever betide,
I'll go where the mariner's going,
And be the mariner's bride.

Yes, mother, the spoiler has reft me
Of reason and self-control ;
Gone, gone is my wretched soul,
And only my body is left me.
The winds, O mother ! are blowing,
The ocean is bright and wide :
I'll go where the mariner's going,
And be the mariner's bride.

TO DON RODRIGO AFTER HIS FINAL DEFEAT

(FROM THE ROMANCERO GENERAL)

O turn those eyes, unhappy King,
O turn those eyes on ruined Spain!
Behold that glory vanishing
That shone so long undimmed by stain:
See how her heroes bleed in vain;
See how the conquering Arabs trample
Her golden fields, her vineyards ample;
See this, and curse thy reckless reign!
(Alas, most wretched land,
Lost for La Cava's lips and hand!)

The memories of a thousand years,
The lustre of the Gothic name,
So wronged, that never blood nor tears
Can wipe away the blighting shame;
And this, to feed thy guilty flame!
O King, thy woes are but beginning:
O King, thou losest by thy sinning
Thy soul and body, crown and fame.
(Alas, most wretched land,
Lost for La Cava's lips and hand!)

DIES IRAE (30)

The day of wrath, the day of woe
Shall lay the world in ashes low:
As David and the Seers foreshow.

What awe must e'en archangels feel
When earth shall make her dread appeal
To God, her Judge for woe or weal!

The marvellous trumpet's mighty tone
Shall thrill the graves from zone to zone,
And wake the dead to face the Throne.

The whole dark ocean of the Past
Shall answer to that earthquake blast,
Till Death and Nature stand aghast.

The accusing record lies unrolled:
And all man thought and wrought of old,
And hidden sins and shames, are told.

Woe! when the rended veil shall fall!
When Truth, in Heaven's own judgment-hall,
Lays bare the shrinking souls of all.

Where then can crime dare turn in trust?
What stay remains for sinful dust,
When fear shall prostrate even the just?

Ah, great good God so long withstood!
I clasp Thy Son's redeeming rood :
My fount of hope is Jesus' blood.

On that dread day, just Judge of men,
Let me not wake for Hell's dark den;
But be, O God! my Saviour then.

Original Poems

I. Those purporting to be Translations
from the Oriental Languages

THE KARAMANIAN EXILE (31)

I see thee ever in my dreams,
Karaman!
Thy hundred hills, thy thousand streams,
Karaman, O Karaman!
As when thy gold-bright morning gleams,
As when the deepening sunset seams
With lines of light thy hills and streams,
Karaman!
So thou loomest on my dreams,
Karaman!
On all my dreams, my homesick dreams,
Karaman, O Karaman!

The hot bright plains, the sun, the skies,
Karaman!
Seem death-black marble to mine eyes,
Karaman, O Karaman!
I turn from summer's blooms and dyes;
Yet in my dreams thou dost arise
In welcome glory to mine eyes,
Karaman!
In thee my life of life yet lies,
Karaman!
Thou still art holy in mine eyes,
Karaman, O Karaman!

Ere my fighting years were come,
Karaman!

Troops were few in Erzerome,
Karaman, O Karaman !
Their fiercest came from Erzerome,
They came from Ukhbar's palace dome,
They dragged me forth from thee, my home,
Karaman !
Thee, my own, my mountain home,
Karaman!
In life and death, my spirit's home,
Karaman, O Karaman !

O none of all my sisters ten,
Karaman !
Loved like me my fellow-men,
Karaman, O Karaman !
I was mild as milk till then,
I was soft as silk till then;
Now my breast is as a den,
Karaman !
Foul with blood and bones of men,
Karaman !
With blood and bones of slaughtered men,
Karaman, O Karaman !

My boyhood's feelings newly born,
Karaman !
Withered like young flowers uptorn,
Karaman, O Karaman !
And in their stead sprang weed and thorn;
What once I loved now moves my scorn;
My burning eyes are dried to horn,
Karaman !

I hate the blessed light of morn,
Karaman !
It maddens me, the face of morn,
Karaman, O Karaman !

The Spahi wears a tyrant's chains,
Karaman !
But bondage worse than this remains,
Karaman, O Karaman !
His heart is black with million stains :
Thereon, as on Kaf's blasted plains,
Shall nevermore fall dews and rains,
Karaman !
Save poison-dews and bloody rains,
Karaman !
Hell's poison-dews and bloody rains,
Karaman, O Karaman !

But life at worst must end ere long,
Karaman !
Azrael [1] avengeth every wrong,
Karaman, O Karaman !
Of late my thoughts rove more among
Thy fields ; o'ershadowing fancies throng
My mind, and texts of bodeful song,
Karaman !
Azrael is terrible and strong,
Karaman !
His lightning sword smites all ere long,
Karaman, O Karaman !

[1] The angel of death.

There's care to-night in Ukhbar's halls,
Karaman!
There's hope, too, for his trodden thralls,
Karaman, O Karaman!
What lights flash red along yon walls?
Hark! hark! the muster-trumpet calls!
I see the sheen of spears and shawls,
Karaman!
The foe! the foe!—they scale the walls,
Karaman!
To-night Muràd or Ukhbar falls,
Karaman, O Karaman! ·

THE WAIL AND WARNING OF THE
THREE KHALANDEERS

THE WAIL

La' laha, il Allah![1]
Here we meet, we three, at length,
Amrah, Osman, Perizad:
Shorn of all our grace and strength,
Poor, and old, and very sad.
We have lived, but live no more;
Life has lost its gloss for us,
Since the days we spent of yore
Boating down the Bosphorus!
La' laha, il Allah!

[1] God alone is all-merciful!

The Bosphorus, the Bosphorus!
Old time brought home no loss for us;
We felt full of health and heart
Upon the foamy Bosphorus!

La' laha, il Allah!
Days indeed! A shepherd's tent
Served us then for house and fold;
All to whom we gave or lent,
Paid us back a thousand fold.
Troublous years, by myriads wailed,
Rarely had a cross for us,
Never, when we gaily sailed
Singing down the Bosphorus.
La' laha, il Allah!
The Bosphorus, the Bosphorus!
There never came a cross for us,
While we daily, gaily sailed
Adown the meadowy Bosphorus.

La' laha, il Allah!
Blithe as birds we flew along,
Laughed and quaffed and stared about;
Wine and roses, mirth and song,
Were what most we cared about.
Fame we left for quacks to seek,
Gold was dust and dross for us,
While we lived from week to week
Boating down the Bosphorus.
La' laha, il Allah!
The Bosphorus, the Bosphorus!
And gold was dust and dross for us,

s

While we lived from week to week
Boating down the Bosphorus.

La' laha, il Allah!
Friends we were, and would have shared
Purses, had we twenty full.
If we spent, or if we spared,
Still our funds were plentiful.
Save the hours we passed apart,
Time brought home no loss for us;
We felt full of hope and heart
While we clove the Bosphorus.
La' laha, il Allah!
The Bosphorus, the Bosphorus!
For life has lost its gloss for us
Since the days we spent of yore
Upon the pleasant Bosphorus!

La' laha, il Allah!
Ah! for youth's delirious hours,
Man pays well in after-days,
When quenched hopes and palsied powers
Mock his love-and-laughter days.
Thorns and thistles on our path
Took the place of moss for us,
Till false fortune's tempest-wrath
Drove us from the Bosphorus.
La' laha, il Allah!
The Bosphorus, the Bosphorus!
When thorns took place of moss for us,
Gone was all!   Our hearts were graves
Deep, deeper than the Bosphorus.

La' laha, il Allah!
Gone is all!   In one abyss
Lie health, youth, and merriment!
All we've learned amounts to this:
Life's a sad experiment!
What it is we trebly feel
Pondering what it was for us,
When our shallop's bounding keel
Clove the joyous Bosphorus.
La' laha, il Allah!
The Bosphorus, the Bosphorus!
We wail for what life was for us,
When our shallop's bounding keel
Clove the joyous Bosphorus!

THE WARNING

La' laha, il Allah!
Pleasure tempts, yet man has none
Save himself t' accuse, if her
Temptings prove, when all is done,
Lures hung out by Lucifer.
Guard your fire in youth, O friends!
Manhood's is but phosphorus,
And bad luck attends and ends
Boatings down the Bosphorus!
La' laha, il Allah!
The Bosphorus, the Bosphorus!
Youth's fire soon wanes to phosphorus,
And slight luck or grace attends
Your boaters down the Bosphorus!

RELIC OF PRINCE BAYAZEED [1]

Slow thro' my bosom's veins their last cold blood is
    flowing;
Above my heart even now I feel the rank grass
    growing. (32)
Hence to the land of naught the caravan is starting;
Its bell already tolls the signal for departing.
Rejoice, my soul, poor bird! thou art at last delivered:
Thy cage is crumbling fast, the bars will soon be
    shivered.
Farewell this troubled world, where sin and crime
    run riot!
For Shahi henceforth rests in God's own house of
    quiet.

ADVICE AGAINST TRAVEL (33)

Traverse not the globe for lore! The sternest
But the surest teacher is the heart;
Studying that and that alone, thou learnest
Best and soonest whence and what thou art.

Time, not travel, 'tis which gives us ready
Speech, experience, prudence, tact, and wit:
Far more light the lamp that bideth steady
Than the wandering lantern doth emit.

[1] Prince Bayazeed, son of Suleiman, was put to death in 1561 by Selim,
Shah of Persia. This poem is said to have been written the night before
his execution.

Moor, Chinese, Egyptian, Russian, Roman,
Tread one common down-hill path of doom;
Everywhere the names are man and woman,
Everywhere the old sad sins find room.

Evil angels tempt us in all places.
What but sands or snows hath earth to give?
Dream not, friend, of deserts and oases!
But look inwards, and begin to live.

ADAM'S OATH

Medreamt I was in Paradise, and there, a-drinking
    wine,
I saw our Father Adam, with his flowing golden hair.
"O Father!" was my greeting, "my heart is faint
    with care:
Tell me, tell me, are the Mooslemin of Aalya sons
    of thine?"
But the noble senior frowned, and his wavy golden hair
Grew black as clouds at evening, when thunder
    thrills the air.
"Nay, the Mooslemin of Aalya I disown for sons of
    mine!"
Then methought I wept, and beat my breast, and
    begged of him a sign.
"O swear it, Father Adam!" So, dilating out, he
    sware:
"If the Mooslemin of Aalyastan be kith or kin of
    mine,
Let dust for ever darken the glory of my hair!"

NIGHT IS NEARING

Allah Akbar!
All things vanish after brief careering:
Down one gulf life's myriad barks are steering.
Headlong mortal! hast thou ears for hearing?
Pause, be wise: the night, thy night, is nearing;
Night is nearing!

Allah Akbar!
Towards the darkness whence no ray is peering,
Towards the void from which no voice comes cheer-
      ing,
Move the countless doomed, none volunteering,
While the winds rise, and the night is nearing,
Night is nearing!

Allah Akbar!
See the palace-dome its pride uprearing
One fleet hour, then darkly disappearing!
So must all of lofty or endearing
Fade, fail, fall: to all the night is nearing,
Night is nearing!

Allah Akbar!
Then, since naught abides, but all is veering,
Flee a world which sin is hourly searing:
Only so mayst front thy fate unfearing,
When life wanes, and death, like night, is nearing.
Night is nearing!

TO MIHRI

My starlight, my moonlight, my midnight, my noon-
    light,
Unveil not, unveil not ! or millions must pine.
Ah, didst thou lay bare
Those dark tresses of thine,
Even night would seem bright
To the hue of thy hair, which is black as despair.

My starlight, my moonlight, my midnight, my noon-
    light,
Unveil not, unveil not ! or millions must pine.
Ah, didst thou disclose
Those bright features of thine,
The Red Vale[1] would look pale
By thy cheek which so glows that it shames the rich
    rose.

My starlight, my moonlight, my midnight, my noon-
    light,
Unveil not, unveil not ! or millions must pine.
Ah, didst thou lay bare
That white bosom of thine,
The bright sun would grow dim
Nigh a rival so rare and so radiantly fair.
My starlight, my moonlight, my midnight, my noon-
    light,
Unveil not, unveil not !

[1] Kuzzil Ragh, the Red Valley : in all probability the Valley of Roses
at Edreen.

THE CITY OF TRUTH

Once I saw a City wide and fair
And the pathways were enamelled all :
He shall never die who enters there !
There he drinks of life's elixirs all.
All the gates thereof are thirty-two,
Wreathèd gates, with stately pillars tall;
All the terraces of gold-bright hue;
Rich the vineyards and the gardens all.
Silver fountain-waters, bright and still,
Into alabaster basins fall;
Musk-scents load the airlets from the hill;
There the garden-bowers are roses all.
There sweet nightingales, like living flutes,
Bind the senses and the soul in thrall;
Then the trees droop under brilliant fruits,
Citrons, dates, pomegranates, peaches all.
This fair City is unseen : it lies
Isolated from one earthly ball,
Ranking higher far than Paradise :
'Tis the goal the angels covet all,
'Tis the City of the Truth alone,
And of Truth's inestimable All.
They whom Allah from the first hath known,
Known and chosen, here are gathered all.
Some drink precious wine, some selsibil [1];
Some in bower, some in palace hall;
All are passed the fear of ail and ill :
Ecstasy-inebriated all !

[1] The waters of life.

Strangers they to passion and to sin ;
Terrors shall no more their hours appal ;
Neither storms without, nor strifes within.
They are tranquil, they are happy, all.
Swords are not for these : their days are free,
Free from bitter feud and angry brawl,
Free from wrangling speech and sophistry ;
For the Holy Spirit dwells with all.
Loving are their words, and honey-sweet,
Unadulterate with envy's gall ;
All their lives are peace : and when they meet,
Oh, they meet indeed as brethren all !
Here are found no lower, higher ranks :
Syrian, Turk, Egyptian, Grecian, Gaul,
Swart and fair, Arabians, Persians, Franks,
Here are linked in common union all.
And as Truth is one, as God is one,
So these denizens, both great and small,
Are combined as one ; and therefore none
Seeks to be the Shah, or slave, of all.
Yet our Prophet never tutored them ;
Neither needed they Mohammed's call !
In the Truth they saw a lovelier gem
Shining through the world alike for all,[1]
So their sect is mankind ; and their creed
Thus is worded : God is all in all !
And His will and wish, where'er they lead
Are their bliss, their glory, and their all.

[1] The author, Mohammed Niazi VI, lies buried in the island of Lemnos, to which he was banished for not speaking the doctrines of Islam strictly by the card. The peculiar character of his heterodoxy may be inferred from these lines.

Never drank they wine from golden bowls,
Never wore the diamond-spangled shawl:
Thus the devil could not spy these souls
Who were shrouded in seclusion all.
Early were they rescued from the abyss
Of the snares and spells that oft enthrall
Man's affections; and the Bird of bliss
Here sits perched upon the heads of all.
They, enraptured, as the holy lyre
Sweetly vibrates at their festival,
Dread not woman, earthquake, storm, nor fire;
Plagues and genii are excluded all.
This securest house, this dome where centre
All delights, where perils ne'er befall
Soul of guest, the houris shall not enter:
Angels form the only tenants all.
Many lamps, refulgent from afar,
Lured them towards the City's lofty wall,
Yet was each a pure celestial star,
And the hand of God had kindled all.
Friend, wouldst thou too gain this glorious goal
When the mourners bear thy funeral pall,
Now by prayer and fasting cleanse thy soul!
Slay thy vanities and vices all.
Look to God! and then, though natural dusk
O'er thy sunless evening sky must fall,
Then, though camphor strew thy head for musk,
He will beautify and brighten all!
We are voyagers on ocean dark,
Yet can never billow, bolt, nor squall,
Damage nor dismay our fragile bark,
If the Lord but pilot us through all!

Heavenly light will bright our path at length,
And that flood shine like another Dall [1]:
God is each one's hope and tower of strength,
And the hope and tower of strength of all.
O stand up ! The serpent and his mates,
But not man, were born to creep and crawl;
Reptile enters not the holy gates.
Knowst thou not the saints look heavenward all ?
How canst grovel in the mire, content
As the brute which wallows in the stall ?
Dost thou then imagine earth was meant
As a burial-den for soul and all ?
Harken to Niazi's warning song !
This is not a poet's idle scrawl:
Thou must one day travel too along
With the last great caravan of all.
May thy road be smooth, and mayst thou see
All the star-lamps on the City's wall
Also beaconing and beckoning thee !
This is his one prayer for thee and all.

AN EPITAPH

Rests within this lonely mausoleum
After life's distraction and fatigue,
Leeh Rewaan, a man to hear and see whom
Monks and princes journeyed many a league.

Yet not Leeh Rewaan himself; but rather
Leeh Rewaan's worn-out and cast-off dress :

[1] Lake of Cashmere.

He, the man, dwells with his Heavenly Father
In a land of light and loveliness.

Shah of song he was; and fond of laughter,
Sweet sharaab,[1] and silver-spangled shawls.
Stranger, mayst thou quaff with him hereafter
Life's red wine in Eden's palace-halls!

GOOD COUNSEL

Tutor not thyself in science: go to masters for per-
    fection,
Also, speak thy thoughts aloud:
Whoso in the glass beholdeth naught besides his own
    reflection
Bides both ignorant and proud.
Study not in one art only: bee-like, rather, at a hundred
Sources gather honeyed lore;
Thou wert else, that helpless bird which, when his
    nest has once been plundered,
Ne'er can build another more. (34)

A GHAZEL

Wonder not thou that the Sultan on earth is alone!
So is the sun that illumines the heavens, alone;
So, tho' a forest of flowers have budded and blown,
Always the garden sultana, the rose, is alone:
The praise be to God!

[1] Shrub, or sherbet.

What is there great among mankind but standeth
   alone?
Lift up the eyes of thy soul to the Ottoman throne,
Turn to the Kaaba,[1] and look at its wonderful Stone;
These, like the rose and the Sultan, are also alone:
The praise be to God!

Wonder not thou that the Sultan on earth is alone:
So is the moon in the hall of the planets alone;
So tho' a hundred rare instruments mingle in tone,
Always the glittering crescent-and-bells is alone:
The praise be to God!

What can the poet accomplish unless when alone,
What, tho' in harness with one who is bone of his
   bone?
Never feels Lamyeh himself that his soul is his own,
Save when he wanders thro' Brusa by moonlight
   alone:
The praise be to God!

Wonder not, then, that the Sultan on earth is alone!
So, on the Balkans, the cedar ariseth alone;
So, tho' a many rich brilliants emblazon thy zone,
Always the emerald, monarch of gems, is alone:
The praise be to God!

So stands the dome of Sophia for ever alone,
Stands without sister since Ephesus' pride was o'erthrown;

[1] The Holy House of Mecca.

Bagdad is fallen, and Balbec a ruin unknown,
Leaving Stamboul and its mosque in their glory alone :
The praise be to God!

Countless are Suleiman's beys, but himself is alone:
Princes are slaves at his gate, yet he still is alone.
So, altho' streams without number flow into the
        Done,[1]
Always that father of rivers himself is alone:
The praise be to God! (35)

THE TIME OF THE ROSES

Morning is blushing; the gay nightingales
Warble their exquisite song in the vales;
Spring, like a spirit, floats everywhere,
Shaking sweet spice-showers loose from her hair,
Murmurs half-musical sounds from the stream,
Breathes in the valley, and shines in the beam.
In, in at the portal that youth uncloses!
It hastes, it wastes, the time of the roses.

Meadows and gardens and sun-lighted glades,
Palaces, terraces, grottoes, and shades
Woo thee; a fairy bird sings in thine ear:
Come and be happy!   An Eden is here.
Knowest thou whether for thee there be any
Years in the future?   Ah, think on how many
A young heart under the mould reposes,
Nor feels how wheels the time of the roses!

----
[1] Danube.

In the red light of the many-leaved rose
Mahomet's wonderful mantle reglows;
Gaudier far, but as blooming and tender,
Tulips and martagons revel in splendor.
Drink from the chalice of joy, ye who may!
Youth is a flower of early decay,
And pleasure a monarch that age deposes,
When past, at last, the time of the roses.

See the young lilies, their scimitar-petals
Glancing, like silver mid earthier metals:
Dews of the brightest, in life-giving showers,
Fall all the night on these luminous flowers:
Each of them sparkles afar like a gem.
Wouldst thou be smiling and happy like them?
O follow all counsel that pleasure proposes!
It dies, it flies, the time of the roses.

Pity the roses! Each rose is a maiden
Pranked, and with jewels of dew overladen:
Pity the maidens! The moon of their bloom
Rises to set in the cells of the tomb.
Life has its winter; when summer is gone,
Maidens, like roses, lie stricken and wan.
Tho' bright as the burning bush of Moses,
Soon fades, fair maids, the time of your roses.

Lustre and odors, and blossoms and flowers,
All that is richest in garden and bowers,
Teach us morality, speak of mortality,
Whisper that life is a sweet unreality.

Death is the end of that lustre, those odors:
Brilliance and beauty are gloomy foreboders
To him who knows what this world of woes is,
And sees how flees the time of the roses!

Heed them not, hear them not!   Morning is blushing,
Perfumes are wandering, fountains are gushing.
What tho' the rose, like a virgin forbidden,
Long under leafy pavilion lay hidden?
Now, far around as the vision can stretch,
Wreaths for the pencil of angels to sketch,
Festoon the tall hills that the landscape discloses.
O sweet, tho' fleet, is the time of the roses!

Now the air, drunk from the breath of the flowers,
Faints like a bride whom her bliss overpowers;
Such and so rich is the fragrance that fills
Ether and cloud, that its essence distils,
As thro' thin lily-leaves, earthward again,
Sprinkling with rose-water garden and plain.
O joyously, after the winter closes,
Returns and burns the time of the roses!

O for some magical vase to imprison
All the sweet incense that yet has not risen,
And the swift pearls that, radiant and rare,
Glisten and drop thro' the hollows of air!
Vain: they depart, both the beaming and fragrant;
So, too, hope leaves us, and love proves a vagrant;
Too soon their entrancing illusion closes:
It cheats, it fleets, the time of the roses!

Tempest and thunder and war were abroad;
Riot and turbulence triumphed unawed;
Suleiman rose, and the thunders were hushed,
Faction was prostrate, turbulence crushed.
Once again peace in her gloriousness rallies;
Once again shine the glad skies on our valleys,
And sweetly anew the poet composes
His lays in praise of the time of the roses!

I, too, Meseehi, already renowned,
Centuries hence by my song shall be crowned;
Far as the stars of the wide heaven shine,
Men shall rejoice in this carol of mine.
Lelia! thou art as a rose unto me:
Think on the nightingale singing for thee!
For he who on love like thine reposes
Least heeds how speeds the time of the roses.

THE TIME ERE THE ROSES WERE BLOWING[1]

Brilliantly sparkle, Meseehi, thy flowing
Numbers, like streams, amid lilies upgrowing;
Yet, wouldst thou mingle the sad and sublime,
Sing, too, the time,
Sing the young time ere the roses were blowing!

Then was the season when hope was yet glowing,
Then the blithe year of the spring and the sowing,

[1] From the Persian of Zazem Zerbayeh, who died at Ispahan in 1541, in reply to Meseehi's *Time of the Roses*.

T

Then the soul dwelt in her own faëry clime;
Then was the time,
Then the gay time ere the roses were blowing.

Soon, ah, too soon came the summer, bestowing
Glory and light, but a light ever showing
In the chill nearness, the autumn's gray rime:
Gone was the time,
Gone the fresh time ere the roses were blowing.

Life is at best but a coming and going,
Now flitting past us on swift, now on slow wing;
Here fair with goodness, there gloomy with crime.
O for the time,
O for the time ere the roses were blowing!

Coldly, ah, coldly goes truth, overthrowing
Fancy's bright palaces, coldly goes mowing
Down the sweet blossoms of boyhood's young prime:
Give us the time,
Give us the time ere the roses were blowing!

I am Zerbayeh, the least of the knowing;
Thou art Meseehi, the golden and glowing.
O when again thou wouldst dazzle in rhyme,
Sing of the time,
Sing of the time ere the roses were blowing!

TO AMINE, ON SEEING HER ABOUT TO VEIL HER MIRROR

Veil not thy mirror, sweet Amine,
Till night shall also veil each star!
Thou seest a twofold marvel there:
The only face so fair as thine,
The only eyes that, near or far,
Can gaze on thine without despair.

THE HOWLING SONG OF AL MOHARA

My heart is as a house of groans
From dusky eve to dawning gray;
(*Allah, Allah hu!*)
The glazed flesh on my staring bones
Grows black and blacker with decay;
(*Allah, Allah hu!*)
Yet am I none whom death may slay:
I am spared to suffer, and to warn,
(*Allah, Allah hu!*)
My lashless eyes are parched to horn
With weeping for my sin alway.
(*Allah, Allah hu!*)
For blood, hot blood that no man sees,
The blood of one I slew,
Burns on my hands: I cry therefore
All night long, on my knees,
Evermore:
Allah, Allah hu!

Because I slew him over wine,
Because I struck him down at night,
(*Allah, Allah hu!*)
Because he died and made no sign,
His blood is always in my sight!
(*Allah, Allah hu!*)
Because I raised mine arm to smite
While the foul cup was at his lips;
(*Allah, Allah hu!*)
Because I wrought his soul's eclipse,
He comes between me and the light.
(*Allah, Allah hu!*)
His is the form my terror sees,
The sinner that I slew ;
My rending cry is still therefore
All night long, on my knees,
Evermore :
Allah, Allah hu!

Under the all-just heaven's expanse
There is for me no resting-spot;
(*Allah, Allah hu!*)
I dread man's revengeful countenance;
The smiles of woman win me not:
(*Allah, Allah hu!*)
I wander among graves where rot
The carcasses of leprous men,
(*Allah, Allah hu!*)
I house me in the dragon's den
Till evening darkens grove and grot.
(*Allah, Allah hu!*)

But bootless all ! Who penance drees,
Must dree it his life through. (36)
My heart-wrung cry is still therefore
All night long, on my knees,
Evermore :
Allah, Allah hu !

The silks that swathe my hall divan
Are damascened with moons of gold;
(*Allah, Allah hu !*)
Musk-roses from my gulistan
Fill vases of Egyptian mould;
(*Allah, Allah hu !*)
The Koran's treasures lie unrolled
Near where my radiant night-lamp burns;
(*Allah, Allah hu !*)
Around me, rows of silver urns
Perfume the air with odors old.
(*Allah, Allah hu !*)
But what avail these luxuries ?
The blood of him I slew
Burns red on all; I cry therefore
All night long, on my knees,
Evermore :
Allah, Allah hu !

Can sultans, can the guilty rich, ·
Purchase with mines and thrones a draught,
(*Allah, Allah hu !*)
From that Nutulian[1] fount of which
The conscience-tortured whilom quaffed ?
(*Allah, Allah hu !*)

[1] Lethean.

Vain dream !   Power, glory, riches, craft,
Prove magnets for the sword of wrath;
(*Allah, Allah hu!*)
Thorn-plant men's last and lampless path
And barb the slaying angel's shaft. (37)
(*Allah, Allah hu!*)
Oh, the blood-guilty ever sees
But sights that make him rue
As I do now, and cry therefore,
All night long, on my knees,
Evermore :
Allah, Allah hu !

SAYINGS AND PROVERBS

I

SAYING OF KEMALLEDIN KHOGENDI

The words of the wise and unknown, quoth Zehir,
    are buds in a garden,
Which flower when summer is come, and are culled
    for the harem by girls;
Or drops of water, saith Saadi, which silently brighten
    and harden,
Till Caliphs themselves exclaim: "They blind me,
    those dazzling pearls ! "

II

I, too, was reared in Djelim's house, and thus his pre-
cepts run and are :
When folly sells the wisdom's crown, 'tis idly gained
and dearly bought ;
Oh, foremost man of all his race, born under some
diviner star
Who, early trained, self-reined, self-chained, can
practise all that Lokman[1] taught !
The joys and cares of earth are snares : heed lest thy
soul too late deplore
The power of sin to wile and win her vision from
the Eight and Four.[2]
Lock up thyself within thyself ; distrust the stranger,
and the fair ;
(The fool is blown from whim to whim by every
gust of passion's gales.)
Bide where the lute and song are mute, and as thy
soul would shun despair,
Avert thine eye from woman's face when twilight
falls, and she unveils.

[1] Lokman flourished about a thousand years before the Christian era. He
is the greatest of the Oriental moralists ; even Mohammed speaks of him in
the Koran with profound reverence. Lokman's wisdom, like Solomon's,
is supposed to have been of divine origin. . . . The maxims of Lokman
are ten thousand in number ; and any one of them, says an Arabian commentator, is of much greater value than the whole world.

[2] The Eight Signs that are to precede the Day of Doom, and the Four
Final Things : Death, Judgment, Hell, Heaven.

Be circumspect, be watchman-like. Put pebbles in
 thy mouth each day :
Pause long ere thou panegyrize; pause doubly long
 ere thou condemn.
Thy thoughts are Tartars, vagabonds : imprison all
 thou canst not slay.
Of many million drops of rain perchance but one
 turns out a gem.

III

A SAYING OF NEDSCHATI

The world is one vast caravanserai
Where none may stay,
But where each guest writes on the wall this word :
O Mighty Lord!

IV

THREE PROVERBS

I

Naught, I hear thee say,
Can fill the greedy eye;
Yet a little clay
Will fill it bye and bye.

II

An hour of good, a day of ill :
This is the lot of mourning man
Who leaves the world whene'er he will,
But goes to Heaven whene'er he can.

III

The steed to the man who bestrides it newly,
The sabre to him who best can wield it,
The damsel to him who has wooed her truly,
And the province to him who refuses to yield it.

LAMENT FROM THE FAREWELL–BOOK
OF AHI

Like a cypress tree
Mateless in a death-black valley,
Where no lily springeth,
Where no bulbul singeth,
Whence gazelle is never seen to sally,
Such am I, woe is me!
Poor, sad, all unknown,
Lone, lone, lone.

Like a wandering bee,
Alien from his hive and fellows,
Humming moanful ditties
Far from men and cities,
Roaming glades the autumn rarely mellows,
Such am I, woe is me!
Poor, sad, all unknown,
Lone, lone, lone.

Like a bark at sea,
All whose crew by night have perished
Drifting on the ocean,
Still with shoreward motion,

Tho' none live by whom hope's throb is cherished,
Such am I, woe is me!
Poor, sad, all unknown,
Lone, lone, lone.

So I pine and dree,
Till the night that knows no morrow
Sees me wrapped in clay-vest.
Thou, chill world, that gavest
Me the bitter boon alone of sorrow,
Give then a grave to me,
Dark, sad, all unknown,
Lone, lone, lone.

LOVE

From eternity the course of love was writ on leaves
    of snow;
Hence it wanders like a vagrant when the winds of
    coldness blow;
And the lamp of love is cold and chill where constancy
    is weak,
And the lily comes to pine upon deserted beauty's cheek.

From eternity the might of love was writ on leaves of
    fire;
Hence the soul of love in spiral flames would mount
    for ever higher.
And the vermeil sun of Eden won, leaves hope no
    more to seek,
And the damask rose ascends her throne on happy
    beauty's cheek.

From eternity the fate of love was writ on leaves of
    gloom,
For the night of its decay must come, and darkness
    build the tomb;
Then the waste of life, a garden once, again is black
    and bleak,
And the raven tresses mourningly o'ershadow beauty's
    cheek.

Ah, the joys of love are sweet and false, are sorrows
    in disguise,
Like the cheating wealth of golden eve, ere night
    break up the skies.
If the graves of earth were opened, O if Hades could
    but speak,
What a world of ruined souls would curse the sheen
    of beauty's cheek!

TRUST NOT THE WORLD, NOR TIME[1]

Trust not the world, nor time; they are liar-mates.
(*Ya Hu!*)[2]
Wealth borrows wings, and woman goes her way.
(*Ya Hu!*)
Into the old house with the ebon gates
(*Ya Hu!*)
Who enters is but guest, and must not stay.
(*Ya Hu!*)

[1] A passage from Hudayi II., a native of Anatolia; he died in 1628,
and lies buried near Constantinople.
[2] The familiar cry of the dervishes.

Look not upon the sun, for that shall die,
(*Ya Hu!*)
Love not the roses, for they must decay;
(*Ya Hu!*)
The child is caught by all that dupes the eye:
(*Ya Hu!*)
The man should gird his loins; he cannot stay.
(*Ya Hu!*)

From moon to moon time rolleth as a river.
(*Ya Hu!*)
Tho' night will soon o'erdark thy life's last ray,
(*Ya Hu!*)
Earth is the prison of the True Believer;
(*Ya Hu!*)
And who in prison stipulates to stay?
(*Ya Hu!*)

Up, dreamer, up! What takest life to be?
(*Ya Hu!*)
Are centuries not made of night and day?
(*Ya Hu!*)
Call now on God while He will list to thee!
(*Ya Hu!*)
The caravan moves on: it will not stay.
(*Ya Hu!*)

Remember Him whom heaven and earth adore;
(*Ya Hu!*)
Fast, and deny thyself; give alms, and pray.
(*Ya Hu!*)

Thy bark drifts hourly toward the phantom shore;
(*Ya Hu!*)
The sails are up, the vessel cannot stay.
(*Ya Hu!*)

As yet the accursing scroll is incomplete,
(*Ya Hu!*)
But Scales and Bridge [1] maintain their dread array.
(*Ya Hu!*)
Now thou art here, now at the judgment-seat,
(*Ya Hu!*)
For death and justice brook no long delay.
(*Ya Hu!*)

Ah, (trust Hudayi!) he alone from birth
(*Ya Hu!*)
Is guided by the Guardian Four [2] alway,
(*Ya Hu!*)
He is alone the friend of God on earth,
(*Ya Hu!*)
Who visits earth, and doth not sigh to stay.
(*Ya Hu!*)

[1] "The scales of Judgment, one of which hangs over Paradise, and the other over Hell. The Bridge is laid over the midst of Hell, and is finer than a hair and sharper than the edge of a sword; and those who cannot pass this bridge fall into Hell." — SALE's *Prelim. Disc.*

[2] The Guardian Four are the four caliphs next in succession to Mahomet : Omar, Ali, Osman, and Abubekhr.

RELIC OF SERVI

When the mourner sits at the feast of woe
The wine is gall, and the lights burn low.
How bounded my heart in my younger years
Ere grief had unlocked the fount of my tears!
Now dead are the roses of hope in their bloom,
And those that I loved are dust in the tomb,
And of all that gave Servi pleasure or pain
His songs and his sorrows alone remain.[1]

JEALOUSY (38)

" My darling tiny little girl,
I'll give thee jewelled shoes and dresses,
I'll give thee zones of silk and pearl;
And tell me who has combed thy hair?
I'll give thee kisses and caresses.
And say : what youth has combed thy hair? "

" O by my word, O by my truth,
O by the life of Ali Shah!
Aminah knows no stranger youth.
By all the times that thou hast kissed her,
Her hair was combed by Zillalah,
Her own beloved sister! "

---

[1] It is a singular coincidence that we find almost the same sentiment in Schutze :

"Und mir ist nichts aus jener Zeit geblieben,
Als nur dies Lied, mein Leiden und mein Liebän."

" My own, my whitest girl, I vow
I'll bring thee sweetmeats sugared newly.
And tell me, only tell me now
Who over-darked thine eyes with *kohl?*
My white Aminah, tell me truly
Who over-darked thine eyes with *kohl?* "

" O by my word, O by my soul,
O by the soul of Ali Shah!
Myself o'er-darked mine eyes with *kohl;*
'Twas given me by my own dear mother,
My whitest mother Fatimah :
I had it from none other."

" My playful girl, I'll give thee rings,
And gold, and gems beyond comparing;
I'll give thee thousand costly things !
And say, who bit those lips of thine ?
Come, tell what Kuzzilbash so daring
Hath bitten those red lips of thine."

" O by my love, O by my life !
'Twas by a bright red rose this morn
Given me by Zayde, my brother's wife,
These guiltless lips of mine were bitten.
(For brightest rose hath sharpest thorn :
This, as thou knowest, is written.) "

" Thou crafty girl, I know thine art !
Dread thou my wrath : I give thee warning.
But if thou wouldst regain my heart
Speak : tell me who has torn thy shawl !

Say what young Galionjee this morning
Tore thus in twain thy scarlet shawl?

O faithless, truthless, worthless jade!
I have tracked thee, then, thro' all thy lying.
Away! No jewels, no brocade,
No sweetmeats shalt thou have of me.
Away, false girl! Thy tears and sighing
Seem worse than even thy lies to be."

THE WORLD: A GHAZEL

To this khan, and from this khan
How many pilgrims came and went too!
In this khan, and by this khan
What arts were spent, what hearts were rent too!
To this khan and from this khan
Which, for penance, man is sent to,
Many a van and caravan
Crowded came, and shrouded went too.
Christian man and Mussulman,
Guebre, heathen, Jew, and Gentoo,
To this khan, and from this khan,
Weeping came, and sleeping went too.
A riddle this since time began,
Which many a sage his mind hath bent to:
All came, all went; but never man
Knew whence they came, or where they went to!

THE TIME OF THE BARMECIDES (39)

My eyes are filmed, my beard is gray,
I am bowed with the weight of years;
I would I were stretched in my bed of clay,
With my long-lost youth's compeers!
For back to the past, tho' the thought brings woe,
My memory ever glides,
To the old, old time, long, long ago,
The time of the Barmecides!
To the old, old time, long, long ago,
The time of the Barmecides.

Then youth was mine, and a fierce wild will,
And an iron arm in war,
And a fleet foot high upon Ishkar's hill,
When the watch-lights glimmered afar;
And as fiery a barb as any I know
That Kurd or Bedouin rides,
Ere my friends lay low, long, long ago,
In the time of the Barmecides.
Ere my friends lay low, long, long ago,
In the time of the Barmecides.

One golden goblet illumed my board,
One silver dish was there;
At hand my tried Karamanian sword
Lay always bright and bare;
For those were the days when the angry blow
Supplanted the word that chides,

U

When hearts could glow, long, long ago,
In the time of the Barmecides;
When hearts could glow, long, long ago,
In the time of the Barmecides.

Thro' city and desert my mates and I
Were free to rove and roam,
Our diapered canopy the deep of the sky,
Or the roof of the palace dome:
O ours was that vivid life to and fro
Which only sloth derides!
Men spent life so, long, long ago,
In the time of the Barmecides;
Men spent life so, long, long ago,
In the time of the Barmecides.,

I see rich Bagdad once again,
With its turrets of Moorish mould,
And the Caliph's twice five hundred men
Whose binishes flamed with gold;
I call up many a gorgeous show
Which the pall of oblivion hides:
All passed like snow, long, long ago,
With the time of the Barmecides;
All passed like snow, long, long ago,
With the time of the Barmecides.

But mine eye is dim, and my beard is gray,
And I bend with the weight of years.
May I soon go down to the house of clay
Where slumber my youth's compeers!

For with them and the past, tho' the thought wakes
    woe,
My memory ever abides;
And I mourn for the times gone long ago,
For the times of the Barmecides!
I mourn for the times gone long ago,
For the times of the Barmecides!

Original Poems

II. Pro Patria

IRISH NATIONAL HYMN

O Ireland, ancient Ireland!
Ancient, yet for ever young,
Thou our mother, home and sireland,
Thou at length hast found a tongue.
Proudly thou, at length,
Resistest in triumphant strength;
Thy flag of freedom floats unfurled;
And as that mighty God existeth,
Who giveth victory when and where He listeth,
Thou yet shalt wake and shake the nations of the
world!

For this dull world still slumbers,
Witless of its wants or loves,
Though, like Galileo, numbers
Cry aloud " It moves! it moves!"
In a midnight dream,
Drifts it down time's wreckful stream.
All march, but few descry the goal.
O Ireland! be it thy high duty
To teach the world the might of moral beauty,
And stamp God's image truly on the struggling soul.

Strong in thy self-reliance,
Not in idle threat or boast,

Hast thou hurled thy fierce defiance
At the haughty Saxon host;
Thou hast claimed, in sight
Of high Heaven, thy long-lost right.
Upon thy hills, along thy plains,
In the green bosom of thy valleys,
The new-born soul of holy freedom rallies,
And calls on thee to trample down in dust thy chains !

Deep, saith the eastern story,
Burns in Iran's mines a gem,
For its dazzling hues and glory
Worth a Sultan's diadem.
But from human eyes
Hidden there it ever lies !
The aye-travailing gnomes alone,
Who toil to form the mountain's treasure,
May gaze and gloat, with pleasure without measure,
Upon the lustrous beauty of that wonder-stone.

So is it with a nation
Which would win for richest dower
That bright pearl, self-liberation :
It must labor hour by hour.
Strangers, who travail
To lay bare the gem, shall fail;
Within itself, must grow, must glow,
Within the depths of its own bosom
Must flower in living might, must broadly blossom
The hopes that shall be born ere freedom's tree can
    blow.

Go on, then, all rejoiceful!
March on thy career, unbowed!
Ireland! let thy noble voiceful
Spirit cry to God aloud!
Man will bid thee speed,
God will aid thee in thy need;
The time, the hour, the power are near:
Be sure thou soon shalt form the vanguard
Of that illustrious band, whom Heaven and man
    guard:
And these words come from one whom some have
    called a seer.

AN INVITATION (40)

Friends to freedom! is't not time
That your course were shaped at length?
Wherefore stand ye loitering here?
Seek some healthier, holier clime,
Where your souls may grow in strength,
And whence love hath exiled fear!

Europe, — Southron, Saxon, Celt,
Sits alone, in tattered robe.
In our day she burns with none
Of the lightning-life she felt,
When Rome shook the troubled globe,
Twenty centuries agone.

Deutschland sleeps: her star hath waned.
France, the thundress whilom, now

Singeth small, with bated breath.
Spain is bleeding, Poland chained;
Italy can but groan and vow;
England lieth sick to death.[1]

Cross with me the Atlantic's foam,
And your genuine goal is won!
Purely freedom's breezes blow,
Merrily freedom's children roam,
By the dædal Amazon,
And the glorious Ohio!

Thither take not gems and gold:
Naught from Europe's robber-hoards
Must profane the western zones.
Thither take ye spirits bold,
Thither take ye ploughs and swords,
And your fathers' buried bones!

Come! if liberty's true fires
Burn within your bosoms, come!
If ye would that in your graves
Your free sons should bless their sires,
Make the far green west your home;
Cross with me the Atlantic waves!

---

[1] "England leidet von einer todtlichen Krankheit, ohne Hoffnung wie ohne Heilung." — England labors under a deadly sickness without hope and without remedy. — NIEBUHR.

SOUL AND COUNTRY

Arise, my slumbering soul, arise!
And learn what yet remains for thee
To dree or do!
The signs are flaming in the skies;
A struggling world would yet be free,
And live anew.
The earthquake hath not yet been born
That soon shall rock the lands around,
Beneath their base.
Immortal freedom's thunder-horn,
As yet, yields but a doleful sound
To Europe's race.

Look round, my soul, and see and say
If those about thee understand
Their mission here;
The will to smite, the power to slay,
Abound in every heart and hand,
Afar, anear.
But, God! must yet the conqueror's sword
Pierce mind, as heart, in this proud year?
O dream it not!
It sounds a false blaspheming word,
Begot and born of moral fear,
And ill-begot!

To leave the world a name is naught;
To leave a name for glorious deeds

And works of love,
A name to waken lightning thought,
And fire the soul of him who reads,
This tells above.
Napoleon sinks to-day before
The ungilded shrine, the single soul
Of Washington;
Truth's name, alone, shall man adore,
Long as the waves of time shall roll
Henceforward on!

My countrymen! my words are weak,
My health is gone, my soul is dark,
My heart is chill;
Yet would I fain and fondly seek
To see you borne in freedom's bark
O'er ocean still.
Beseech your God, and bide your hour:
He cannot, will not, long be dumb;
Even now His tread
Is heard o'er earth with coming power;
And coming, trust me, it will come,
Else were He dead!

A HIGHWAY FOR FREEDOM

" My suffering country shall be freed,
And shine with tenfold glory!"
So spake the gallant Winkelried
Renowned in German story.

"No tyrant, though of kingly grade,
Shall cross or darken my way!"
Out flashed his blade; and so he made
For freedom's course a highway.

We want a man like this, with power
To rouse the world by one word;
We want a chief to meet the hour,
To march the masses sunward.
But chief or none, thro' blood and fire
My fatherland lies thy way!
The men must fight who dare desire
For freedom's course a highway.

Alas, I can but idly gaze
Around, in grief and wonder;
The people's will alone can raise
The people's shout of thunder.
Too long, O friends! you faint for fear
In secret crypt and byway;
At last, be men! Stand forth, and clear
For freedom's course a highway.

You intersect wood, lea, and lawn
With roads for monster wagons,
Wherein you speed like lightning, drawn
By fiery iron dragons.
So do: such work is good, no doubt.
But why not seek some high way
For Mind, as well? Path also out
For freedom's course a highway!

Yes, up! and let your weapons be
Sharp steel, and self-reliance.
Why waste a burning energy
In void and vain defiance,
And phrases fierce and fugitive?
'Tis deeds, not words, that I weigh:
Your swords, your guns, alone can give
To freedom's course a highway!

TO MY NATIVE LAND

Awake, arise, shake off thy dreams!
Thou art not what thou wert of yore.
Of all those rich, those dazzling beams
That once illumed thine aspect o'er,
Show me a solitary one
Whose glory is not quenched and done.

The harp remaineth where it fell,
With mouldering frame and broken chord;
Around the song there hangs no spell,
No laurel wreath entwines the sword;
And startlingly the footstep falls
Along thy dim and dreary halls.

When other men in future years
In wonder ask how this could be,
Then answer only by thy tears
That ruin fell on thine and thee,

Because thyself wouldst have it so,
Because thou welcomedst the blow

To stamp dishonor on thy brow
Was not within the power of earth.
And art thou agonized, when now
The hour that lost thee all thy worth,
And turned thee to the thing thou art,
Rushes upon thy bleeding heart?

Weep, weep, degraded one: the deed,
The desperate deed, was all thine own;
Thou madest more than maniac speed
To hurl thine honors from their throne.
Thine honors fell; and when they fell,
The nations rang thy funeral knell.

Well may thy sons be seared in soul,
Their groans be deep by night and day!
Till day and night forget to roll,
Their noblest hopes shall morn decay;
Their freshest flowers shall die by blight;
Their brightest sun shall set ere night.

The stranger, as he treads thy sod
And views thy universal wreck,
May execrate the foot that trod
Triumphant on a prostrate neck;
But what is that to thee? Thy woes
May hope in vain for pause or close.

Awake, arise, shake off thy dreams!
'Tis idle all to talk of power
And fame and glory; these are themes
Befitting ill so dark an hour.
Till miracles are wrought for thee,
No fame nor glory shalt thou see.

Thou art forsaken of the earth,
Which makes a byword of thy name.
Nations, and thrones, and powers whose birth
As yet is not, shall rise to fame,
Shall flourish, and may fall: but thou
Shalt linger, as thou lingerest now.

And till all earthly power shall wane,
And time's gray pillar, groaning, fall,
Thus shall it be! and still in vain
Thou shalt essay to burst the thrall
Which binds, in fetters forged by fate,
The wreck and ruin of what once was great.

HYMN FOR PENTECOST (41)

Pure Spirit of the alway-faithful God,
Kindler of Heaven's true light within the soul!
From the lorn land our sainted fathers trod,
Ascends to Thee our cry of hope and dole.
Thee, Thee we praise;
To Thee we raise
Our choral hymn in these awakening days:

O send us down anew that fire
Which of old lived in David's and Isaiah's lyre.

Centuries had rolled, and earth lay tombed in sleep,
The nightmare-sleep of nations beneath kings;
And far abroad o'er liberty's great deep
Death's angel waved his black and stilling wings.
Then struck Thine hour!
Thou, in Thy power,
But breathedst, and the free stood up, a tower;
And tyranny's thrones and strongholds fell,
And men made jubilee for an abolished hell.

And she, our mother-home, the famed, the fair,
The golden house of light and intellect,
Must she still groan in her intense despair?
Shall she lie prone while Europe stands erect?
Forfend this, Thou
To whom we vow
Souls even our giant wrongs shall never bow:
Thou wilt not leave our green flag furled,
Nor bear that we abide the byword of the world.

Like the last lamp that burned in Tullia's tomb
Through ages, vainly, with unwaning ray,
Our star of hope lights but a path of gloom
Whose false track leads us round and round alway.
But thou canst ope
A gate from hope
To victory! Thou canst nerve our arms to cope
With looming storm and danger still,
And lend a thunder-voice to the land's lightning-will.

x

Descend then, Spirit of the Eternal King!
To thee, to Him, to His avenging Son,
The Triune God, in boundless trust we cling:
His help once ours, our nationhood is won.
We watch the time
Till that sublime
Event shall thrill the free of every clime.
Speed, mighty Spirit! speed its march,
And thus complete for earth mankind's triumphal arch.

Original Poems

III. Those on Miscellaneous Subjects

POMPEII (42)

The heralds of thy ruin and despair
Thickened and quickened as thy time drew nigh:
What prodigies of sound convulsed the air!
How many a death-flag was unfurled on high!
The sullen sun went down, a globe of blood,
Rayless, and coloring every heart with gloom,
Till even the dullest felt and understood
The coming of an overwhelming doom,
The presage of a destiny and fall,
A shock, a thunder-shock, for thee, for them, for all.

The sullen sun went down, a globe of blood
Rayless, and coloring every soul with gloom;
And men's imagination, prone to brood
Over the worst, and summon from the womb
Of unborn time the evil and the dark,
Launched forth in fear upon that shoreless ocean
Whose whirlpool billows but engulf the barque.
Conjectural dread, and each fresh-felt emotion,
Like spectral figures on a magic mirror,
Seemed wilder than the last, and stronglier stung with
        terror.

We shrink within ourselves when night and storm
Are darkly mustering; for to every soul
Heaven here foreshadows character and form
Of Nature's death-hour.   Doth the thunder roll,

The wild wave boil, the lightning stream or strike,
Flood, fire, and earthquake devastate, in vain?
Or is there not a voice which peals alike
To all, from these, conjuring up that train
Of scenes and images that shall be born
In living naked might upon the Judgment Morn?

If thus we cower to tempest and to night,
How feltest thou when first the red bolt broke,
That seventeen suffocating centuries might
Enshroud thine ashes in time's midnight cloak?
Where wert thou in that moment?   Was thy power
All a funereal phantom? thy renown
An echo? thine the triumph of an hour?
Enough! I rave: when empires, worlds, go down
Time's wave to dissolution, when they bow
To fate, let none ask *where*, but simply *what* wert
    thou!

The desolated cities which of yore
Perished by flooding fire and sulphury rain,
Where sleeps the Dead Sea's immemorial shore,
Lie, blasted wrecks, below that mortar plain. (43)
They fell, thou fellest!   But, renounced of earth,
Blotted from being for eternal years,
Their image chills the life-blood: thine gives birth
Even while we shudder, to some human tears.
Hadst thou less guilt?   Who knows?   The book of
    time
Bears, on each leaf alike, the broad red stamp of
    crime.

TWENTY GOLDEN YEARS AGO (44)

O the rain, the weary, dreary rain,
How it plashes on the window-sill!
Night, I guess too, must be on the wane,
Strass and Gass¹ around are grown so still.
Here I sit, with coffee in my cup:
Ah! 'twas rarely I beheld it flow
In the tavern where I loved to sup
Twenty golden years ago!

Twenty years ago, alas! — (But stay:
On my life, 'tis half-past twelve o'clock!
After all, the hours do slip away.
Come, here goes to burn another block.
For the night, or morn, is wet and cold,
And my fire is dwindling rather low:
I had fire enough, when young and bold,
Twenty golden years ago.)

Dear! I don't feel well at all, somehow:
Few in Weimar dream how bad I am.
Floods of tears grow common with me now,
High Dutch floods, that reason cannot dam.
Doctors think I'll neither live nor thrive
If I mope at home so; I don't know!
Am I living now? I was alive
Twenty golden years ago.

¹ Street and lane.

Wifeless, friendless, flagonless, alone,
Not quite bookless, tho', unless I choose;
Left with naught to do, except to groan,
Not a soul to woo, except the muse; —
O but this is hard for me to bear,
Me, who whilom lived so much *en haut*,
Me, who broke all hearts like chinaware,
Twenty golden years ago!

Perhaps 'tis better time's defacing waves
Long have quenched the radiance of my brow;
They who curse me nightly from their graves,
Scarce could love me were they living now.
But my loneliness hath darker ills:
Such dun duns as Conscience, Thought and Co.,
Awful Gorgons! worse than tailor's bills
Twenty golden years ago!

Did I paint a fifth of what I feel,
O how plaintive you would ween I was!
But I won't, albeit I have a deal
More to wail about than Kerner has!
Kerner's tears are wept for withered flowers,
Mine for withered hopes; my scroll of woe
Dates, alas, from youth's deserted bowers,
Twenty golden years ago!

Yet, may Deutschland bardlings flourish long!
Me, I tweak no beak among them; hawks
Must not pounce on hawks: besides, in song
I could once beat all of them by chalks.

Though you find me, as I near my goal,
Sentimentalizing like Rousseau,
Ah, I had a grand Byronian soul
Twenty golden years ago!

Tick-tick, tick-tick! — Not a sound save time's,
And the wind-gust as it drives the rain.
Tortured torturer of reluctant rhymes,
Go to bed, and rest thine aching brain!
Sleep! no more the dupe of hopes or schemes.
Soon thou sleepest where the thistles blow:
Curious anticlimax to thy dreams
Twenty golden years ago!

TO LAURA (45)

The charm that gilded life is over!
I live to feel I live in vain,
And worlds were worthless to recover
That dazzling dream of mine again.
The idol I adored is broken,
And I may weep its overthrow;
Thy lips at length my doom have spoken,
And nothing now remains but woe.

And is it, indeed, we sever,
And hast thou, then, forgotten all?
And canst thou cast me off for ever,
To mourn, a dark and hopeless thrall?
O perfidy! In friend or foe,
In stranger, lover, husband, wife,

Thou art the blackest drop of woe
That bubbles in the cup of life.

But most of all in woman's breast
Triumphant in thy blasting power,
Thou reignest like a demon-guest
Enthroned in some celestial bower.
Oh, cold and cruel she, who while
She lavishes all wiles to win
Her lover o'er, can smile and smile,
Yet be all dark and false within.

Who, when his glances on another
Too idly and too long have dwelt,
Will sigh as if she sought to smother
The grief her bosom never felt;
Who, versed in every witching art
That e'er the warmest love would dare,
First having gained her victim's heart,
Then turns him over to despair!

Alas, and can such treachery be?
The worm that winds in slime along,
Is nobler, better far than she
Who revels in that heartless wrong!
Go now, and triumph in thy guilt,
And weave thy wanton spells anew;
Go, false as fair, and, if thou wilt,
Again betray the fond and true.

Yet this, my last and long farewell,
Is less in anger than in sorrow;

Mine is the tale which myriads tell
Who loathe to-day, and dread to-morrow.
Me, Frances! me thou never knewest,
Nor sawest, that if my speech was cold,
The love is deepest oft, and truest
That burns within the breast untold.

My soul was formed for love and grief;
These both were blended at my birth;
But lifeless as a shrivelled leaf,
Lie now my dearest hopes in earth.
I sigh, when none my sighs return;
I love, but am not loved again:
Till life be past this heart must burn,
With none to soothe or share its pain.

Farewell! In life's gay giddy whirl
Soon wilt thou have forgotten me;
But where, O most dissembling girl!
Where shall I from thine image flee?
Farewell! for thee the heavens are bright,
And flowers along thy pathway lie;
The bolts that strike, the winds that blight
Will pass thy bower of beauty by.

But when shall I find rest? Alas,
Soon as the winter winds shall rave
At midnight, thro' the long dark grass
Above mine unremembered grave.

SONNET

Bird that discoursest from yon poplar bough,
Outweeping night, and in thy eloquent tears
Holding sweet converse with the thousand spheres
That glow and glisten from night's glorious brow,
O may thy lot be mine! that, lonely now,
And doomed to mourn the remnant of my years,
My song may swell to more than mortal ears,
And sweet as is thy strain be poured my vow.

Bird of the poets' paradise! by thee
Taught where the tides of feeling deepest tremble,
Playful in gloom, like some sequestered sea,
I too amidst my anguish would dissemble,
And tune misfortune to such melody,
That my despair thy transports should resemble.

CURTAIN THE LAMP

Curtain the lamp, and bury the bowl,
The ban is on drinking;
Reason shall reign the queen of the soul
When the spirits are sinking.
Chained lies the demon that smote with blight
Men's morals and laurels,
Then hail to health, and a long good night
To old wine, and new quarrels!

Nights shall descend, and no taverns ring
To the roar of our revels;

Mornings shall dawn but none of them bring
White lips and blue devils.
Riot and frenzy sleep with remorse
In the obsolete potion,
And mind grows calm as a ship on her course
O'er the level of ocean.

So should it be! for man's world of romance
Is fast disappearing,
And shadows of changes are seen in advance,
Whose epochs are nearing.
And the days are at hand, when the best shall require
All means of salvation.
And the souls of men shall be tried in the fire
Of the final probation!

And the witling no longer or sneers or smiles,
And the worldling dissembles,
And the black-hearted sceptic feels anxious at whiles,
And marvels and trembles;
And fear and defiance are blent in the jest
Of the blind self-deceiver;
But hope bounds high in the joyous breast
Of the childlike believer!

Darken the lamp then, and shatter the bowl,
Ye faithfullest-hearted!
And as your swift years travel on to the goal
Whither worlds have departed,
Spend labor, life, soul, in your zeal to atone
For the past and its errors:
So best shall you bear to encounter alone
The Event! and its terrors.

THE DYING ENTHUSIAST (46)

Speak no more of life!
What can life bestow
In this amphitheatre of strife
All times dark with tragedy and woe?
Know'st thou not how care and pain
Build their lampless dwelling in the brain,
Even as the stern intrusion
Of our teachers, time and truth,
Turn to gloom the bright illusions
Rainbowed on the soul of youth?
Could I live to find that this is so?
Oh! no, no.

As the stream of time
Sluggishly doth flow,
Look, how all of beaming or sublime
Sinks into the black abysm below!
Yea, the loftiest intellect
Earliest on the strand of life is wrecked.
Naught of lovely, nothing glorious,
Lives to triumph o'er decay;
Desolation reigns victorious:
Mind is dungeon-walled by clay:
Could I bear to feel mine own laid low?
Oh! no, no.

Restless o'er the earth,
Thronging millions go:
But behold how genius, love, and worth,
Move like lonely phantoms to and fro.

Suns are quenched, and kingdoms fall,
But the doom of these outdarkens all !
Die they then ?   Yes, love's devotion,
Stricken, withers in its bloom;
Fond affections, deep as ocean,
In their cradle find their tomb :
Shall I linger, then, to count each throe ?
Oh ! no, no.

Prison-bursting death !
Welcome be thy blow !
Thine is but the forfeit of my breath,
Not the spirit, nor the spirit's glow.
Spheres of beauty, hallowed spheres
Undefaced by time, undimmed by tears,
Henceforth hail !   Oh, who would grovel
In a world impure as this,
Who would weep in cell or hovel,
When a palace might be his ?
Wouldst thou have me that bright lot forego ?
Oh ! no, no.

TO JOSEPH BRENAN (47)

Friend and brother, and yet more than brother,
Thou endowed with all of Shelley's soul !
Thou whose heart so burneth for thy Mother,
That, like his, it may defy all other
Flames, while time shall roll !

Thou of language bland, and manner meekest,
Gentle bearing, yet unswerving will!
Gladly, gladly, list I when thou speakest:
Honored highly is the man thou seekest
To redeem from ill!

Truly showest thou me the one thing needful!
Thou art not, nor is the world, yet blind.
Truly have I been long years unheedful
Of the thorns and tares that choked the weedful
Garden of my mind!

Thorns and tares which rose in rank profusion
Round my scanty fruitage and my flowers,
Till I almost deemed it self-delusion,
To attempt or glance at their extrusion
From their midnight bowers.

Dream and waking life have now been blended
Long time in the caverns of my soul;
Oft in daylight have my steps descended
Down to that dusk realm where all is ended,
Save remeadless dole!

Oft, with tears, I have groaned to God for pity,
Oft gone wandering till my way grew dim;
Oft sung unto Him a prayerful ditty,
Oft, all lonely in this throngful city,
Raised my soul to Him!

And from path to path His mercy tracked me:
From a many a peril snatched He me;

When false friends pursued, betrayed, attacked me,
When gloom overdarked, and sickness racked me,
He was by to save and free!

Friend! thou warnest me in truly noble
Thoughts and phrases: I will heed thee well.
Well will I obey thy mystic double
Counsel, through all scenes of woe and trouble,
As a magic spell!

Yes! to live a bard, in thought and feeling:
Yes! to act my rhyme, by self-restraint,
This is truth's, is reason's deep revealing
Unto me from thee, as God's to a kneeling
And entrancèd saint!

Fare thee well! We now know each the other;
Each has struck the other's inmost chords;
Fare thee well, my friend and more than brother:
And may scorn pursue me, if I smother
In my soul thy words!

LINES ON THE DEATH OF C. H. (48)

I stood aloof: I dared not to behold
Thy relics covered over with the mould;
I shed no tear, I uttered not a groan,
But Oh, I felt heartbroken and alone.

Y

How feel I now?   The bitterness of grief
Has passed, for all that is intense is brief.
A softer sadness overshades my mind,
But there thine image ever lies enshrined.

And if I mourn, (for this is human, too,)
I mourn no longer that thy days were few,
Nor that thou hast escaped the tears and woe,
And deaths on deaths the living undergo.

Thou fadedst in the springtime of thy years :
Life's juggling joys and spirit-wasting fears
Thou knewest but in romance : and to thine eyes
Man shone a god, the earth a paradise.

Thou diedst ere the icy breath of scorn
Froze the warm feelings of thy girlhood's morn,
Ere thou couldst learn that man is but a slave,
And this bleak world a prison and a grave.

Thy spirit is at peace : peace! blessed word
Forgotten by the million, or unheard.
But mine still struggles down this vale of death,
And courts the favor of a little breath.

Thro' every stage of life's consuming fever
The soul too often is her own deceiver,
And revels, even in a world like this,
In golden visions of unbounded bliss.

But he who, looking on the naked chart
Of life, feels nature sinking at his heart,

He who is drugged with sorrow, he for whom
Affliction carves a pathway to the tomb,

He will unite with me to bless that Power
Who gathers and transplants the fragile flower
Ere yet the spirit of the whirlwind storm
Comes forth in wrath to prostrate and deform.

And if it be that God Himself removes
From peril and contagion those He loves,
Weep such no more; but strew with freshest roses
The hallowed mound where innocence reposes.

THE WORLD'S CHANGES

The solemn Shadow that bears in his hands
The conquering scythe, and the glass of sands,
Paused once on his flight where the sunrise shone
On a warlike city's towers of stone;
And he asked of a panoplied soldier near :
" How long has this fortressed city been here ? "
And the man looked up, man's pride on his brow :
" The city stands here from the ages of old ;
And as it was then, and as it is now,
So will it endure till the funeral knell
Of the world be knolled,
As eternity's annals shall tell."

And after a thousand years were o'er,
The Shadow paused over the spot once more.

And vestige was none of a city there,
But lakes lay blue, and plains lay bare,
And the marshalled corn stood high and pale,
And a shepherd piped of love in a vale.
" How," spake the Shadow, " can temple and tower
Thus fleet like mist from the morning hour ? "
But the shepherd shook the long locks from his brow :
" The world is filled with sheep and corn !
Thus was it of old, thus is it now :
Thus, too, will it be while moon and sun
Rule night and morn,
For Nature and life are one."

And after a thousand years were o'er,
The Shadow paused over the spot once more.

And lo ! in the room of the meadow-lands
A sea foamed far over saffron sands,
And flashed in the noontide, bright and dark ;
And a fisher was casting his nets from a barque.
How marvelled the Shadow !   " Where, then, is the
        plain ?
And where be the acres of golden grain ? "
But the fisher dashed off the salt spray from his brow :
" These waters begirdle the earth alway ;
The sea ever rolled, as it rolleth now.
What babblest thou about grain and fields ?
By night, by day,
Man looks for what ocean yields."

And after a thousand years were o'er,
The Shadow paused over the spot once more.

And the ruddy rays of the eventide
Were gilding the skirts of a forest wide;
The moss of the trees looked old, so old !
And, valley and hill, the ancient mould
Was robed in sward, an evergreen cloak :
And a woodman sang as he felled an oak.
Him asked the Shadow : " Rememberest thou
Any trace of a sea where wave those trees ? "
But the woodman laughed.   Said he : " I trow
If oak and pine do flourish and fall,
It is not amid seas !
The earth is one forest all."

And after a thousand years were o'er,
The Shadow paused over the spot once more.

And what saw the Shadow ?   A city again ;
But peopled by pale mechanical men,
With workhouses filled, and prisons, and marts,
And faces that spake exanimate hearts :
Strange picture, and sad ! was the Shadow's thought ;
And turning to one of the ghastly, he sought
For a clue in words to the when and the how
Of the ominous change he now beheld.
But the man uplifted his careworn brow :
" Change ?   What   was   life   ever   but   conflict   and
          change ?
From the ages of eld,
Hath affliction been widening her range."

" Enough ! " said the Shadow, and passed from the spot :
" At last it is vanished, the beautiful youth

Of the earth, to return with to-morrow;
All changes have checkered mortality's lot,
But this is the darkest; for knowledge and truth
Are but golden gates to the temple of sorrow."

THE DEPARTURE OF LOVE (49)

Spirit of wordless love, that in the lone
Bowers of the poet's musing soul doth weave
Tissues of thought hued like the skies at eve
Ere the last glories of the sun are flown!
How soon, almost before our hearts have known
The change, above the ruins of thy throne
Whose vanished beauty we would fain retrieve
With all earth's thrones beside, we stand and grieve,
But weep not: for the world's chill breath has bound
In chains of ice the fountains of our tears,
And ever-mourning memory thenceforth rears
Her altars upon desecrated ground,
And always, with a low despondful sound,
Tolls the disastrous bell of all our years.

BEAR UP

Time rolleth on; and with our years
Our sorrows grow and multiply,
Our visions fade;
With late remorse and withering fears,

We look for light to days gone by :
But all is shade.
Our dear fond friends have long been gone,
No moon is up in heaven above ;
The chill winds blow.
The dolorous night of age comes on :
The current of our life and love
Moves low, moves slow.

Yet earth hath still a twofold dower :
On desert sands the palm-trees rise
In greenest bloom ;
The dawn breaks at the darkest hour ;
Stars brightliest shine when midnight skies
Are palled in gloom ;
The deep hath treasures unrevealed
Of gold and gems and argosies
And gallant ships ;
The sword strikes hurtless on the shield ;
And from the once plague-laden breeze
Health greets thy lips !

Thou, therefore, man, shalt never droop,
Shalt never doubt, shalt always trust
The power of God :
Thou art not heaven's or nature's dupe !
This fleshly hull shall rot in dust,
A trodden clod.
But wilt thou cower, tho' death draw nigh ?
The mouldering frame, the eternal soul,
Which, say, is best ?
Thou canst not live unless thou die,

Thou must march far to reach thy goal
Of endless rest.

Bear up, even tho' thou be like me
Stretched on a couch of torturing pain
This weary day;
Tho' heaven and earth seem dark to thee,
And thine eye glance around in vain
For one hope-ray!
Tho' overborne by wrong and ill,
Tho' thou hast drained even to the lees
Life's bitter cup,
Though death and hell be round thee, still
Place faith in God: He hears, He sees.
Bear up!   Bear up!

TWO SONNETS TO CAROLINE

I

Have I not called thee angel-like and fair?
What wouldst thou more?   'Twere perilous to gaze
Long on those dark-bright eyes, whose flashing rays
Fill with a soft and fond, yet proud, despair
The bosoms of the shrouded few, who share
Their locked-up thoughts with none.   Thou hast
        their praise;
But Beauty hears not their adoring lays
Which tremble when but whispered to the air.
Yet think not, altho' stamped as one of those,

Ah, think not thou this heart hath never burned
With passion deeply felt and ill-returned.
If ice-cold now, its pulse no longer glows,
The memory of unuttered love and woes
Lies there, alas, too faithfully inurned.

II

For once I dreamed that mutual love was more
Than a bright phantom thought; and when mankind
Mocked mine illusion, then would I deplore
That ignorance, and deem them cold and blind;
And years rolled on, and still did I adore
The unreal image loftily enshrined
In the recesses of mine own sick mind.
Enough : the spell is broke, the dream is o'er,
The enchantment is dissolved; the world appears
The thing it is, a theatre, a mart.
Genius illumines, and the wand of art
Renews the wonder of our childish years;
Power awes, wealth shines, wit sparkles; but the
        heart,
The heart is lost, for love no more endears.

ENTHUSIASM

Not yet trodden-under wholly,
Not yet darkened,
O my spirit's flickering lamp! art thou:
Still, alas, thou wanest, tho' but slowly,

And I feel as if my heart had hearkened
To the whispers of despondence now.

Yet the world shall not enthrall me.
Never, never!
On my briary pathway to the grave
Shapes of pain and peril may appal me,
Agony and ruin may befall me,
Darkness and dismay may hover ever;
But, cold world, I will not die thy slave.

Underneath my feet I trample
You, ye juggles:
Pleasure, passion, thirst of power and gold.
Shall I, dare I, shame the bright example
Beaming, burning, in the deeds and struggles
Of the consecrated few of old?

Sacred flame which art eternal,
O bright essence,
Thou, enthusiasm! forsake me not.
Ah, tho' life be reft of all her vernal
Beauty, ever let thy magic presence
Shed its glory round my clouded lot.

THE LOVELY LAND: ON A LANDSCAPE PAINTED BY MACLISE

Glorious birth of mind and color!
Gazing on thy radiant face,
The most lorn of Adam's race
Might forget all dolor!

What divinest light is beaming
Over mountain, mead, and grove!
That blue noontide sky above,
Seems asleep and dreaming.

Rich Italia's wild-birds warble
In the foliage of those trees :
I can trace thee, Veronese,
In these rocks of marble!

Yet, no!   Mark I not where quiver
The sun's rays on yonder stream?
Only a Poussin could dream
Such a sun and river.

What bold imaging!   Stony valley,
And fair bower of eglantine;
Here I see the black ravine,
There the lilied alley.

This is some rare climate olden,
Peopled, not by men, but fays;
Some lone land of genii days,
Storyful and golden!

O for magic power to wander
One bright year through such a land!
Might I even one hour stand
On the blest hills yonder!

But—what spy I? . . .   Here by noonlight
'Tis the same! the pillar-tower
I have oft passed thrice an hour,
Twilight, sunlight, moonlight.

Shame to me, my own, my sireland,
Not to know thy soil and skies!
Shame, that through Maclise's eyes
I first see thee, Ireland!

Nay, no land doth rank above thee
Or for loveliness or worth:
So shall I, from this day forth,
Ever sing and love thee.

FRONTI NULLA FIDES

Beware of blindly trusting
To outward art,
And specious sheen;
For vice is oft encrusting
The hollow heart
Within, unseen.
See that black pool below thee!
There heaven sleeps
In golden fire.
Yet whatsoe'er it show thee,
The mirror's deeps
Are slime and mire.

SIBERIA (50)

In Siberia's wastes
The ice-wind's breath
Woundeth like the toothèd steel:

Lost Siberia doth reveal
Only blight and death.

Blight and death alone.
No summer shines;
Night is interblent with day;
In Siberia's wastes, alway
The blood blackens, the heart pines.

In Siberia's wastes
No tears are shed,
For they freeze within the brain :
Naught is felt but dullest pain,
Pain acute, yet dead;

Pain as in a dream,
When years go by
Funeral-paced, yet fugitive;
When man lives and doth not live,
Doth not live, nor die.

In Siberia's wastes
Are sands and rocks.
Nothing blooms of green or soft,
But the snow-peaks rise aloft,
And the gaunt ice-blocks.

And the exile there
Is one with those;
They are part, and he is part !
For the sands are in his heart,
And the killing snows.

Therefore, in those wastes
None curse the Czar.
Each man's tongue is cloven by
The north blast, that heweth nigh
With sharp scimitar.

And such doom each drees,
Till, hunger-gnawn,
Cold-slain, he at length sinks there;
Yet scarce more a corpse than ere
His last breath was drawn.

A VISION OF CONNAUGHT IN THE THIRTEENTH CENTURY

("Et moi, j'ai été aussi en Arcadie." — And I, I, too, have been a dreamer. — *Inscription on a Painting by Poussin.*)

I walked entranced
Through a land of morn;
The sun, with wondrous excess of light,
Shone down and glanced
Over seas of corn
And lustrous gardens aleft and right.
Even in the clime
Of resplendent Spain,
Beams no such sun upon such a land;
But it was the time,
'Twas in the reign,
Of Cahal Mor of the Wine-red Hand.[1]

[1] The Irish and Oriental poets agree in attributing favorable or unfavorable weather, and abundant or deficient harvests, to the good or bad qualities of the reigning monarch. *Mor* means great.

Anon stood nigh
By my side a man
Of princely aspect and port sublime.
Him queried I,
" O my Lord and Khan ! [1]
What clime is this, and what golden time ? "
When he : " The clime
Is a clime to praise,
The clime is Erin's, the green and bland ;
And it is the time,
These be the days,
Of Cahal Mor of the Wine-red Hand ! "

Then saw I thrones,
And circling fires,
And a dome rose near me, as by a spell,
Whence flowed the tones
Of silver lyres,
And many voices in wreathèd swell ;
And their thrilling chime
Fell on mine ears
As the heavenly hymn of an angel-band :
" It is now the time,
These be the years,
Of Cahal Mor of the Wine-red Hand ! "

I sought the hall,
And behold ! a change
From light to darkness, from joy to woe.
Kings, nobles, all,

---

[1] *Ceann*, the Gaelic title for a chief.

Looked aghast and strange;
The minstrel group sat in dumbest show.
Had some great crime
Wrought this dread amaze,
This terror? . . . None seemed to understand.
'Twas then the time,
We were in the days,
Of Cahal Mor of the Wine-red Hand.

I again walked forth;
But lo, the sky
Showed flecked with blood, and an alien sun
Glared from the north,
And there stood on high,
Amid his shorn beams, a skeleton![1] . . .
It was by the stream
Of the castled Maine,
One autumn eve, in the Teuton's land,
That I dreamed this dream
Of the time and reign
Of Cahal Mor of the Wine-red Hand.

[1] "It was but natural that these portentous appearances should thus be
exhibited on this occasion, for they were the heralds of a very great calamity
that befell the Connacians in this year; namely, the death of Cahal of the
Red Hand, son of Torlogh Mor of the Wine, and King of Connaught, a
prince of most amiable qualities, and into whose heart God had infused more
piety and goodness than into the hearts of any of his contemporaries." —
Annals of the Four Masters, A.D. 1224.

THE SAW–MILL

My path lay towards the Mourne again;
But I stopped to rest by the hillside
That glanced adown o'er the sunken glen,
Which the saw-and-water-mills hide,
Which now, as then,
The saw-and-water-mills hide.

And there, as I lay reclined on the hill,
Like a man made by sudden qualm ill, (51)
I heard the water in the water-mill,
And I saw the saw in the saw-mill. ·
As I thus lay still,
I saw the saw in the saw-mill.

The saw, the breeze, and the humming bees
Lulled me into a dreamy reverie,
Till the objects round me, hills, mills, trees,
Seemed grown alive all and every;
By slow degrees
Took life, as it were, all and every!

Anon the sound of the waters grew
To a mournful ditty,
And the song of the tree that the saw sawed through
Disturbed my spirit with pity,
Began to subdue
My spirit with tenderest pity!

" O wanderer! the hour that brings thee back
Is of all meet hours the meetest.

z

Thou now, in sooth, art on the track,
Art nigher to home than thou weetest;
Thou hast thought time slack,
But his flight has been of the fleetest!

For thee it is that I dree such pain
As, when wounded, even a plank will;
My bosom is pierced, is rent in twain,
That thine may ever bide tranquil,
May ever remain
Henceforward, untroubled and tranquil.

In a few days more, most lonely one!
Shall I, as a narrow ark, veil
Thine eyes from the glare of the world and sun,
'Mong the urns in yonder dark vale,
In the cold and dun
Recesses of yonder dark vale!

For this grieve not!   Thou knowest what thanks
The weary-souled and the meek owe
To Death!" . . .   I awoke, and heard four planks
Fall down with a saddening echo.
I heard four planks
Fall down with a hollow echo.

THE ONE MYSTERY

'Tis idle ! we exhaust and squander
The glittering mine of thought in vain ;
All-baffled reason cannot wander
Beyond her chain.
The flood of life runs dark ; .dark clouds
Make lampless night around its shore :
The dead, where are they ?   In their shrouds !
Man knows no more.

Evoke the ancient and the past ;
Will one illumining star arise ?
Or must the film, from first to last,
O'erspread thine eyes ?
When life, love, glory, beauty, wither,
Will wisdom's page, or science' chart,
Map out for thee the region whither
Their shades depart ?

Supposest thou the wondrous powers
To high imagination given,
Pale types of what shall yet be ours,
When earth is heaven ?
When this decaying shell is cold,
Ah, sayest thou the soul shall climb
That magic mount she trod of old,
Ere childhood's time ?

And shall the sacred pulse that thrilled,
Thrill once again to glory's name ?

And shall the conquering love that filled
All earth with flame,
Reborn, revived, renewed, immortal,
Resume his reign in prouder might,
A sun beyond the ebon portal
Of death and night?

No more, no more! . . . With aching brow,
And restless heart, and burning brain,
We ask the when, the where, the how,
And ask in vain.
And all philosophy, all faith,
All earthly, all celestial lore,
Have but one voice, which only saith:
Endure, adore.

THE NAMELESS ONE

Roll forth, my song, like the rushing river
That sweeps along to the mighty sea;
God will inspire me while I deliver
My soul of thee!

Tell thou the world, when my bones lie whitening
Amid the last homes of youth and eld,
That once there was one whose veins ran lightning
No eye beheld.

Tell how his boyhood was one drear night-hour,
How shone for him, through his grief and gloom,
No star of all heaven sends to light our
Path to the tomb.

Roll on, my song, and to after ages
Tell how, disdaining all earth can give,
He would have taught men, from wisdom's pages,
The way to live.

And tell how trampled, derided, hated,
And worn by weakness, disease, and wrong,
He fled for shelter to God, who mated
His soul with song;

With song which alway, sublime or vapid,
Flowed like a rill in the morning-beam,
Perchance not deep, but intense and rapid :
A mountain stream.

Tell how this Nameless, condemned for years long
To herd with demons from hell beneath,
Saw things that made him, with groans and tears, long
For even death.

Go on to tell how with genius wasted,
Betrayed in friendship, befooled in love,
With spirit shipwrecked, and young hope blasted,
He still, still strove,

Till, spent with toil, dreeing death for others,
(And some whose hands should have wrought for him,
If children live not for sires and mothers,)
His mind grew dim;

And he fell far through that pit abysmal,
The gulf and grave of Maginn and Burns,
And pawned his soul for the devil's dismal
Stock of returns;

But yet redeemed it in days of darkness,
And shapes and signs of the final wrath,
When death, in hideous and ghastly starkness,
Stood on his path.

And tell how now, amid wreck and sorrow,
And want, and sickness, and houseless nights,
He bides in calmness the silent morrow
That no ray lights.

And lives he still, then? Yes! Old and hoary
At thirty-nine, from despair and woe,
He lives, enduring what future story
Will never know.

Him grant a grave to, ye pitying noble,
Deep in your bosoms: there let him dwell!
He, too, had tears for all souls in trouble
Here, and in hell.

Notes by the Editor

NOTE 1, page 115. If our dear friend, Master Edmund Spenser, had had his way in the south of Ireland, we should hardly have occasion to be thankful for a contemporary poet in the north, and his *Roisin Dubh*. In *A View of the Present State*, Spenser puts in the mouth of Irenæus a plea for the extermination of the bards, already greatly injured by the penal statutes under Elizabeth. "I have caused divers of them to be translated unto me that I might understand them, and surely they savored of sweet wit and good invention . . . sprinkled with some pretty flowers of their own natural device, which gave good grace and comeliness unto them. . . . But they seldom use to choose unto themselves the doings of good men for the ornaments of their poems; but whomsoever they find to be most licentious of life, most bold and lawless in his doings, most dangerous and desperate in all parts of disobedience and rebellious disposition, him they set up and glorify in their rhymes, him they praise to the people, and to young men, make an example to follow." Had they but sung Gloriana !

2, p. 128. The illustrious Colonel Owen Roe O'Neill, nephew of the Earl of Tyrone, had, like most Irish exiles to Spain, seen service in Flanders. He returned home in 1642, and headed the revolt in Ulster. The royalist war was crushed by Cromwell, but O'Neill was already dead (1648).

3, p. 129. Donogh Mac Con-Mara (a name sometimes incorrectly given as Macnamara), a native of County Waterford, wrote this very lovely lyric in Gaelic, while he was keeping a boys' school in Hamburg. He was a great traveller, and had a most adventurous life. He was born in 1738, and dying in 1814, was buried at home.

4, p. 131. The peculiarly eighteenth-century Irish note of this characteristic poem is reason enough for its inclusion. The "marble" brow, the grave genealogical details, and the unavoidable reference to Helen of Troy, are most hedge-schoolmasterly touches.

5, p. 135. Neillidhe Bhán is an anonymous production. Its vehemence and incoherence stamp it as genuinely felt, as well as genuinely conceived. The lover boasts, in the first stanza, how gladly he would "breast the Shannon's waters" to reach the North, and in the third mentions "the flooding Shannon" as the reason of his absence!

6, p. 137. This O'Hussey is an undiscovered genius. In the *Ode for Cuconnaught in the North with Hugh* (his same chief, Hugh Maguire) occur some magnificent apostrophes, which should have adorned *Lyra Celtica*: —

> "Thou joy, thou promise, thou sprightly salmon!
> Thou beauteous azure ocean-wave!
> Thou pourer of panic into the breasts of heroes!"

The close of the *avran* in the poem translated by Mangan will appeal to every reader, in its concentrated passion.

7, p. 141. "No Irish pilgrim," says a sympathetic writer, "ascends the Janiculum without thinking of Mangan, and mentally repeating, 'O Woman of the Piercing Wail.'" The celebrated poem has an intense monotony, comparable to Homer's catalogue, in its imagination of scenes and circumstances which might have comforted by corroboration the Lady Nuala O'Donnell, and brought to her side a host of fellow-mourners. From this very Celtic circumstance it draws much of its powerful effect. It was included, long ago, in Gavan Duffy's *Ballad Poetry of Ireland* (the best anthology of the sort extant), and deeply impressed one of the finest of

English critics. Concerning the book, Lord Jeffrey wrote to Mrs. Empson : "There are some most pathetic and many most spirited pieces, and all, with scarcely an exception, so entirely *national.* Do get the book and read it. I am most struck with *Soggarth Aroon,* after the first two stanzas, and a long, racy, authentic-sounding dirge for the Tyrconnell Princes."

8, p. 150. Mangan made this translation in the early part of 1847. "I have not been able," he says, "to dis-cover the name of the author." There seems to be a great deal of Mangan in it, as it stands. In general character, however, it reminds one both of Neillidhe Bhán (Ellen Bawn) and the last three stanzas of the second part of *The Coolun,* a ballad put into enchanting English by Sir Samuel Fergu-son : —

"O had you seen the *coolun*
Walking down by the cuckoo's street !"

9, p. 152. Eoghan O'Sullivan the Red, an interesting Gaelic poet, cousin to Gaolach (Timothy) O'Sullivan, more celebrated than himself, died in 1784.

10, p. 156. "Dathi, nephew to Niall by his brother Fiachra, was the last pagan king of Ireland, and reigned twenty-three years. His proper name was Fearadhach ; but he was surnamed Dathi, from the rapidity with which he used to put on his armor : 'Daitheadh,' in the Irish lan-guage, signifying swiftness. He pillaged Gaul and carried his arms even to the Alps, where he was suddenly struck dead by a thunderbolt from heaven, thus expiating his sacri-legious cruelty to Parmenius, a man highly distinguished for sanctity, A.D. 428, A.M. 5627." — From *Cambrensis Ever-sus, seu Potius Historica Fides in Rebus Hibernicis Giraldo Cambrensi Abrogata,* by Gratianus Lucius (John Lynch), 1662.

11, p. 162. Sarsfield commanded a division of the loyal

Irish forces, nominally under King James the Second, at the battle of Boyne Water, 1688. "Change kings," he said in the bitter moment of his defeat, "and let us fight it over." He went into exile with the other Irish nobles and gentry, (the first of the never-forgotten "Wild Geese" of popular ballads), entered the service of France, and closed a most chivalrous career by a death on the battlefield of Landen (1693), where Luxembourg was victorious over the Allies. This most remarkable of the, *Farewells* to the Earl, at the time of his going over sea, is full of unique and vehement expressions, which will repay the study of any humanist.

12, p. 166. "Donegal Castle," says Thomas D'Arcy M'Gee, "the chief seat of the princely family of the O'Donnells, stands now in ruins, in the centre of the village of the same name, at the head of Donegal Bay. It was built in the fifteenth century, and shows, even in its decay, royal proportions." It now belongs to the Lord Arran. Hugh the Red O'Donnell, Earl of Tyrconnell, fired it before leaving for Spain, A.D. 1607, lest it should be defiled by English occupation. The original poem must have been composed by some one perfectly familiar with the castle interior, prior to the Elizabethan wars, but the bard's name has not come down to us. He may even be the same to whom we owe *Roisin Dubh*.

13, p. 173. *Kathaleen Ny-Houlahan* and all the poems which follow, in this division, except the *Dirge for O'Sullivan Beare*, are relics of the Jacobite insurrections, chiefly of the immortal '45. "The King's son" is, of course, Prince Charles Edward. "The Irish Jacobites claimed the Stuarts as of the Milesian line, fondly deducing them from Fergus." The popular lyrics of that day, which were written in Ireland, in the English tongue, have the tang of novelty and wildness, but lack, in many instances, the odd exquisite tenderness of *Shule Aroon* and *The Blackbird*. As in Scotland, some of the sweetest of the Jacobite lyrics date from a gen-

eration or more after the event ; so nothing written under
the Georges, who hated " boets," is so good an English
poem out of Ireland as its modern successors : Callanan's spirited *Avenger*, or *The Wild Geese*, and a few other lyrics of
Katharine Tynan (Mrs. Hinkson). The Gaelic compositions
of the loyalists were very much more numerous, and of superior
quality. Mangan translated a great many, among which I have
endeavored to choose the best. They cannot for a moment,
however, be compared to the simpler, briefer songs floating contemporaneously about the Highlands of Scotland. Mr. Edward Hayes, in the introduction to his collected *Ballads of Ireland*, remarks : " The poets of the last century looked forward
more to a religious than to a political deliverer, whence their
effusions were more dynastic than national, more Jacobite
than Irish. When they sang of Ireland, it was in connection with the fallen dynasty. They longed for the union of
Una and Donald, in other words, Ireland and the Stuart.
They addressed their country as a beloved female, to disguise
the object of their affection. Sometimes it was Sabia from
Brian Boru's daughter of that name ; sometimes it was
Sheela Ni Guira, or Cecilia O'Gara ; Maureen Ni Colle-
nan, Kathleen Ny Houlahan, Roseen Dhuv ; more frequently Granu Weal, or Grace O'Malley, from a princess of
Connaught who rendered herself famous by her exploits and
adventures. The poet beheld his beloved in a vision, and
wandering in remote places, bewailed the suffering of his
country. He rests himself beneath the shade of forest trees,
and seeks refuge from his thoughts in calm repose. There
appears to his rapt fancy one of those beautiful creatures we
have named. Language is not sufficiently copious to describe all her charms. He addresses her, and asks her if she
be one of the fair divinities of old, or an angel from heaven
to brighten his pathway through life and restore peace to his
afflicted country. She replies that she is Erin of the Sorrows,
once a queen, but now a slave. After she enumerates all the

wrongs and iniquities which she is enduring, she prophesies
the dawn of a brighter day, when her exiled lord shall be
restored to his rightful inheritance. This was the style
adopted by most of the Jacobite poets of the last century, to
express the sufferings of their country and their hope of
deliverance from oppression. We question if imagination
could originate a style of song more pathetic in its allusions
or more powerful in its results.''

Not every one will agree with Mr. Hayes' estimate.
The allegorical style surely seems to readers of to-day a most
mistaken, far-fetched, and ineffective device. It led to
indescribable sameness and conventionality, exactly what
was to be expected of the curious brood of pedants who
gave Ireland her Della Cruscan eighteenth-century literature.
Says Mrs. Hinkson very neatly, in her preface to *Irish Love
Songs*: ''Some of these were laborers, some peddlers, some
hedge-schoolmasters, — all alike touched with genius, wit,
fire, and learning (for it was a time when the Irish peasant
had the dead languages at his fingers' ends); all alike
scamps, in a simple and virtuous age, and adding to their
scampishness a Voltairean spirit much out of its due time
and place.'' Scotland had also her lesser dash of pseudo-
classicism, which went far towards ruining some of her
invaluable Prince Charlie songs. Of ''the lad that I'll
gang wi','' the romantic lad with ''phillabeg aboon the
knee,'' we are told in almost the next breath that ''you'd
tak him for the god o' war.'' In Egan O'Rahilly's *Vision*,
rendered by Mangan, who reported only what he found,
the distressed virgin, the Brightest of the Bright, has crystals
for eyes, a mirror for a bosom, crimson glories for cheeks ;
and she looked, as was inevitable, like ''a daughter of the
Celestial Powers.'' There is no ''highfalutin'' of this sort
in *Kathaleen Ny-Houlahan*. The ballads under that name
are almost as good as the group entitled *Roisin Dubh*, which
are a century and a half earlier. From John Mitchel we

·receive an explanatory passage regarding them, and Mangan's felicitous handling of them.   "In these translations, as well as those from the German, Mangan did not assume to be literal in words and phrases.   Nor, indeed, in general, was there any uniform unvarying version of the original poems, to which he could be literal, because they lived, for the most part, only in the memories of the illiterate peasantry ; and Gaelic scholars, in their researches for authentic originals, usually found three or four different ballads, on the same subject and under the same name, having some lines and verses identical, but varying in the arrangement ; always, however, agreeing in cadence and rhythm, in general scope and spirit.   To this scope and spirit he was always faithful.''

Here is a second *Kathaleen,* from our translator's pen, in *The Poets and Poetry of Munster :* —

> In vain, in vain we turn to Spain : she heeds us not,
> Yet may we still, by strength of will, amend our lot ;
> O yes ! our foe shall yet lie low ; our swords are drawn
> For her, our queen, our Caitilin Ny Uallachain.
>
> Yield not to fear : the time is near.   With sword in hand
> We soon will chase the Saxon race far from our land.
> What glory then to stand as men on field and bawn
> And see, all sheen, our Caitilin Ny Uallachain !
>
> How tossed, how lost, with hopes all crossed we long have been !
> Our gold is gone ; gear have we none, as all have seen.
> But ships shall brave the ocean wave, and morn shall dawn
> On Eiré green, on Caitilin Ny Uallachain !
>
> Let none believe this lovely Eve outworn or old ;
> Fair is her form, her blood is warm, her heart is bold.
> Tho' strangers long have wrought her wrong, she will not fawn,
> Will not prove mean, our Caitilin Ni Uallachain !
>
> Her stately air, her flowing hair, her eyes that far
> Pierce thro' the gloom of Banba's doom, each like a star ;
> Her songful voice that makes rejoice hearts grief hath gnawn,
> Prove her our queen, our Caitilin Ni Uallachain !

We will not bear the chains we wear, not bear them long !
We seem bereaven, but mighty heaven will make us strong :
The God who led thro' Ocean Red all Israel on,
Will aid our queen, our Caitilin Ni Uallachain !

A word as to Ny-Houlahan. " Ny " is the correct Gaelic
substitute, in a female name, for the tribal " Mac " or " O."
As Mr. Conor MacSweeny reminds his countrywomen : " A
lady who writes ' O ' or ' Mac ' to her name calls herself
' son ' instead of ' daughter.' What should we say of a
Hebrew lady who would write herself ' Esther, son of
Judah ? ' I therefore advise every Irish lady to substitute
' Ni ' (pronounced ' Nee ') for ' O ' or ' Mac.' . . . In
Irish we never use ' O ' or ' Mac ' with a woman's name ;
and why must it be done in English ? "

Among the love-names for Ireland just quoted from Hayes'
Ballads are several which have been from the beginning associated with the most beautiful wild old airs : notably *Moirin
Ni Chuillionain* (Little Mary Cullenan) and *Sighile Ni Gara*
(Celia O'Gara). To the second version of *Roisin*, quoted
in the introduction to this book, " Since last night's star,"
etc., belongs also a strangely lovely air in A minor, full of
rushing sixteenth notes, which may be found, unharmonized,
in *The Poets and Poetry of Munster*. " The Silk o' the
Kine," one of the most touching phrases on the lips of the
Irish of bygone rebellion, has been exquisitely celebrated by
Mr. Aubrey de Vere.

" The silk o' the kine shall rest at last :
    What drove her forth but the dragon-fly ?
In the golden vale she shall feed full fast,
    With her mild gold horn, and her slow dark eye."

There is no " genuine " Irish Jacobite poetry more quiet,
tender, and convincing than that.

14, p. 174. William Heffernan, surnamed Dall, or the
Blind, of Shronehill, County Tipperary, wrote this poem just

before Culloden.   *The Song of Gladness,* which follows *Welcome to the Prince,* has its justification in the extraordinary energy of the close.

15, p. 179.   "Shieling," defined as a poor cabin or shelter for a shepherd or fisher, is familiar to ballad-lovers, and occurs contemporaneously with Lochiel's muster of the Camerons : —

> "Then up the wild Glennevis,
> And down by Lochy's side,
> Young Donald left his shieling,
> And Malcolm left his bride."

16, p. 182.   Geoffrey Keating, born in 1570, died in 1650.

17, p. 184.   "The words to this spirited air are the production of a violent Jacobite.   By leathering away with the wattle, he implies his determination to decide political differences by an appeal to physical force.   The wattle was a stout cudgel or *ailpin.*"   Cotter has the courage to be antiquarian and national in his pretty poem ; and yet he cannot leave out the She

> — "that launched a thousand ships,
> And burnt the topless towers of Ilium."

18, p. 190.   Muircheartach Oge, of the Barony of Beara, called in English Murtagh, or Mortimer, The Young O'Sullivan, was a disaffected chieftain descended from Donal of the Ships, who occupied himself ten years after Culloden in raising troops (the celebrated Wild Geese) for France, the ally of the Stuarts against England.   He had served with distinction at Fontenoy, and was received with open arms by the people of the south, on his return to recruit for the French cause.   His story, a strange, grimly romantic one, was cut short by his betrayal and assassination in 1756.   This is the substance of Mangan's note, too long for incorporation.   The Gaelic manuscript of the poem was found in

Castletown about 1825 by Jeremiah Joseph Callanan, who made a close translation of it. Compare with Mangan's more imaginative passage (in the last stanza but one) : —

> " Dear head of my darling !
> How gory and pale
> These aged eyes see thee
> High-spiked on the jail !
> That cheek in the summer sun
> Ne'er shall grow warm,
> Nor that eye e'er catch light
> But the flash of the storm.''

The *caoine* is a fine specimen of the terrible Hebraic invective of the race ; the original is supposed to be the composition of The O'Sullivan's old nurse, upon whose lips the lament is placed. The passages in parentheses may be taken to be the customary chorus of women, as at a "wake," repeating, with swayings of their bodies, the melancholy word and tone of the keener. Mangan has used his favorite refrain here with ghastly effect. The penultimate stanza, the weak one among the nine, seems to have had no warrant in the original, as it is not in the Callanan transcription.

19, p. 199. Something in the impression of heard music which this lyric leaves, reminds one of Wordsworth's *Highland Reaper*. It may be worth while to append Rückert's poem, for the pleasure of comparison. Which is lovelier, it would take Apollo, expert among Sicilian reeds, to decide.

DAS EINE LIED

> Ich weiss der Lieder viele
> Und singe was ihr liebt.
> Das ist wohl gut zum spiele,
> Weil Wechzel Freude giebt ;
> Doch hätte Lieb' und Friede
> Genug an einem Liede,
> Und fragte nicht, wo's hundert giebt.

Jüngst sah ich einen Hirten
Im stillen Wiesenthal,
Wo klare Bächlein irrten
Am hellen Sonnenstrahl.
Er lag am schatt'gen Baume,
Und blies als wie im Traume
Ein Lied auf einem Blättlein schmal.

Das Lied, es mochte steigen
Nur wenig Tön, hinauf,
Dann musst' es hin sich neigen
Und nahm denselben Lauf.
Es freut' ihn immer wieder ;
Gern hätt ich meine Lieder,
Geboten all dafür zum Rauf.

Er blies sein Lied, und liess es,
Und sah sich um in Hag,
Hub wieder an und blies es,
Ich schaute wie er lag :
Er sah bei seinem Blasen
Die stillen Lämmlein grasen,
Und langsam fliehn der Sommertag.

20, p. 211. " Battle droops his clotted wing '': a line worthy of Keats.

21, p. 215. This poem of Herder's is founded on a fragment of folk-lore very general in Europe, and at its best, perhaps, in the wonderful Breton ballad of *Seigneur Nann*. All English readers will recall it as nearly identical with *Lord Ronald my Son*, although this has no direct mention of supernatual interference, nor is its "true love" a fay.

22, p. 220. There is no line-repetition in *Wenn die Rosen blühen*. It ends : —

" Ewig nun genesen,
Wirst du neu erglühn
Wirst ein himmlich Wesen,
Wenn die Rosen blühn.''

2 A

23, p. 220.

UHLAND'S FRISCHE LIEDER

Wie wenn ein Strom, ben lange
Ein Winter eingezwängt,
Im Lenzhauch mit Gesange
Verjüngt die Fesseln sprengt;

Wie wenn nach Jahr und Tagen
Ein Baum, einst blüthenreich,
Fängt Blüthen an zu tragen
Den alten gänzlich gleich;

Wie wenn ein Wein, verschlossen
Im Fasse Jahre lang,
Kommt wieder frisch geflossen,
Ein dustender Gesang;

Wie wenn auf einmal wieder
Ein rief'ger Dom ertönt,
Dem Ohr, an Vogellieder,
Seit Jahren nur gewöhnt,

Schien mir's, ist mir's geworden,
Als jüngst nach Jahren lang,
Du Haupst von Liederorden!
Frisch tönte dein Gesang.

24, p. 221. Emerson's

"Then will yet my Mother yield
A pillow in her greenest field,
Nor the June daisies scorn to cover
The clay of their departed lover,"

is in the same key as these stanzas of Kerner's *Sängers Trost.*
Mangan has somehow missed the simplicity of the ending : —

"Blumen, Hain, und Ane,
Stern und Mondenlicht,
Die ich sang! vergessen
Ihres Sängers nicht."

25, p. 226. *The Ride Around the Parapet* is placed as the first of a group of five which are called translations, for mere convention's sake. They are, rather, voluntaries of an extraordinary sort on German themes; elaborate, jocose embroideries on provided cloth-of-frieze. The Lady Eleanora von Alleyne is a very magnificent presentation, circa 1840, of the New Woman. Compare

> "Nun warte bis ein andrer kommt wieder, der es kann,
>   Das Fraulein Kunigunde von Kynast!
> Ich habe schon Weib und Kinder, und werde nicht dein Mann,
>   Das Fraulein Kunigunde!"

with Mangan's extremely pointed and *espiègle* enlargement of it : —

> "Mayest bide until they come, O stately Lady Eleanor,
>   O Lady Eleanora von Alleyne!
> Mayest bide until they come, O stately Lady Eleanor!
> And thou and they may marry; but for me, I must not tarry:
> I have won a wife already out of Spain,
>   Virgin Lady Eleanora,
>   Virgin Lady Eleanora von Alleyne!"

And again, the pleasing specifications about the forfeit, at the close, are hardly to be traced to the plain statement : —

> "Müss er mit Geld sich lösen wenn er nicht küsst die Braut,
>   Das Fraulein Kunigunde!"

Besides, the whole much-extended poem is crowded throughout with enriching detail of all kinds, and every new stroke tells. "It is a very fine ballad," Rückert might say, "by my friend Mangan."

26, p. 234.

SEHNSUCHT

(CONRAD WETZEL)

> Kennt ihr das schöne Eiland
> Weit draussen im Meer so wüst,
> Wo der Morgenrothe Reigen,
> Und der Sonnen Ausgang ist?

O dahin möcht ich ziehen
Dahin steht mir mein Sinn !
Dahin wer kann mich führen ?
Wer weiss den Weg dahin ?

27, p. 235.   August Kopisch :   *Des Kleinen Volkes Ueberfahrt.*

28, p. 238.   Enough has been said of this fantasia in the Introduction, as also of Rückert's beautiful ghazel which follows it.

29, p. 244.   For

" Ambi nemici sono, ambi fu servi,"

this is certainly a clouded rendition.

30, p. 248.   This translation of the eternally-translated *Dies Irae* occurs in Mangan's rendering of *Das Nordlicht von Kazan.*

31, p. 253.   The Karamanian Exile.   See the note on Joseph Brenan.

32, p. 260.   Relic of Prince Bayazeed.   The second line is almost too reminiscential of Keats' dying saying: " I feel the flowers growing over me."   The third and fourth refer to a very ancient custom mentioned by most Oriental poets : the bell rung for the starting of the caravan, and the cry raised of *Ar Rahil, Ar Rahil!* (Depart, Depart).

33, p. 260.   A late corroboration of the known opinion of dear old Roger Ascham, as also of Dr. Johnson.

34, p. 268.   Says Thomas Fuller :   " Keep a commonplace book : for he that with Bias carries all his learning about him in his head, will utterly be beggared and bankrupt, if a violent disease, like a merciless thief, should rob and strip him."

35, p. 270.   In this ghazel, the second line and the line next to the last foreshadow Arnold's great and well-known two : —

" Alone the sun arises, and alone
Spring the great streams."

36, p. 277. "Dree," to endure, to undergo ; a word set down in the dictionaries as "Scotch or obsolete," but in common use with Mangan and other Irish poets, and with most people in Ireland; to this day.

37, p. 278. The recurrent sounds of ā, ă, ā, â, in this concluding stanza of a splendid poem, are atrocious, and show an almost inconceivable carelessness on the part of their author. They are hardly outdone by that musical passage in *How we brought the Good News from Ghent to Aix* : —

"Rebuckled the cheek-strap, chained slacker the bit ! "

38, p. 286. *Jealousy* is very close akin to Victor Hugo's *La Voile ;* somewhat less so to Mr. Charles De Kay's powerful *Ulf in Ireland.*

39, p. 289. *The Time of the Barmecides.* Rejected readings : —

Line 1, "Mine eyes are dimmed, my hair is gray."
Line 15, "And a barb as fiery as any I know."
Lines 17, 19, 27, 29, "'Twas a long, long time back, long ago."
Line 33, "Whose armor glowed like gold."

Mangan was always an admirable reviser.

40, p. 297. This and the following poem were written some time before the first great Irish famine (1847) drove countless immigrants to America. A number of Mangan's exhortations were proved prophetic by the event, in this as in other matters.

41, p. 304. First printed in *The Irish Tribune,* in 1848, hence named by the author *The Tribune's Hymn for Pentecost.*

42, p. 309. A couple of stanzas from a poem by John Edmund Reade are worth printing in connection with Pompeii.

"O thou Vesuvius ! that risest there,
Image of drear eternity, alone
Seated in thy own silent fields of air ;
Titan, whose chainless struggles have but shown

The annihilating powers are still thine own,
Parent of lightnings, and the tempest's shroud,
Crowning, or round thy giant shoulders thrown
In majesty of shadow, ere the cloud
Break on the nether world in fulmined wrath avowed.

Grave of dead cities thou ! thy heart is fire,
Thy pulse is earthquake ; from thy breast are rolled
The flames in which shall penal earth expire ;
Thy robes are of the lava's burning fold,
Thine armèd hand the thunderbolt doth hold,
Thy voice is as the trump that calls to doom ;
Creator and destroyer ! who hath told
What world of life lies buried in thy womb,
What mightiest wrecks are sunk in thy absorbing tomb ? ''

This is the very twin of Mangan's poem, and both echo Byron to the life.

43, p. 310.   The fourth line in the fifth verse of *Pompeii* seemed to have suffered from the printers.   There are but two possible readings ; that given in the text, and one only less likely : —

"Like blasted wrecks, bestrew that mortar plain."

44, p. 311.   From the German of "Selber" !
45, p. 313.   From "Cascagni," forsooth.   Rejected readings (from a shorter version) : —

Line 1, "The life of life is gone and over."
Lines 37, 38, "Go thou, exulting in thy guilt,
                        And weave thy wanton web anew."

And the last stanza : —

"But where shall I find rest ?   Alas,
When first the winter wind shall wave
The pale wildflower, the long dark grass,
Above mine unremembered grave ! "

This poem has borne two other titles : *To Frances*, and *The Last Reproach*.   Its author was apparently also under the

Shakespearean shadow in those days. "Less in anger than in sorrow" is popularly supposed to spring from *Hamlet*, Act I., Scene v., and

> — "smile and smile
> Yet be all dark and false within,"

has possibly been heard of before, in the second scene of the same act.

46, p. 318. Written in 1832, in Mangan's twenty-ninth year. Entitled variously by him *The Dying Enthusiast, The Dying Enthusiast to his Friend, The Dying Enthusiast to his Child.*

47, p. 319. This touching poem, addressed to a friend who had not then attained his majority, marks for us one of Clarence Mangan's moods of bitter awakening and self-reproach, — moods often renewed, often outworn, as years passed. He revered Brenan, not without reason. Born in Cork, in 1828, "all of Shelley's soul" got fitly and promptly into the National Movement twenty years later, and suffered for it in Kilmainham Jail. In the October of 1849, Brenan went to New York, and did some journalistic work there; his marriage followed, with a sister of his old colleague, John Savage, and presently he moved to New Orleans, attaching himself first to the staff of *The New Orleans Delta*, then becoming editor of *The New Orleans Times*. He died in May of 1857, at Shelley's own early age. Joseph Brenan's verses have never been collected, but they have singular beauty; one of them, a pæan for Charlotte Corday, is sometimes met with in the anthologies. It is to him, in a measure, that we Americans owe one of our few fine sectional songs: *Maryland, my Maryland*. The following extract is copied from *Fifty Years among Authors, Books, and Publishers*, by Derby, New York, 1884: "James Ryder Randall, who wrote *Maryland, my Maryland*, when a young man was a schoolmaster in Louisiana, but was born in Baltimore, Maryland. . . . The editor of *The New Orleans Delta*, who encouraged young Randall's efforts at poetry, gave him a volume of the poems of James Clarence Mangan, and the weird melodies and wasted life and melancholy death of the unfortunate Irish poet made an indelible impression on his mind. He was especially struck with the rhythm of one poem, purporting to be translated from the Ottoman, and entitled *The Karamanian Exile*. One day, while the melody of *The Karamanian Exile* was running through his brain, Mr. Randall rode to the Mississippi River, seven miles distant, to get his mail. Among it was a copy of the *Delta* containing an account of the passage of the Massachusetts troops through Baltimore, and of the riot which occurred there, which he read with the deepest interest. Agitated by the thrilling news, indignant at what he considered an outrage on his native city, and anxious about relatives and friends, there was no sleep for Randall that night. For some unaccountable reason, as he kept thinking of these events in Baltimore, the stirring melody of *The Karamanian Exile* seemed to run through his head ; so much so, that he appeared possessed with its spirit, and in a moment the whole scheme of his *Maryland, my Maryland* was formed in his brain. He sat down at his desk, and in less than an hour the poem was completed. Next day he read it to his scholars, the most of whom were Creoles, and it fired them to such a degree of enthusiasm that he decided to send it to the *Delta* for publication. Its success was electrical."

The "book of Mangan's poems" mentioned as given to Mr. Randall must have been Mitchel's edition, printed just before Brenan's death. Up to that very time, *The Karamanian Exile* would have been inaccessible, except in newspaper or manuscript form. The author of *Maryland, my Maryland* is still living.

48, p. 321. "From the Irish."

49, p. 326. Another reading (September, 1835) : —

"Spirit of wordless Love, that in the lone
Bowers of the poet's museful soul doth weave
Tissues of thought, hued like the robes of eve
Ere the last glories of the sun have shone !
How soon, almost before our hearts have known
The change, above the ruins of thy throne,
Whose trampled beauty we would fain retrieve
By all earth's thrones beside, we stand and grieve !
We weep not, for the world's bleak breath hath bound
In triple ice the fountains of our tears ;
But ever-mourning Memory thenceforth rears
Her altars upon desecrated ground,
And always, with a low despairful sound,
Heavily tolls the bell of all our years.''

The altered version (1841) is much superior to this one ;
but neither sonnet has the octette perfect in form, as the sixth,
seventh, and eighth lines seem to have changed places. It is
singular that Mangan's seeing eye (a "regardful" eye, as he
might have preferred to call it) allowed the irregularity to
pass uncorrected.

50, p. 332. There is a truly Slavic gloom about this
too intense little poem.

51, p. 337. The "man made by sudden qualm ill" is
too bad ! We have reason to fear, too, that it was inten-
tional. It is not the only grotesque touch in a most original
lyric.

www.ingramcontent.com/pod-product-compliance
Lightning Source LLC
Chambersburg PA
CBHW030910270326
41929CB00008B/638